MAKE
ELEPHANTS FLY

MAKE ELEPHANTS FLY

The Process of Radical Innovation

STEVEN S. HOFFMAN

CENTER
STREET

New York Nashville

Center Street
Hachette Book Group
1290 Avenue of the Americas, New York, NY 10104
centerstreet.com
twitter.com/centerstreet

First Edition: November 2017

Center Street is a division of Hachette Book Group, Inc. The Center Street name and logo are trademarks of Hachette Book Group, Inc.

The publisher is not responsible for websites (or their content) that are not owned by the publisher.

The Hachette Speakers Bureau provides a wide range of authors for speaking events. To find out more, go to www.HachetteSpeakersBureau.com or call (866) 376-6591.

Library of Congress Cataloging-in-Publication Data has been applied for.

ISBNs: 978-1-4789-9294-3 (hardcover), 978-1-4789-9293-6 (ebook)

Printed in the United States of America

LSC-C

10 9 8 7 6 5 4 3 2 1

To Mike & Sharna Hoffman and Naomi Kokubo

Contents

Captain's Log

My goal in writing this book is to expose the process of innovation behind the world's startup factory and its ability to reshape our lives and fortunes. I've spent the past decade in San Francisco working with hundreds of startup founders, helping them understand the underlying methods, models, and mind-set of Silicon Valley and put those to use in coming up with breakthrough products and services. What I can tell you is that innovation isn't straightforward. It's not linear. It's an unpredictable, impractical, and incredibly difficult process, which is why so many people and companies fail at it. It's like trying to make an elephant fly. But it's also responsible for most of the wealth creation today, and if you aren't innovating, you're going to miss out.

Whether you work for yourself or someone else, in today's world you will need to innovate to stay competitive. It doesn't matter if you're a startup founder, corporate executive, small business owner, freelancer, or professional, there's a technology out there that's going to upend your industry. And if you aren't able to harness it to your advantage, someone else will. Innovation is no longer an option—it's the price of admission into the business world.

Almost every major company today has made innovation its number one priority. Yet fewer than one in four executives believe their organizations are effective innovators. The pressure to innovate and the price paid for failure keeps rising, while most companies haven't progressed at all. They are still using the same antiquated techniques pioneered decades ago.

This is why some of the biggest corporations in the world manage to lose entire markets to startups they've never heard of.

As the Captain of Founders Space, one of the leading incubators and accelerators in the world, I've been on the front lines of innovation. They call me Captain Hoff, and I work hands-on with startups in Silicon Valley, helping them develop their business models, create breakout products, raise capital, and scale their companies. Throughout this process, the founders are constantly experimenting, failing, and learning from their mistakes. As their teacher and mentor, I've gained valuable insights into exactly how successful teams take rough, half-formed ideas and transform them into the next blockbusters.

In this book, I'm going to show you the process by which successful startups and established corporations come up with new products and services, as well as answer the critical questions every innovator needs to know:

- How do Silicon Valley entrepreneurs innovate?
- Why do some of the smartest companies fail during the process of innovation?
- What's the best way to structure innovation teams?
- Who should be on those teams and what skills should they possess?
- How can innovation be put into practice inside larger organizations?
- Which methodologies and processes yield lasting results?
- How do you identify the next billion-dollar opportunity?

Finding answers to these questions isn't easy. Innovating is complex, messy, and often opaque. That said, I'm going to explain this process step-by-step and show exactly what it takes to replicate it inside your company. I'll make clear how you can take these lessons and apply them to any established organization, from startups and family-owned businesses to multinational corporations.

The reason I believe I'm a good teacher is because I have done the work myself. I cofounded three different venture-funded startups. I've been in the trenches struggling to find the right path for my companies. I know how hard it can be. I witnessed the rise and collapse of the dot-com bubble. I lived through the 2008 financial crisis. I rode several of the biggest tech waves, and I've taken all my experience, successes, and travails and used them as the foundation for my teaching.

I've also worked for large, public companies, including Infospace and SEGA; coached managers from multinationals, like IBM, Fujitsu, and Huawei; and helped numerous family-owned companies across Asia. Because of my diverse background, I'm able to look at innovation from both the perspective of a bootstrapped entrepreneur and a corporate executive. In this book, I approach innovation from both points of view. I show how innovation works in startups as well as in some of the world's largest conglomerates.

So what is Founders Space? Founders Space is an incubator and accelerator for startup companies. Most people don't understand exactly what incubators and accelerators do, so I will explain.

Incubators, like Bill Gross's Idealab, typically begin with their own ideas and then put together the team, funding, resources, and relationships necessary to transform a concept into a successful business.

Accelerators don't form companies. Instead, they recruit already existing companies which are at an early stage in their development, and provide them with the mentoring, resources, relationships, training, and funding necessary to accelerate their growth.

How did I get started forming my own incubator and accelerator? Five years ago, after I'd finished my third venture-funded startup, I was taking a break. At this time, many of my friends were launching their own startups in Silicon Valley, and they came to me for assistance. "Steve, you have to help me!" my friends would say. "How do I get funded? How do you put together a business plan? Who should I have on my board of advisors?"

I was happy to answer their questions on fund-raising, product development, design, and go-to-market strategy. After a couple months of this,

I realized that most entrepreneurs have the same questions, so I posted answers to those questions on my blog. Some of the posts went viral. Soon new startup founders, whom I didn't know, began asking me for help. That was when Founders Space was born.

My colleagues and I started holding meetups in San Francisco and Silicon Valley. Our events and roundtables became so popular that they spread to Los Angeles, New York, Texas, and as far away as Singapore. Over the years, Founders Space grew from a part-time hobby and labor of love into a more than full-time global business. Founders Space has more than fifty strategic partners around the world. Our headquarters are in San Francisco. Our first goal was to help startups from all over the world to tap into the Silicon Valley ecosystem. As we expanded, so did our mission. We are now an international organization with those strategic partners in twenty-two countries. We believe innovators need to think globally, and Founders Space has become an educational and knowledge-sharing hub for worldwide entrepreneurship.

Europe has been a big focus for us, and now we're expanding rapidly in Asia. We run in-depth courses across China, Taiwan, and Korea, and we launched a Founders Space Incubator in Shanghai with plans to open up in Japan and Germany. Our mission is to continue expanding globally with Southeast Asia and Latin America next on our list. Within the past two years, we've had thousands of startups attend our seminars and more than four hundred entrepreneurs go through our incubator program. Our success includes one of the fastest growing organic food delivery startups and the top-grossing virtual reality game developer, as well as startups using artificial intelligence, big data, and the Internet of Things to remake our homes, workplaces, and lives.

So why did I feel compelled to write this book? Although there are plenty of innovation books on the market, none of them takes the processes and methodologies used inside a Silicon Valley incubator and shows how these techniques can be adapted for all businesses, from global behemoths to garage startups. This, combined with my personal experience, has allowed me to gain a deep insight into how innovation takes place across diverse organizations, cultures, and business environments, and then distill this experience down to something everyone can use. My goal is to help you understand what it means to put the ideas, energy, and ingenuity of Silicon Valley to work within your company, so you can outthink and outmaneuver the competition. By the time you've digested this book, I sincerely hope you can take your impossibly big idea and make it fly!

MAKE
ELEPHANTS FLY

Section One

THE ESSENCE OF INNOVATION

Chapter 1

Innovation Vector

"Once a new technology rolls over you, if you're not part of the steamroller, you're part of the road."

—Stewart Brand, creator of
The Whole Earth Catalog

Innovation isn't new. We've been doing it since prehistoric times. The first major innovation was when humans stumbled upon fire and figured out how to use it to keep warm, cook meat, fend off enemies, and see in the dark. Not much has changed since then. We're still going through the same process, although with more knowledge, better tools, and improved collaboration.

Arguably the most important innovation in all of history was Johannes Gutenberg's printing press. It appears so simple in hindsight: movable type. However, the impact was enormous. This single innovation enabled the dissemination of knowledge and exchange of ideas on an unprecedented scale. The free flow of information set in motion momentous changes, including the Renaissance, Reformation, and Scientific Revolution. This unprecedented explosion in knowledge sharing has formed the basis of our modern world.

Our progress for tens of thousands of years was linear, but the ability to organize, share, and use information on a global scale propelled us from the Dark Ages into the Age of Enlightenment and beyond. If you look at innovation over time, the invention of moveable type was the point where we first started to see exponential growth. This acceleration has continued with the Industrial Revolution and Information Age, as more information and resources have become available to more people than in the entire preceding millennia. Today, Second and Third World countries can access the identical knowledge base as the First World. Enterprising students at the University of Nairobi can tap into the same online forums, discussion groups, and information as those in New York, Berlin, and Tokyo.

Now we are about to take the next great stride forward. We are on the cusp of the Cognitive Era, where artificial intelligence will enable machines to start thinking and acting autonomously as they process vast amounts of data, make complex decisions, and communicate on a scale never seen before. Decision-making will migrate from human beings to computers as we outsource routine and complex decisions. Within the next few decades, we will have microprocessors embedded in all parts of our bodies, extending our lives, our cognitive abilities, and our power to manipulate the world. Human-computer symbiosis will rapidly reach a level where parts of our decision-making will reside not in our heads but in the cloud. Our brains will be plugged directly into the Internet 24/7.

If this sounds like a fantasy, it's not. Already, scientists in labs have inserted wireless chips into the brains of monkeys so that they can control a robotic arm with their thoughts and feed themselves. In another experiment, the monkeys were placed in electric wheelchairs, and just by thinking, they could drive the wheelchairs around a room. If monkeys can do this, so can human beings. If they put a wireless chip in my brain today, I would be capable of turning on and off the lights in my home, answering my phone, and steering a vehicle with my thoughts.

That's not all. Scientists recently trained a rat how to gain access to special food. The training took a bit of work, because the rat had to learn exactly how to access the food. The scientists then hooked the rat's brain up to the Internet and connected it directly to another rat's brain in a different location. Instantly, that second rat understood how to get the food without any training. In other words, scientists managed to transfer information directly from one living brain to another.

This may sound like science fiction, but it's happening today, and if we look into the future, we can easily imagine a time when we'll no longer need to go to school. We will be able download all the knowledge into our heads. We'll even be able to download other people's thoughts, memories, and emotions. This type of technology may not even require chips in our brains. We may be able to do it all noninvasively in the future with electroencephalography-based brain-computer interfaces or similar technology, and just like most people today cannot imagine living without smartphones, in the future we won't be able to imagine living without a direct brain-to-Internet connection.

If you combine these advances in technology with the progress being made in DNA editing, robotics, nanotechnology, big data, and artificial intelligence, we will be living in a completely different world in twenty years. This may sound scary, but it shouldn't. If you took one of our prehistoric ancestors and beamed them into the present-day world, it would be unfathomable to them, but to us, it's quite normal. Remember, it wasn't that long ago that 90 percent of the world's population toiled on farms doing all the work with only the assistance of animals. Soon the idea of people working in factories and service jobs will seem antiquated. Advances in technology will free people up for more creative work and enable us to experience and do things we never imagined possible. It will also help solve some of the world's most pressing problems, like climate change, food supply, habitat destruction, and disease outbreaks. And it will open up new ways to view ourselves and our universe. Technological innovation is not only the next step in our evolution as a species, but it's the key to our survival. Without radical innovation, we can't sustain our current way of life.

Fortunately, with each leap forward, our capacity to innovate will continue to rise exponentially. It's similar to Moore's Law, which states that the number of transistors present in new integrated circuits will double approximately every two years—meaning that computing power will increase exponentially over time. The observation was made by Gordon Moore, the cofounder of Intel, and it has held true for decades. Recently, Moore's Law has failed to deliver on its promise because it was too narrowly

INNOVATION CURVE GRAPH

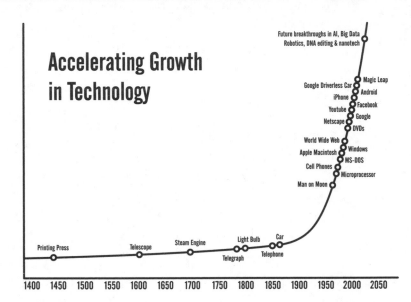

defined. It was only applied to the processing power of microchips with their physical limitations. Instead, Moore should have expanded his law to innovation itself. It's not as easy to quantify the rate of innovation, but if you look at our progress over the past two millennia, it's clear we're experiencing more than a linear progression.

Imagine moving up the innovation curve in the coming decades. No matter what you do for a living, you are part of this massive change taking place, and it will transform your job, your life, and your image of yourself. The changes will be both profound and revelatory. What we call work today will no longer be the domain of humans, and what we think of as our own personal thoughts and experiences will be intertwined with those of machines, extending beyond the current physical limitations of our brains and bodies. All this will happen within our children's lifetimes, and those of us who push the boundaries of science, technology, and business will reap the rewards and have a chance to shape the future.

MYTH: INNOVATION IS STEADILY PROGRESSING

Even I fall prey to this myth when I over simplify the innovation curve, showing a smooth progression upward toward exponential growth. The truth is that history moves in fits and starts. There is one step backward, then two forward, then three backward. Political turmoil, wars, famine, and natural catastrophes can all impact the steady march of progress.

If we look back at the ancient Greeks, they actually came up with many innovations and theories that were lost until the Renaissance. Take, for example, the Greek philosophers Leucippus and Democritus. They developed the concept of the atom in the fifth century BCE. However, their theory ran counter to both Aristotelian and Christian dogma, and so it was suppressed until the sixteenth and seventeenth centuries. The same thing happened when the Greeks proposed the idea of a spherical Earth back in the sixth century BCE.

Even with these major setbacks, if we look at the macro picture, things are progressing. It looks more like a jagged line than a smooth curve, but the overall direction is up and the rate of innovation is accelerating.

Chapter 2

Technology Isn't the Answer

Any new technology tends to go through a twenty-five-year adoption cycle.

—Marc Andreessen, venture capitalist at
Andreessen Horowitz

One of the biggest misconceptions is that innovation is all about technology. It's not. Technology plays just one part in the innovation process, and it's not always the most important part for the entrepreneur. The fact is that most new inventions don't become viable businesses for decades. You can look at any invention throughout history, from the combustible engine to the lightbulb to the computer, and you'll see a significant lag time from the original invention to the birth of the industry.

When I travel the world with Founders Space, I'm always meeting politicians and industry leaders who believe the way to replicate Silicon Valley is to develop or import new technologies. They are often willing to spend billions to accomplish this task. This is flawed thinking. While technology is important, it's not the answer. If you analyze most successful startups, you can see that most of them had little or no proprietary technology when they began. Just take a look at the high-flying companies listed below. They are called unicorns because their valuation after investment was over a billion dollars, which is supposed to be very rare, just like the mythical unicorn:

- Uber—ride sharing
- Airbnb—home sharing

- WeWork—coworking space
- Spotify—music
- Snapdeal—online shopping
- Zenefits—online HR software
- SoFi—student loans
- Vice Media—media & journalism
- Credit Karma—free credit scores
- Delivery Hero—online food-ordering service
- Wish—online shopping
- Houzz—design your home
- Blue Apron—ready-to-cook meals
- Dropbox—online file sharing
- Instacart—groceries delivered to your door
- SurveyMonkey—online surveys
- BuzzFeed—online news
- Jet—online shopping
- Thumbtack—hiring professionals for projects
- Eventbrite—event ticketing and discovery
- Evernote—mobile note taking
- Warby Parker—shop for online glasses
- Nextdoor—neighborhood social network
- Kabbage—small business loans
- Udacity—online courses
- Box—online file sharing for businesses

None of these companies developed their own proprietary technology when they launched. Instead, they used existing technology in new ways, while focusing on business model and design innovation. The technologies that most successful startups employ are typically off-the-shelf or open-source. These are readily available to anyone anywhere in the world. They aren't restricted to Silicon Valley. So when I hear governments insist on developing or importing technology from Silicon Valley to spur innovation, I can't help but think they are focusing on the wrong problem. What technology are they talking about? The technology they need doesn't have to be imported. Most of it is publically available as open-source or is easily licensed from private companies, universities, and research centers.

Look at the iPhone. We think of it as a technological marvel, but the real genius behind Apple is its design innovation. Steve Jobs understood the power of creating a unique and compelling user experience. The technology in the iPhone isn't that special. Most of it isn't even made by Apple. The hardware and chips tend to come from third parties, including Apple's competitors, like Samsung. What Apple brings to the table is a deep understanding of the customers and what they need and want out of a product. Apple's major innovation was in the design of the user experience and the app ecosystem.

This is where the brilliance of Steve Jobs and Jony Ive truly shines. Users fall in love with the product, invest their time and energy, and don't want to give that up. So even if an iPhone costs two or three times as much as an Android phone, most of its users won't switch. Just look at the App Store. When it launched, it was a breakthrough in design and business model innovation. The store made it easy and fun to browse, install, purchase, and manage software, while providing an ongoing revenue stream and binding the user ever closer to Apple. Each time a user installs software, they invest more time, and often more money, into the ecosystem. If they leave, they give it all up. This is where the value of Apple resides—not in the hardware or technology.

In Silicon Valley, more value has been created through design innovation than any other way. If you look at most startups that begin with proprietary technology but no clear understanding of the customer, they have a harder time creating value than those who start with nothing but a hypothesis. Have you ever heard of a solution in search of a problem? As soon as a company has its own technology, it can limit its ability to explore the market. The business becomes married to the technology, and if an opportunity is not readily apparent, the company may wind up searching for one that fits the technology. This is what I call the technology trap.

I see startups at Founders Space fall into this trap all the time. A

European startup came to us recently after spending years and millions of dollars developing a new technology for displaying 3D images without requiring 3D glasses. The problem was that they'd spent most of their money and still hadn't productized the tech, let alone figured out the business model. We struggled to help them find a product-market fit that Silicon Valley investors could get behind. I can tell you that it would have been far better if they'd validated the market before spending millions on R & D.

It's easy to believe your technology will give you a distinct advantage, when in fact it's hindering your progress and limiting opportunity. Companies burdened with proprietary technology but having no clear business opportunities tend to come up with solutions that fit their technology. The hitch is that these solutions, more often than not, solve a problem for the customer that doesn't exist.

Let's face it. It's hard to identify a bona fide customer problem that is large enough to justify starting a business, let alone one that meets the requirements and limitations of a specific technology. Bitcoin, the virtual currency that was supposed to replace cash and credit cards, is a great example of this. The blockchain, upon which Bitcoin was built, is a marvel of technology, but almost no one wanted to use Bitcoin in place of credit cards. Bitcoin was a classic solution to a problem that didn't exist for consumers. I remember startups raising huge amounts of capital from some of the top venture capitalists in the valley, including Andreessen Horowitz, only to cast about searching for a problem to solve. The problem was that there wasn't any problem to solve. People were pretty happy with the status quo.

I didn't invest in a single Bitcoin company despite all the hype. I'm not saying that digital currency isn't the future. I believe someday paper money will disappear and all currency will be digitized. However, at the time Bitcoin launched, my analysis was simple: My credit card was easy, convenient, trustworthy, and paid me 2 percent cash back on every purchase, while Bitcoin was difficult, inconvenient, subject to volatility, and paid me nothing. The only thing it had going for it was blockchain technology, an open, distributed ledger that can record transactions between two parties, which I couldn't care less about as a consumer. I have to admit, as a techno geek I was excited about Bitcoin, but the consumer in me won out. Sometimes Silicon Valley drinks its own Kool-Aid, and it's usually when a new technology comes out that is so sexy everyone falls in love with it, only to find the infatuation is short-lived.

Google, which is hell-bent on developing new technologies, is known for killing more projects than almost anyone else. Many of Google's initiatives, including Google Glass, Google Wave, Google Buzz, and Google+, have been solutions in search of problems. It's no accident that Google's moonshot projects lost $859 million in the second quarter of 2016. We will see this same thing repeated with the next wave of virtual reality and augmented reality apps. Upward of 90 percent will be solutions to problems that simply don't exist. But the technology is so dazzling that investors are flocking to it without distinguishing between what makes a good business and what looks good in a PowerPoint. VR (virtual reality) and AR (augmented reality) are classic examples of putting the technology cart in front of the business horse. The business always needs to drive the adoption of technology, not vice versa.

I'm a big fan of reading history, especially the biographies of famous inventors, and as history shows us, most inventors don't wind up making the big bucks or building new industries. Just look at Nikola Tesla's amazing life. He invented fluorescent bulbs, radio, remote control, the electric motor, the laser, and wireless communications, but wound up dying penniless and ignored. How was it possible for someone to develop so many earth-shattering technologies and die without a cent to his name? Unfortunately, Tesla wasn't alone. Here are other inventors who died in poverty after making stupendous leaps forward in technology:

- Johannes Gutenberg—the printing press
- Edwin H. Armstrong—the FM radio
- Antonio Meucci—the telephone
- Rudolf Diesel—the diesel engine
- Geoffrey Dummer—the integrated circuit
- Charles Goodyear—vulcanization

And the list goes on...

I'm not trying to discourage anyone from becoming an inventor. Inventors play an invaluable role in our society. I just want to make it crystal clear that translating new inventions into a viable business isn't easy. It's incredibly hard. The big breakthroughs tend to come from the next generation of entrepreneurs, who just focus on the opportunities and aren't wed to any specific technology, unless it serves their purposes.

As an angel investor, I see startups all the time who have some proprietary technology that they feel compelled to use, usually because they've spent loads of money and time developing it, only to discover that finding a product-market fit for their creations is harder and more expensive than all the research and development they've done. Whenever a startup comes to me with new technology but no proof of customer demand, I cringe. It's typically a death warrant. It's like being handed a key but not knowing if it opens anything worthwhile. Far better to start with a treasure chest and find a way to pick the lock. That's what smart entrepreneurs do.

Large corporations aren't much better at monetizing their technology, especially when it falls outside their core business. Bell Labs had an unparalleled string of world-rocking inventions, including the first transistor, solar cell, and high-definition television, but they weren't the ones to reap the most profit from these breakthroughs. The profits went in large part to entrepreneurs who licensed Bell Lab's technology and built new industries around them.

Xerox PARC, which Xerox Corporation founded in 1970 to help spur innovation, is an even more telling example. They invented the Ethernet, graphical user interface, bitmapped displays, icons, pop-up menus, overlapping windows, the mouse, and object-oriented programming. None of these added much to Xerox's bottom line or prevented the company's decline. The fact is that it's typically not the company or individual who comes up with the technology who benefits; it's the innovator who sees the opportunity and jumps on it. Take Steve Jobs, for example. He took Xerox's most prized inventions and used them to create the Macintosh.

Thomas Edison is another good example. He wasn't the first to invent the lightbulb, movie camera, power generator, storage battery, or telegraph, but he did identify the business opportunity and innovated his way to success. He was a genius at recognizing an opportunity, pulling all the pieces together, and figuring out how to bring a product to market, while stealing all the credit. This is what true innovators do.

Edison epitomizes the difference between an inventor and an innovator. Innovations unlock business opportunities, while inventions bring new science and technology into the world. If you're reading this book, it's probably not because you want to bury yourself in a research lab. It's because you want to use what's out there already to transform your industry. So let's make a deal. Don't go down the path of spending huge sums on research and development with no idea what the end result will be. Instead, look at the world and its problems, then take existing technologies, modify them to suit your purposes, test the markets to see if there's demand, and then exploit those opportunities.

MYTH: THE LONE INVENTOR

People love to romanticize the role of the lone genius: the hero that single-handedly, against all odds, transforms the world. The truth is that great innovations don't happen in a vacuum. They are the culmination of all the work that precedes them. Sir Isaac Newton summed this up eloquently when he said, "If I have seen further, it is by standing on the shoulders of giants."

If you examine the life of any great innovator, you'll see a deep level of collaboration and exchange of ideas. Thomas Edison, who took credit for a ceaseless stream of new inventions, actually collaborated intensely with others. Despite his desire to hog the fame, many of his patents have the names of his coworkers on them, which means they did most of the work.

Albert Einstein, Wolfgang Mozart, and Sigmund Freud also worked closely with others. Although they tend to get all the credit, their ideas were part of a collaborative process, where they exchanged, stole, modified, and built upon existing bodies of thought and scientific research. Einstein relied heavily upon the experimental research of his peers; Mozart's father, a composer and conductor in his own right, was his son's teacher and collaborator; and Freud formed his own discussion group, where many of his greatest ideas were born.

T. S. Eliot famously said, "Immature poets imitate; mature poets steal; bad poets deface what they take, and good poets make it into something better, or at least something different." Whether it takes the form of collaboration, cooperation, or thievery, most geniuses don't come up with their best ideas alone.

Chapter 3

Inventive Ecosystems

I'm a Silicon Valley guy. I just think people from Silicon Valley can do anything.

—Elon Musk, CEO of Tesla and SpaceX

If technology isn't the key to Silicon Valley's success, what is? Certainly not our intelligence. It's not our brains that give us the edge. It's something much more powerful: momentum and diversity. Silicon Valley began with a bunch of misfits, hackers, hippies, artists, and technologists all coming together. These included Stewart Brand, who founded *The Whole Earth Catalog*; Steve Jobs, who was a fruitarian and didn't bathe regularly; Douglas Engelbart, who put on "the Mother of All Demos," Buckminster Fuller, who popularized the term "Spaceship Earth"; Ken Kesey and the psychedelic Merry Pranksters; and Gordon French, cofounder of the Homebrew Computer Club—just to name a few.

The key to Silicon Valley's creative explosion was that you could have an MBA, an artist, a nerdy scientist, and an LSD-experimenting hippie together in the same room bouncing wild ideas off each other. These types of encounters led to more than one world-changing business. The sheer concentration of creative minds in one place during the chaotic and free-loving 1960s and '70s led to a revolution in what people thought was possible. To change the world wasn't just an abstract idea; it was a mission and a reality that permeated the air everyone breathed. Risk taking, experimentation, spiritual awakening, and new technology all blended together to form a mind-expanding brew that fueled and altered the character of Silicon Valley entrepreneurs and inventors. It didn't matter if they were ex–Wall Street suits, academics, researchers, marketers, designers, or hackers. They became converted to the Silicon Valley religion that anyone can make an elephant fly.

These roots in diversity, free thinking, and irrational optimism are what still drive most of Silicon Valley's innovation today. To quote Steve Jobs, people here "think different!" We enjoy being rebels, pushing back, questioning the status quo, and going down the path less traveled. The lines between art and science are continually blurred. The vanguard of Silicon Valley are all spiritual children of luminaries like Ada Lovelace, who wove art and mathematics together in 1842 to conceptualize the first general-purpose computer—well before anyone had ever heard of a transistor, let alone an operating system or a programming language.

Leonardo da Vinci is another spiritual role model. Who else can legitimately claim to be an inventor, a painter, a sculptor, an architect, a scientist, a musician, a mathematician, an engineer, an anatomist, a geologist, an astronomer, a botanist, a writer, a historian, a poet, and a cartographer? The technological renaissance that began in Silicon Valley in the 1960s is still running strong. Reid Hoffman, cofounder of LinkedIn, sums it up nicely when he says, "Silicon Valley is a mind-set, not a location."

That was why I personally came back to the Bay Area, long before it was the world's epicenter of innovation. I remember walking the streets of San Francisco in the midnineties and seeing multiple subcultures flourishing within miles of each other. Haight-Ashbury had the rebels, rockers, freaks, and runaways. Castro had the free-loving, gloriously gay, never-ending party. South of Market was being transformed as artists, geeks, and yuppies piled in. The financial district was abuzz with investment bankers, traders, institutional investors, and assorted suits. The Mission was drenched in Latino culture. Chinatown was a gritty leftover from the '70s, while the new, business-savvy Chinese rolled into the Richmond District and helped reinvent the city. And just south of the city lay Silicon Valley, with its wealth of tech giants and venture dollars. I knew this place was ready to explode with creativity, and I had to be a part of it!

Now that Silicon Valley has attained near-mythical status, with its streets paved in venture dollars and unicorns dancing on its suburban lawns, the momentum continues, as thousands of the brightest minds from every corner of the globe flock to California to make their names and fortunes. This modern-day Gold Rush brings ever more diversity of thought, with the world's most brilliant brains converging and mingling in one small geographic region. When I go out to an event in Silicon Valley, I'm often the only California native in a room. At a single mixer, I may wind up exchanging ideas with an Indian investment banker, a Korean neuroscientist, an Estonian designer, a Chilean botanist, a Chinese venture capitalist, an Egyptian mathematician, and a Thai entrepreneur. Each of these adventurers brings with them their own unique cultural perspectives, points of view, experiences, and approaches to problem solving.

Think of what that means for startups. When you open up shop in the Valley, you have a wealth of talent from all over the globe to choose from. If you choose right, your company can feast on a melting pot of new ideas and ways of doing business. This kind of diversity is at the heart of what makes Silicon Valley so dynamic. According to a study by the Center for Talent Innovation, employees at companies with both inherent diversity, based on gender, ethnicity, and sexual orientation, and acquired diversity, based on learning, are 45 percent likelier to grow their market share over the previous year and 70 percent likelier to capture a new market than companies that lack this diversity.

Silicon Valley has another cultural advantage. Unlike in most other countries, respect isn't automatically granted to authority figures. It has to be earned. Californian culture dictates that everyone has something to contribute, everyone has a role, and everyone's opinion has a right to be heard. The boss is not always right. In fact, if the boss isn't open to new ideas, the best talent will jump ship and join another startup. It's an egalitarian meritocracy. It doesn't matter who you know or what your past is. It's what you do that counts. "Success in Silicon Valley, most would agree, is more merit-driven than almost any other place in the world," says Michael Arrington, founder of TechCrunch. "It doesn't matter how old you are, what sex you are, what politics you support or what color you are. If your idea rocks and you can execute, you can change the world and/or get really, stinking rich!"

It's precisely this nonconformity and heterogeneity that is Silicon Valley's strength. Our racial and cultural diversity, openness to immigrants, and acceptance of differences give us a significant competitive advantage over other countries. I travel a lot in Asia, and I can tell you the Chinese, Koreans, and Japanese are just as talented as anyone in California. They have incredible technologists and some of the most entrepreneurial businesspeople I have ever met. But what they lack is Silicon Valley's willingness to challenge the status quo, cultural diversity, and openness to unconventional ideas and points of view. Most parents in Asia encourage their children to study engineering and business over other subjects. The result is that the majority of people working in high tech have engineering degrees or MBAs—or both. Students enter the workforce equipped with roughly the same ideas and experience, and for that reason alone, they are at a disadvantage when it comes to thinking differently.

Innovation is about creating something new, something the world has never seen before, something that has never been tried. Doing this with a team of like-minded individuals that have all been through the same rigid educational system is a lot to ask. In the rush to be competitive and ensure their success, many countries have missed out on an opportunity. They've limited their ability to build a diverse ecosystem. The educational system and parents should be encouraging their youth to follow their passions— not the norms. If a student is interested in music, sculpture, ethnography, creative writing, religion, or philosophy, the student should be applauded for taking the path less traveled.

I'm not saying that countries with more traditional values and educational systems, like China, India, Japan, and Korea, can't innovate. They are already innovating and will continue to do so at an ever more rapid pace. They are global players, rich in talent, culture, history and ideas.

But there's an opportunity to accelerate growth and ignite a renaissance of creativity, invention, and discovery. Having a wide variety of backgrounds and knowledge is an essential part of building a truly innovative ecosystem. Most big leaps forward come out of interdisciplinary collaborations. Cross-pollination between anthropology, linguistics, and computer science can lead to amazing things. It's when a musician gets together with a computer hacker and they start talking about the possibilities that new ideas are born. This is Silicon Valley's secret sauce. It is what gives us an unfair advantage.

I was in Beijing last year, and a mother showed me the paintings her son in elementary school had created. I was blown away. They were incredible, and I told her he should be an artist. This triggered in her an instant negative reaction. She clearly admired her son's work but didn't want him to pursue something so frivolous. How could he make money? What type of career was that? What type of life would he have? Her dream was for him to become an investment banker.

This type of narrow thinking is a problem worldwide, and it's a detriment to long-term competitiveness and progress. In America, public funding for the arts by federal, state, and local governments has declined by 15 percent, when adjusting for inflation, over the past twenty years. Unfortunately, things are only going to get worse, not better, with the National Endowment for the Arts on the chopping block at the time of writing this book. We must realize that if a nation is going to build a true innovation ecosystem, it has to have all the elements in place: creativity and diversity of thought, culture, and education being essential catalysts.

Chapter 4

Watch the Waves

A lot of the best tech startups are ideas that have been around for years but the time is finally right.

—Chris Dixon, venture capitalist at
Andreessen Horowitz

What's the biggest factor in the success of any startup? Surprisingly, it's not any of the things we've been talking about. It's not creativity, the team, the customer, product, or technology. It's *timing*. Having the right thing at the right time is essential. Just ask any Hollywood producer. They can do everything right: have a star roster, a big brand, and a talented director; but the movie can flop. Or they can make a subpar film, but if it strikes a chord with the public, it's a hit. *Citizen Kane* versus *Snakes on a Plane* says it all. The same is true in nearly every business. Just ask a restaurant owner, a stockbroker, an electronics manufacturer, a banker, or a real estate developer. It's nearly impossible to succeed if your timing is off.

So how do you time a successful product? You need to watch the waves. Everything in our society happens in waves, whether it's the Beanie Babies toy craze, the housing bubble, the Billboard Top 40, the adoption of a new technology, or the fashions we all wear. Even in the stodgy corporate and banking worlds, waves dictate how people think, act, and do business. Right now, there's a big innovation wave, and that's why I'm writing this book. Everyone from the CEO of General Electric to the head of a family-owned textile factory in Hangzhou are thinking about how to modernize and remake their businesses so they aren't left eating some startup's dust.

I tell everyone who comes to Founders Space that if you're going to innovate, you need to watch all the waves. There are many different types of waves running through society. A recent one is the fitness wave. This wave has made the fortunes of many startups. Crossfit, a gym franchise, hopped on this wave to launch its intensive workout program. Fitbit, a wearable for tracking your exercise, rode this wave all the way to an initial public offering (IPO). Tough Mudder, a competition where men and women participate in insanely hard races, has tapped the macho fitness craze. Lululemon leveraged the Yoga wave to launch a worldwide brand of clothing and accessories.

Part of catching a wave lies in speed. You need to paddle fast enough at just the right time or you'll miss it. Just ask any surfer. This is why most successful startup founders don't develop their own technology. Developing proprietary technology is nice, but it takes time. In that time, the startup will probably miss whatever wave was on the horizon. This is why most smart entrepreneurs, if given a choice, opt to use existing off-the-shelf technology and open-source whenever possible. This enables them to move fast and catch a wave just before it crests.

The power of a wave to take a tiny startup and propel it into a world-changing business can't be underestimated. A startup with an idea, no matter how innovative, that's too early or too late is practically doomed. It doesn't matter if the startup has the best management team, a war chest full of venture capital, and all the right connections; if the world isn't ready for what they are offering, it won't go anywhere. Just look at Webvan, the online grocery store launched during the dot-com bubble. It raised close to $800 million from Benchmark Capital, Sequoia Capital, Softbank, Goldman Sachs, and Yahoo. The company also raised $375 million from its initial public offering of stock. It was a promising idea, just too early. No one was ready to buy their groceries online in 1999. The wave wasn't there yet, so this elephant of an idea couldn't get off the ground.

When venture capitalists (VCs) in Silicon Valley insist on seeing traction, they are saying that they want to see proof of the wave. That traction can be sales, user engagement, press, social capital, or all of the above. The more evidence of a wave, the more excited venture investors get, because they know from experience that if you catch a wave, it can take you all the way to IPO or acquisition—even if what you have isn't that incredible.

Look at Zynga, the game publisher. They caught the social gaming wave. It carried them to IPO and then crashed right after they went public. Too bad for all the game companies in their wake, but not so bad for the VCs who sold their stock early and made a sweet return. Nest is another example. They caught the Internet of Things (IoT) wave right at the beginning. Their smart thermostat was so beautifully designed and inventive that it caught the imagination of geeks worldwide. Nest turned a blasé home appliance into a coveted showpiece, and their name became synonymous with the future of smart devices in the home. The wave was so big that Google acquired Nest for $3.2 billion. Since the acquisition, Nest's sales haven't met expectations, but this doesn't matter to the VCs. As a venture investment, Nest was a home run, and it's due in large part to perfect timing.

This is why you see most of the top venture capitalists, who have offices on the prestigious Sand Hill Road in Menlo Park, California, invest in the same thing at the same time. It's not just that they are lemmings heading off a cliff. They see the waves, and they want to catch them at just the right time. There was a wave of enterprise software investments, followed by a wave of social network investments, followed by a wave of game investments, and so on. Some of these waves crash too soon and leave the investors underwater. Just look at Bitcoin, the virtual currency no one wanted, and clean energy technology (cleantech), which got killed by falling oil prices. Other waves carry their startups all the way to the promised land. This includes social networking, with hits like Facebook, Twitter, LinkedIn, and Snapchat.

Let's examine one of the biggest waves to sweep Silicon Valley in the last few decades. That's the mobile wave led by Apple. The introduction of the iPhone at just the right time caught the world's imagination and was the ship that launched ten thousand startups. Everyone from grandparents to their grandkids felt compelled to buy a smartphone. Even if they didn't know what it would do for them, they had to have one. The media hopped on the bandwagon and drove demand. There were stories about a guy who made a million dollars with a silly app that simulated a match lighter. There was Angry Birds, the adorable mobile game that became the poster child for indie developers, capturing the hearts and minds of everyone. There were countless startups making millions and then billions with their mobile apps. What a wave it was!

This wave, too, has crested. It's much more difficult to just put out an app and have it dazzle the world. The public and press have heard the story too many times. There are just too many apps, and competition is too intense. You have to have something truly special to cut through the noise. I'm sorry, but the low-hanging fruit has been picked clean. Just ask any app developers today. They know how much harder it is to have a hit app than a few years ago. So, what's my advice to all you innovators? Look for the next wave, of course!

What investors care about more than anything are technologies that can disrupt existing markets and create new ones. The big technology waves that are coming into shore are robotics, artificial intelligence, big data, and financial technology, to name just a few. This is where the money is going right now in Silicon Valley. Will all these waves pan out? Time will tell. But the odds of success are much higher when you bet on a wave than against it.

This is one reason that having a diverse team is so essential. It's hard to spot waves before they are big. Often they are just ripples on the horizon. You won't even see one unless you know what you're looking for. One way to identify them early is to have people on your team who are intensely curious and interested in things beyond just their work.

Palmer Luckey, the founder of Oculus, spotted the virtual reality wave by being a geek who was fascinated with the possibilities of VR. It was his passion and hobby. I guarantee you that if he hadn't come up with Oculus

Rift, the first virtual reality headset to capture the world's imagination, someone else would have. The timing was right. The technology was there. The novel and intense experience of being immersed in a virtual world resonates with so many people that it was bound to happen. Luckey didn't even invent the technology. It was all open-source code developed by the University of Southern California. He just created a compelling video at the right time and put it on Kickstarter. Luckey was lucky. But you can't get lucky unless you have these types of people on your team.

But who are these wave catchers? They tend to be people who obsessively invest time and energy into hobbies and interests outside of their jobs. That's how they spot the trends that are about to reshape society. I become worried when I talk to a founding team and they do nothing but work. That's a huge red flag. This problem is particularly acute in Asia. I meet startup founders all the time who are complete workaholics. They believe that if they work harder than anyone else, they will succeed. This is true to a degree, but if taken too far, it can actually hurt their chances of success, because they lack the ability to put together the pieces to see what's coming next.

Here's an example of what I mean. I was in Beijing having drinks with a startup founder in my hotel at 9:00 p.m. After we were done, I asked, "So you're heading home?" She looked up in surprise. "No, I'm going back to the office. All my managers are waiting for me. We are going to work until 2:00 a.m." To make matters worse, most of these highly ambitious startup founders don't have time for hobbies. I asked another ambitious young woman if she had time to go to any museums. "Museums? No way. I have to work on the weekends." To me this type of narrow focus on work is a severe handicap that many founders don't even realize they have. It sounds crazy to a fun-loving Californian like me, but many entrepreneurs are so focused on their work that they don't read novels, go to the theater, take weekends off to explore nature, or even have relationships outside of work.

I've been told more than once by startup founders that they don't have time for a boyfriend or girlfriend. This isn't healthy. And it isn't good for business. Only by opening up your mind can you experience life and see what's actually happening in the world and society. To close everything off is to miss out not only on the incoming waves but also on life itself. I challenge every startup founder and innovator out there to spend at least one day a week doing something completely pointless and unrelated to anything in your business. Focus on something that intensely interests you but has no immediate benefits outside the experience itself. Go hang gliding; study oceanography; join an improv group. That's how you spot waves.

MYTH: TOP INNOVATORS DISRUPT EXISTING MARKETS

This isn't always true. Yes, it pays to disrupt large markets with new innovations, but many innovators create entirely new markets that never existed before. Think of Nest with smart homes, Dropbox with cloud storage, and Snapchat with messaging. Innovation isn't always about disrupting the existing markets: Innovators can create new ones.

POWER OF THE WAVES

The beauty of waves is that they can totally reshape the business landscape. Every time a new wave rolls past it undermines everything in its path, which creates opportunity. Let's take technology waves. When the mobile wave came, it rewrote the rules for practically every industry on the planet. We are still seeing the repercussions of this wave, as one business after another moves to mobile or is left behind to die. Big data—the ability to access massive amounts of data and analyze it to gain insights into behaviors and processes—is doing the same. So is artificial intelligence. With each of these waves, thousands of big corporations are rendered obsolete, and most of them don't even realize it until it's too late. They continue to do business thinking nothing has changed. But all it takes is for one startup to figure out how to use technology to tilt the playing field in their favor, and the incumbents are no longer competitive.

My advice to every innovator out there is to focus on these waves, whether they are technological, social, political, or economic. They are the determining factor. But don't get too attached to any single wave. The wave itself doesn't matter. If you miss it, there will always be another wave coming. Far better to focus on the next wave than chase one that's already passed.

I see this time and again with struggling startups. Many are just a bit too late, and no matter how hard they try, they can't catch up. They just wear themselves out trying. It doesn't matter how much time and money you've invested in your project. That won't save you if you're heading in the wrong direction. Instead, turn around, look out on the horizon, and focus on the incoming waves. That's where opportunity lies. That's what can take your business to the next level. Looking back to shore at the older waves is pointless. It doesn't matter how big they are. They've passed. Innovation lies in the future.

Chapter 5

Copying vs. Creating

Originality is nothing but judicious imitation.
—Voltaire, philosopher and writer

Silicon Valley types hate to admit it, but copying is a brilliant business strategy. If you look at many of the most successful startups, they were essentially copying their predecessors and then innovating on top. Facebook was copied from Friendster and MySpace, the two pioneering social networks, then innovated on the user experience. LinkedIn copied from Facebook but adapted it to business users. Uber copied Lyft, which had figured out that having nonprofessional drivers was key, then moved faster and smarter. Steve Jobs built the Mac by borrowing from Xerox PARC, and Bill Gates copied Steve Jobs to develop Windows, then leveraged Microsoft's superior market position with business customers.

Why invent something new and risky when you can copy something you know will work? Inventing and innovating is incredibly hard and prone to failure. The only reason anyone in Silicon Valley attempts to innovate is because they know that copying alone isn't enough. If everyone in Silicon Valley could simply copy the best ideas from someone else and make a fortune, they would. It would be crazy not to.

China, known for copying everything it can from Silicon Valley, has been able to exploit this strategy because of its insular market combined with the lag time between Silicon Valley innovations and Chinese adoption. This gap created an opportunity for entrepreneurs, and that opportunity led to enormous value creation. Just look at the Chinese giants: Baidu, Alibaba, and Tencent. They were all born from copying but have become much more. Baidu is a search engine that originally imitated Google; Alibaba is an e-commerce platform that combined elements from Amazon, eBay, and PayPal; and Tencent created WeChat, the dominant Chinese messaging app, which took its inspiration from ICQ and Kakao Talk. The irony now is that all three companies are innovating beyond expectations, and their products are now blazing new ground, which others are copying. Facebook now routinely copies WeChat. The point being: Copy when you can, and innovate when you can't.

Unfortunately, when you're the world's leader, like Silicon Valley, there's often no one to copy, so you are forced to innovate. A "me too" product in Silicon Valley goes nowhere. It's DOA: dead on arrival. The competition is so fierce and markets move so fast that it's nearly impossible to catch up, unless you have something of unique value to offer. This is why entrepreneurs in Silicon Valley work so hard to innovate. It's not that they like to innovate. Innovation is difficult, costly, brutal, and painful. But there is no other path to success in the Valley. It's either innovate or stay a small fry.

There are thousands of copycats in Silicon Valley, but few of them amount to anything. Just adding an extra feature or a function to a product doesn't make it innovative. True innovators need to identify a customer need and meet that need in a way that no competitor can match. Only by identifying new opportunities and understanding the underlying value proposition can someone get ahead in a highly competitive environment.

The Chinese are experiencing this now. Copying was golden a few years back, but increasingly it has become difficult to copy and succeed— even in China's insular market. The problem is that there are so many Chinese startups looking for the latest ideas to surface in Silicon Valley that even if you copy quickly, you'll wind up competing against dozens of other Chinese copycats. It's not like the days when Jack Ma and Pony Ma could take an idea from abroad, move quickly, and dominate the market without intense local competition. The odds of this strategy working today are becoming slimmer every month.

This is good news for China. I hear politicians and businesspeople lament all the time about how Chinese startups aren't innovative enough. Some groups are trying to figure out complex solutions to help their entrepreneurs come up with more inventive and original ideas. Most of these efforts aren't necessary, because the problem will solve itself. Chinese will begin to innovate because they have to. As the old saying goes: Necessity is the mother of invention. The Chinese will stop copying as soon as it no longer works. That's what we did in Silicon Valley, that's what the Japanese did, and that's what the Koreans did. As an economy matures and businesses want to move up the value chain, they will have to innovate to compete.

MYTH: BUILD A BETTER MOUSETRAP

Building a great product does not mean customers will come flocking to your door. The product itself is only one part of a complex equation that includes marketing, timing, public perception, competition, distribution, and more. Without the other pieces in place, the innovation will often go unrecognized. Think of the hundreds of thousands of apps in the App Store that hardly anyone knows exist. I'm certain some of them are better mousetraps.

Let me be clear. All innovations start off as copies of something that preceded them. That's how we learn. The difference is that great entrepreneurs not only copy, they make the copy their own. It's like Picasso said, "Good artists copy, great artists steal." Every genius in Silicon Valley, from William Shockley to Mark Zuckerberg to Elon Musk, stole to get started. William Shockley tried to get Bell Labs to patent the transistor exclusively under his own name, ignoring the contributions of his colleagues

John Bardeen and Walter Brattain, but failed. Mark Zuckerberg took from Friendster, MySpace, HarvardConnection.com, Hot or Not, and Harvard's online facebooks but made it his own. Elon Musk is often given most of the credit for starting Tesla, but it was actually Martin Eberhard and Marc Tarpenning who cofounded the company, with Eberhard acting as CEO. Musk joined later as an investor, board member, and cofounder. The point isn't to diminish Shockley's contribution to the transistor, Zuckerberg's development of the social network, or Musk's transformation of Tesla. It's to make clear that brilliant minds tend to latch on to something, then innovate on top, often reaching the point where they're given the lion's share of the credit. So copy and make it your own!

Section Two

THE ENTREPRENEURIAL
APPROACH

Chapter 6

Think Small

Great things are done by a series of small things brought together.
—attributed to Vincent
Van Gogh, painter

Many people believe that to innovate, you need to think big. If you're the head of a large corporation, you must implement a massive innovation program that encompasses your entire organization. Everyone must be on board. Money should be no object because this is the future of your business, and the next billion-dollar revenue stream will come from innovating.

Nothing could be further from the truth. To truly innovate, you can't think big. You need to *think small*. Most big innovation projects fail. They fail precisely because they require big budgets, big teams, and big results. When innovating, it's often the smallest ideas that have the power to change an industry. Think of the Post-it note, Velcro, or disposable razors. These are all simple ideas that revolutionized their industries.

In hindsight, sticky paper seems like something so basic anyone could have thought of it. But no one did. In fact, the whole thing came about because of a mistake. A scientist at 3M, Dr. Spencer Silver, was attempting to develop a superstrong adhesive. However, he accidentally came up with a "low-tack," reusable, pressure-sensitive adhesive. For the next five years, Dr. Silver tried to get 3M to make a product using his invention. But no one cared until a colleague, who had attended one of his seminars, came up with the idea of using this new adhesive to anchor his bookmark in his hymnbook. This series of little insights is what led to Post-it notes.

If you look at the process by which most great innovations happen, the path isn't that different. Great ideas typically don't come from big visions but from small experiments and chance discoveries. The big visions come later, when the story of their discovery is rewritten in the media and the minds of the public.

The same holds true for tech startups. Let's take an example with which we're all familiar. YouTube didn't start out with a grand vision of building a new global broadcast network with millions of videos, creators, and viewers. YouTube was originally something entirely different. It began life as a video dating site called Tune In Hook Up, a copy of Hot or Not with video. When that experiment failed to gain traction, the founders began casting about for other ideas.

The spark didn't come from a world-changing vision but from two small frustrations. First was when Jawed Karim, a cofounder, became irritated that he couldn't find video of Janet Jackson's "wardrobe malfunction" online. The second was when Chad Hurley and Steve Chen, the other cofounders, got annoyed at not being able to share videos of their dinner party with friends due to the limitations of e-mail attachments.

The combination of these two small frustrations gave birth to YouTube as we know it. The key insight was that people needed a simple way to share videos online. Once they built a simple mechanism for sharing videos, everything else followed. Within a short time, several videos went viral and YouTube's traffic exploded, making it the destination for video content.

The emergence of YouTube as the world's number one online broadcast network wasn't the result of a grand vision or plan but a small innovation that produced an enormous effect. I would even go so far as to argue that if the founders had set out to build a broadcast network, they would have never succeeded in creating YouTube. Just look at the history of startups, like Digital Entertainment Network, which wanted to bring TV-style programming to the Internet in the dot-com days. They tried the big-vision approach and failed. It was too expensive to produce the content, and the ad model wasn't there.

It's a common mistake many startups make. For example, I was working with a company from Taiwan that wanted to create a universal app that would unlock any smart device, from smart bicycle locks to automobiles, doors, and filing cabinets. They knew they couldn't charge for this, so they were preparing to give it away for free and build a social network within their app. They wanted to partner with everyone from automobile to IoT manufacturers. To complicate matters, the devices required specific hardware to work, which everyone would have to adopt. I could see there was no way they were going to get something this big and complex off the ground with their approach.

I told them rather bluntly, "You have to think small. Pick one customer that highly values your solution and focus on that." I suggested they target companies that valued security and sell them a security solution that would allow them to control access throughout their organization to all critical access points, including doors, desks, filing cabinets, and storerooms, with a single smartphone app. They could charge for the service based on the number of smart locks deployed and provide added-value services. This was far simpler than their original plan, had a single customer type, and clear revenue model. It's still too early to tell if their pivot will succeed, but I'm keeping my fingers crossed.

Whether you have a three-person startup or a three-hundred-thousand-person multinational corporation, the process for innovation is similar. You need to create an environment and structure where teams can think small.

Chapter 7

Small Teams

A good, quick, small team can beat a big, slow team any time.
—attributed to Paul Bryant,
American football coach

As I mentioned, I'm writing this book for everyone from startup founders to managers in large corporations who want to innovate. With this in mind, it's important to talk about team size. Most startups begin with small teams, because that's all they can afford. It's usually just the founders and a few part-timers. Corporations, on the other hand, have the luxury of assembling large innovation teams from the get-go. That is a big mistake, and I'll explain why.

From my experience both running Founders Space and consulting for global corporations, I've found that the ideal team ranges in size from two to eight people. This is because smaller groups collaborate, communicate, and cooperate better and more intimately. They can bond in a way that's impossible for larger groups. With a small team, everyone knows everyone, understands each other's strengths and weaknesses, and can form deeper relationships. This all leads to better teamwork and more intense collaboration.

Inversely, the larger the group, the more careful and guarded people tend to become. I even find myself editing what I say in front of larger groups. I don't want to make a mistake and appear stupid. We've all been in these situations where communication grows more formalized, with fixed schedules, structured meetings, a web of complex interpersonal relationships, and roles for each member. The entire process changes from individual to group dynamics.

Our desire to fit into social groups is ingrained in who we are and how we act. It's impossible for most people to behave the same in a large group as they would in a small one. As the group size changes, members' psychology adapts to the new structure. Big groups tend toward hierarchical structures, which are ideal for organizing and directing larger numbers of people, but they're not the best for unleashing creativity and free thinking that might upset the order of things.

The smaller the group, the more egalitarian the structure. With intimate teams, people are naturally more inclined to act as partners, rather than leader and followers. This dynamic is essential for innovation. To be creative, people need to collaborate deeply and share ideas openly. With smaller groups, this becomes easier for everyone—especially those who are shy, introverted, or cautious.

Another reason small teams work better is that when a team has more than ten people, things slow down. Larger groups simply can't move as fast, especially when testing new ideas. Innovation requires rapid iteration, where the team needs to reach decisions quickly without continually excluding or alienating a portion of its members. From my experience, the key to successful teams is a structure whereby all team members can fully contribute to the process. However, the larger the team the more difficult it is to give everyone a voice. Just try getting a dozen people in a room to agree on anything. It can be painful.

Voting on the best ideas is one way to give everyone a voice, but it doesn't necessarily allow or encourage others to contribute fully. Voting often brings out divisions inside the group, with certain parties being consistently voted down. The result tends to be factionalism, and the last thing you want is an innovation team splintering into factions, where politics take over the process. Another potential downside to voting is that some members may go along with the majority decisions, even when they don't agree, simply because they want to avoid alienating others.

An alternative for large teams is a hierarchical structure with the leaders choosing the best ideas. But unless the team leader is skilled at giving everyone a voice, this won't promote true collaboration where everyone on the team feels equally empowered to contribute their ideas and share in the decision-making process. What you typically wind up with is a small number of people actively innovating, while the rest of the group follows. The larger the group, the smaller the percentage of people involved in the innovation process, which defeats the whole purpose of forming innovation teams.

No matter what the structure, the ideal innovation team should be an intimate group where everyone actively contributes to the process and participates in the decision-making. Jeff Bezos, one of my heroes, summed it up with his two-pizza rule: If a team can't be fed with two pizzas, it's too big. I'm a big eater. I can eat half a pizza by myself, so four people like me is all you want!

TEAM'S DNA

What's the recipe for the perfect innovation team? At Founders Space we have a simple formula:

- **The Hustler**—We like to see that at least one person on the team has a thorough understanding of the business, the customers, and the market. In most startups, this person is called the CEO. This person is also the one who typically sells the vision and the product to the world. So this person should be a great leader and communicator.
- **The Hacker**—Someone who knows the latest technology inside and out and can use this to transform the business. Having a techie on the team from the start is essential. Innovation usually rides a wave of new technologies that disrupt both business and society. The innovation team needs someone who understands how these technologies can be used to reshape and disrupt the world. This technical wizard must also be willing to roll up her sleeves and do the grunt work, like coding and testing. On a small team, there's no room for delegators. The team needs people willing

to do the actual work. In a typical startup, this person would be the lead developer and CTO.

■ **The Hipster**—This is the creative lead. The importance of design thinking in successful startups can't be overestimated. Design is often at the heart of innovation. Small changes in design can have huge impacts. Any good innovation team needs a designer on board from the beginning. YouTube, Slideshare, Etsy, Flickr, Gowalla, Pinterest, Jawbone, Airbnb, Flipboard, Android, and Square all had designers as cofounders. Dave McClure, cofounder of accelerator 500 Startups, is fond of saying every team needs a hustler, hacker, and hipster. I like to add a fourth one.

■ **The Hotshot**—It helps to have a domain expert on the team, especially if you're attempting something highly technical. This is someone who understands, at the deepest level, the specific problem the team is trying to solve. This is typically a researcher with a PhD or someone with years of experience in the field. Having someone on board with an in-depth knowledge, beyond your typical manager, can make all the difference when it comes to realizing the critical breakthrough. Elon Musk's SpaceX could have never gotten his satellites into orbit without hiring domain experts. The same is true for Craig Venter's mission to build the world's largest database of whole genome, phenotype, and clinical data.

We've found that startups with these four skill sets have a much higher success rate. This doesn't mean every innovation team must have four people. Some of the best startups have only two founders, but often each founder fills more than one role. Look at Mark Zuckerberg. He was a strong coder, completely understood his business, and was a domain expert. He also knew how to design a product. But Mark didn't do it alone. He put together a team, and the team made Facebook such an outstanding success.

When a startup comes into Founders Space missing a key team member, the first thing I do is tell them, "Your number one job right now is to fill this position. Nothing else will matter as much to your startup's success as getting the right people on board from the start!" I then go on to share the story of when I was raising capital for one of my startups called

RocketOn, a virtual world spread across the entire Internet. You could create an avatar and walk on top of any website: Google, Amazon, CNN, Adult Swim—you name it. You could chat with friends, play games, listen to music, and talk about the news on practically every web page in the world. After three months of pitching, I had no luck closing a round. I couldn't understand why I wasn't getting funded with such a cool idea. Then I suddenly realized I was missing a key member of the team: my head of product. That was why all the VCs were passing. They saw the gap, but none of them told me.

I made filling the position my priority. Fortunately, my friend had just left his job and was the perfect fit. A day after bringing him on board, we went out to pitch together. The presentation was identical to all my previous pitches. The only difference was that I had my new cofounder sitting beside me. After hearing my pitch, the first venture firm said they wanted to bring us back for a partner meeting. This was a good sign. The second firm we pitched that day agreed to fund us then and there. That's the power of having the right team.

CORPORATE INNOVATION TEAMS

If you're inside a larger organization, in addition to the Hustler, Hacker, Hipster, and Hotshot, you'll need a few other talents to get the job done.

- **The Politician**—This is the main one you need, someone who can champion the project within the larger organization, secure resources, and coordinate efforts across departments. Without a politician on board, most projects will never see the light of day.
- **The Organizer**—In addition to drumming up and maintaining support for the innovation effort, you'll need someone to manage the project and day-to-day overhead that any larger organization requires of its staff.

As for the rest of the team, don't hire based on rank, title, or years of experience. Hire based on expertise, drive, and curiosity. Those will count for much more at the end of the day. You need hungry, ambitious, open-minded team members who are willing to challenge company orthodoxies and aren't afraid to push the boundaries and fail along the way.

SOLO INNOVATORS

We've found that startups with a single founder don't do nearly as well as startups founded by teams. Why is this? The reason is multifaceted. To begin with, you can never build a large business alone. What is the last billion-dollar business you saw with a single employee? The key to taking on any great endeavor is bringing on board the talent necessary to achieve the goal. Most successful CEOs are exceptionally good at recognizing and attracting talent.

In addition, people tend to be more creative when they can bounce their ideas off peers, as well as when their peers question their assumptions. Socrates is a wonderful example of this. He made his fellow Athenians question everything they did. No question was too sacred to ask. As I've personally learned, the Socratic method of questioning why things are the way they are is an essential part of the innovation process. At Founders Space, I often find myself playing Socrates to my startups, asking them endless questions to get at the truth. By creating teams with diverse members who are free to challenge one another and the status quo, startups can engineer a team dynamic that is much more conducive to innovation. When there's a single founder, this is harder to do.

Does this mean that a single-member innovation team won't work? Absolutely not. With the right individual, it may wind up producing strong results. However, most of the time, well-constructed teams will out-perform any single individual. As any chemist knows, different combinations of substances will yield drastically different results. Having a diverse team creates the opportunity for unique reactions to take place. What you want is the fusion of each individual's ideas, background, and knowledge creating a spark that none of them would have generated independently.

Another benefit of having more than one person is that a team can get more done. Coming up with a new idea is just the first step. The hard part is proving that the concept actually yields the desired results. A team can work together to speed up the testing and validation process. There's also the social aspect of a team. It's easy for a solo founder to get stuck at a certain point, become discouraged, and simply walk away at the first onerous roadblock, while startups with multiple founders feel obligated to keep going. I see this all the time at Founders Space. Even when it seems impossible, a team tends to fight on because no one wants to let their mates down.

This spirit is exemplified by Hashplay, a startup at Founders Space, which was dead set on creating a virtual reality gaming network similar to Twitch. Twitch, which sold to Amazon for $970 million, enables players to easily share gaming videos online. Why not do the same thing for VR? I have to admit that I was skeptical. Building a virtual reality version of Twitch is incredibly hard. It's not like simply recording a video and sharing it. VR is an immersive experience with numerous technical challenges and hardware requirements. However, I saw an exceptionally strong team. So I chose to bet on the team, not their product.

Any solo founder or weaker team would have crashed and burned, but these guys were so amazing that they just kept going. They pivoted and experimented until they found a model that worked for them. Despite all the difficulties, they are still pushing forward. They're all in it together. It's the power of teams.

Groups also tend to be more productive than solo founders for the simple reason that if one member is working hard, the other members feel like they can't slack off. If the innovation team is comprised of just a single person, there isn't the peer pressure that is often needed to spur someone to do his or her best. Having a team in place from the beginning sets the right tone. It forces everyone to think of the endeavor as a group effort, rather than a personal project. This is key, because the innovation team and its culture will often form the nucleus of the new business, and that culture needs to be one of inclusion and cooperation.

In the context of a larger organization, a solo innovator can be much harder to integrate back into the company than a well-functioning team. For example, an individual who comes up with a breakthrough idea may think, "I did this all myself. Why should I share it with the company? They didn't do anything!"

If you look at Silicon Valley's history, small teams have led the technology revolution that we're experiencing right now: Intel, Hewlett Packard, Apple, Google, Amazon, Stripe, Zenefits, Airbnb—and the list goes on. Larger, established companies have also benefited from fostering small teams inside their organizations. IBM reinvented itself by enabling a small team within their organization to develop the AS/400. Lockheed Martin's famous Skunk Works empowered small, autonomous teams to develop some of the most innovative aircraft in history, including the SR71. Steve Jobs is famous for saying, "The Macintosh team was what is commonly known as intrapreneurship . . . a group of people going, in essence, back to the garage, but in a large company."

For all these reasons, when forming an innovation team inside a larger organization, I prefer teams of two to eight people. I've found this is the ideal number. That said, you can experiment with solo innovators and teams of ten or more people and see how it works. There will always be exceptions to the rule. A lot depends on your industry, the size of the project, the technical complexity, and the personalities of the people involved. The key is to be flexible. If someone insists on working alone, let them have a shot at it. If another group says it needs to have a dozen team members, let them try and carefully measure the results. If the teams are productive, let them continue. If not, dissolve them and start over.

Chapter 8
Small Budgets

We embrace the shoestring budget. We like being limited by the constraints. It inspires creativity.

—Charles Lincoln "Link" Neal III, cocreator of
Good Mythical Morning

Why is it easier to innovate on a small budget? You'd think that a larger budget means more resources, more people, faster progress, and better results. But this isn't necessarily true. In fact, chances are if an innovation team requests a large budget, they will probably need to submit a proposal to justify the spending. If the company approves this proposal, the innovation team will feel compelled to execute on the plan and deliver results, instead of being free to go down new paths that may open up during the process.

The narrowing of focus too early can be detrimental. Innovation is about exploration, but as soon as you submit a detailed proposal, you're committing to a plan, when in reality, you don't know enough to make the right plan, let alone stick to it. Instead of opening up new possibilities, you wind up closing them off.

Another downside is that big budgets tend to mean bigger teams. Team leaders need to begin setting goals, creating schedules, assigning tasks, and tracking progress. This compels the team to pin things down instead of leaving options open. And it is exactly the opposite of what an innovation team needs to do in the early stages, where the focus should be on discovery and experimentation.

Locking down ideas and building a plan to implement a project is the antithesis of the innovation process, which is all about keeping an open mind, testing out new possibilities, hitting dead ends, learning from mistakes, and wandering off into the woods to see what you can find. As soon as your innovation team is saddled with employees who need direction and support, the leaders become managers. The last thing you want is for your key innovators to turn into project managers. Those are two entirely different roles.

The larger the team grows, the more reluctant both managers and employees become about switching directions, even when data shows they are headed down the wrong path. Pivoting rapidly is the heart of innovation. That's how you learn and make difficult breakthroughs. The bigger the budget, the bigger the commitment, and the harder pivoting becomes.

Just look at your typical startup. Most of its biggest innovations happen when the company has no funding at all. Once the money starts pouring into startups, they usually stop innovating and focus on scaling their business. This works if the startup has figured out a viable business model. But if the business model is still embryonic, it can prevent it from reaching maturity.

Let's look at a few examples. Color was a startup that raised $41 million for a new photo-sharing app based around events. The problem was that Color didn't actually have an innovation that worked—just a grand vision. They raised the money too soon. Most startups would be thrilled to have $41 million in the bank, but the money actually hurt Color. They weren't free to experiment. With $41 million in cash, the venture capitalists expected Color to execute on their vision—not just sit on the money. This was the beginning of the end. After a string of failed pivots, Color wound up selling its assets to Apple in a fire sale.

We see this pattern over and over again. Startups raise too much money too soon and fail spectacularly. Fab is another example. This online retail startup burned through $200 million without ever finding a sustainable business model. I'd argue that if they had less money, they might have actually found a business model that worked. But their money cloaked the fact that they were failing. They could afford to spend enormous amounts on customer acquisition, without facing the reality that customers weren't sticking around.

"We spent $200M in the past two years. $200M!" said Jason Goldberg, the CEO of Fab, in a now famous letter. "And we have not proven that we know precisely what our customers want to buy."

Goldberg isn't the only one. It's common for startups to fool themselves and their investors by spending money to cover up harsh realities. They think they're buying themselves time for things to work out, but in reality, they're in denial. The money just allows them to avoid addressing the problem. Heck, it's easy to do when you raise capital ahead of finding a true product-market fit.

I'm working with a startup right now that raised millions from investors to build a next-generation Internet of Things device. Because they have so much money, they've hired up a large team and been able to ignore fundamental problems in their business, such as figuring out who their customer is and exactly what they want. I've told them to their face that they need to stop doing R & D and start engaging potential customers. But the more money they raise, the easier it is for them to ignore the problem. They feel the investment dollars are a validation that having the best technology is all that matters.

MYTH: BIG LAUNCHES HELP

We all remember the much hyped launches of Google+, Google Glass, and Google Wave. Even with the power of Google behind them, they flopped. These were innovative products, but sometimes it's better to play down the hype and focus on the customer. Where innovation is concerned, big launches lead to big expectations and often bigger disappointments.

I can tell you that it's really hard to convince startup founders who just raised a sizable round that their idea isn't going anywhere. Flush with cash, entrepreneurs, who tend to be naturally optimistic, don't want to hear that they're on the wrong track. They raised this money based on their plan, and they don't see why they need to change plans now that the money is in the bank.

This isn't entirely the entrepreneur's fault. Part of the blame lies with investors, many of whom have been throwing money at startups without demanding any proof of concept. They go on faith rather than facts. It's lazy investing, and it hurts the entrepreneurs as much as it does the investors. Sadly, it's often easier to raise money on a vision pitch than a validated business model. That's because the majority of business models never appear as promising as when they are just ideas.

Webvan epitomized this phenomenon. Their vision was to create the world's first online supermarket that would deliver fresh produce and groceries to your home. This was back in the dot-com days, 1995 to 2001. They had the right idea, but the devil is always in the details. After burning through their cash, they were forced to give up the dream. Ironically, over a decade later, this same dream lives on in a crop of new startups, as well as in established players like Amazon.

Other notable failures include 38 Studios, the defunct video game company that lost $75 million; Boo.com, the online retailer that raised $135 million and sold for $372,500; and Quirky, a platform for inventors that raised $180 million but tragically had a flawed business model. The list goes on and on.

Nils Bunger, who founded the startup Pano Logic, sums it up nicely: "Too much capital is toxic. Too much capital early in a company's life can hamstring a company and its options. When you raise a lot of capital, you're effectively saying you've found your business model, and it's time to scale it. But if you do that before you've truly figured it out, you'll run into a lot of problems because your board expects you to scale the business while you're still working out what your business actually is."

Pano Logic, which developed virtual desktop infrastructure, wound up going bankrupt despite being well funded and positioned. "When you have too much money, there's intense pressure to spend it," Bunger elaborates, "and to spend it prematurely or in ways that are overly influenced by outside forces."

Conversely, having a limited budget can actually encourage innovative thinking. The financial constraints and lack of resources help to inspire entrepreneurs, especially ambitious ones, to think in radical new ways. They tend to move quickly and try things others might overlook or dismiss as impossible. They can't think conventionally, because they don't have the time or resources to execute on conventional plans.

This is similar to the feeling you get when you're trying to fix something around the home quickly, but you don't have the right parts and can't afford to spend the time to go to the hardware store. With enough thought, you can usually come up with a new way to fix it. The constraints actually force you to be creative.

The same is true with startups. Because of their lack of money, they often can't afford to invent new technologies, so they opt to use existing technologies and tools in new ways. Out of this process comes innovation. They wind up combining existing technologies and services to create new ones that can be brought to market faster and cheaper than anything they could develop independently.

The advantages you gain from using off-the-shelf technologies are numerous:

- You don't have to spend time doing research and development.
- Most of the glitches have been identified.
- You don't have to worry about manufacturing.
- They tend to be far cheaper than if you developed them yourself.
- They usually have extensive documentation both online and off.
- If you get stuck, you can find others who can help you solve problems.
- You can often pay for support from professionals.
- You can avoid wasting precious time reinventing the wheel.

Another key advantage is that the existing technologies are more likely to spread faster and further than new ones. This is because they are well tested and familiar to users, allowing people to easily adopt them. Imagine if Uber had invented its own ride-hailing device instead of using the smartphone. It would never have been as successful. There's a huge advantage in using technologies that are already proven and in the marketplace.

Here's an example of constrained resources inspiring innovation. In Mexico, public health-care providers are in short supply and difficult for people to access, so most Mexicans pay for private health care out of their own pockets. The problem is that private health care is expensive. That was what inspired Pedro Yrigoyen, who was running call centers in Mexico City, to think of ideas on how to lower costs.

Pedro's concept was to take an existing call center and staff it with medically trained people, who were supported by the same diagnostic computer systems used by many of the best hospitals in the world. He didn't invent any of this. Instead, he took existing services and put them together in a new way.

Pedro decided to charge only $5 a month for anyone to access his medical call centers whenever they need it. This small innovation revolutionized health care in Mexico. Today, 62 percent of medical issues are resolved on the phone. If it's a difficult issue, the team connects patients with medical specialists. This not only helps the patient but earns a referral fee, a portion of which is passed on to the patient in the form of a discount. It's a win-win for the patients and Pedro's company, Medicall Home.

The health-care industry could have done this long ago, but it took an outsider with a unique background and limited resources to come up with the solution. This example is emblematic of why limited budgets often produce better results. Pedro didn't have an R & D budget or any real experience in the health-care business. This forced him to think creatively and offer value to health-care customers in an entirely new way.

When it comes to some of the largest corporations in the world, spending more on R & D doesn't necessarily translate into innovation. "Innovation has nothing to do with how many R & D dollars you have," said Steve Jobs. "When Apple came up with the Mac, IBM was spending at least one hundred times more on R & D. It's not about money. It's about the people you have, how you're led, and how much you get it." This sentiment is backed up by data from Booz & Company. It identified one thousand companies with the largest research-and-development budgets and invited six hundred executives from those companies to rate which ones they thought were the most innovative. Apple was ranked as most innovative. However, their R & D budget was seventieth. Google came in second, but their R & D budget wasn't even in the top twenty.

Back in 2004 and 2007, Nokia's total R & D budget was over $20 billion, while Apple's was $2.5 billion. During this same time period, Apple developed and launched the iPhone, and Nokia set the stage for their precipitous decline. The lesson here is that having a large budget relative to your competitors doesn't always help innovation, and in some cases it may hurt. So whether you work in a multinational corporation or a tiny startup, remember this: Having a limited budget can counter the "not invented here" syndrome and inspire your team to bring its products to market faster, explore new ideas, and think more creatively.

Chapter 9

Small Time

If you spend too much time thinking about a thing, you'll never get it done.

—Bruce Lee, martial
artist and actor

Parkinson's law (not the disease) states that "work expands so as to fill the time available for its completion." If you give someone six months to create a business plan, they'll take six months. If you give them six days, they'll find a way to get it done in six days.

The Koreans are all too familiar with Parkinson's law. They require their employees to consistently work overtime as a test of loyalty and dedication. Koreans are fond of saying they work harder and longer than anyone else in Asia. So why wasn't Korea near the very top in productivity for all OECD nations? The answer is simple. Koreans take longer to do the same job. If they know they have to stay at the office until 10:00 p.m., why get the work done by 5:00 p.m.?

Likewise, if your startup teams think they have three months to build a prototype, why get it done in three weeks? If you're going to have innovation teams, you need to create a sense of urgency. There is almost a 100 percent chance that a competitor somewhere in the world is working on the same project at the same time. In today's world, if your team moves slowly, they'll lose the market.

This is part of the reason why, at Founders Space, we prefer to run short, intensive incubator programs. Many of our competitors run programs that can last up to six or more months. I'm sorry, but that's just too long. There's little point in dragging out the process. We take the opposite approach. We often condense our programs down to a month or less, where we flood the startups with ideas, education, mentoring, and opportunities. Founders Space is an "accelerated" accelerator, where every day from morning until evening, the startups are being given a crash course in some vital topic, hands-on workshops, and plenty of feedback.

By limiting the time, we can up the intensity and provide an experience more akin to a prolonged hack-a-thon than a traditional three- or four-month incubator. Our two-week programs are the most popular right now, with overseas startups coming to Silicon Valley because they want to get up and running right away. Many of them don't want to wait months to pitch investors at Demo Day, which typically comes at the end of the program. Their time in the Valley is limited, and they need to figure it out fast.

Steve Jobs was famous for creating a sense of urgency. He wielded his "reality distortion field," where he'd give his teams a seemingly impossible task and a ridiculous deadline, and then convince them it could and must be done. Miraculously, they'd find a way to meet his outsized expectations.

Most successful startups practice some form of reality distortion. It's the only way to compete when you have a tiny team with virtually no budget and you're up against a world full of competitors, including titans like Google, Facebook, and Amazon with massive resources at their disposal. The value of deadlines cannot be underestimated.

A perfect example of this is hack-a-thons, where groups of entrepreneurs, coders, and designers are typically given twenty-four to forty-eight hours to come up with a new product or service. After staying up one or two nights in a row, brainstorming, designing, coding, and recoding their projects, the results can be impressive. For example, mobile marketplace app Carousell and taxi app EasyTaxi are a few of the many success stories. Other hack-a-thon wins include:

- GroupMe—acquired by Skype for $80 million
- Airpost.io—acquired by Box

- Appetas—acquired by Google
- SlickLogin—acquired by Google

INNOVATION SPRINTS

Short, intense sprints, similar to hack-a-thons, can provide a number of benefits:

- Creates a sense of urgency
- Gives the team a mission and a way to bond under pressure
- Work becomes more meaningful and important
- Able to focus on one activity to the exclusion of all else
- Heightened communication and collaboration
- Team members are challenged to do their very best
- Sense of accomplishment at achieving the goals

Shutterstock, a startup that is now a publicly traded company on the New York Stock Exchange, hosts an annual twenty-four-hour hack-a-thon to generate new ideas and stimulate collaboration between its employees. With over 50 million royalty-free stock photos, vector graphics, and illustrations, as well as videos and music, Shutterstock is a content giant. One of the best ideas to come out of its hack-a-thon was Spectrum, a tool that allows users to search all the photos by color.

Facebook also throws hack-a-thons. Out of one of its caffeine-fueled events emerged the Awesome button, which we now fondly call the Like button. The point is that when teams are forced into an adrenalized, hypercreative state in a compressed amount of time, their neurons start flashing and they can come up with ideas and innovations they might otherwise never have thought of. They can also come together as a team and work in ways they otherwise would not be able to do in a normal office environment.

Naturally, this pace can't be sustained, but if used effectively, these short bursts of innovation tied to stringent deadlines can produce superior results. The key is to structure the deadlines so teams can sprint, create, and then recover.

Here is my formula for *innovation sprints*, as I've dubbed them. First, break the process up into well-defined sprints. Each sprint should be focused on a distinct goal. For example, you may do an innovation sprint with the goal of identifying a customer need, validating a business model, or coming up with a prototype. Any single step in the startup process can be turned into a sprint. Here are a few examples of sprints:

- Brainstorm on possible areas of innovation.
- Come up with a new product idea.
- Develop a viable business model.
- Validate and size the market.
- Build a workable prototype.
- Get customer feedback.
- Prove a product-market fit.
- Design a marketing campaign.
- Line up business leads.
- Create a sales pitch.

Once you have a theme for your innovation sprint, you can assemble your innovation teams, set a hard deadline, and let them go at it. The deliverables at the end should be clearly articulated so that everyone knows exactly what's expected of them.

If you want to tap into the competitive nature of your teams, you can turn the innovation sprint into a contest. This is what most hack-a-thons do. They are essentially competitions, where the teams vie for prizes and recognition. You can do the same inside your company, and you can use these to motivate and stimulate your entire organization. The judges can come from all parts of your business, and they can play a role in providing feedback and ideas on top of what the innovation teams produce.

Most important, make it fun! The sprints should be a positive challenge, not a grueling exercise that your team members have to suffer through. At hack-a-thons, they provide food, drinks, music, and plenty of prizes. This celebratory environment both motivates and rewards the participants.

THE POWER OF DEADLINES

Any student knows that as an exam approaches, the pressure to stop procrastinating and get some studying done increases. The psychological tension resulting from the impending exam can be enough to stimulate students, who otherwise wouldn't study, to actually crack a book. The classic example is pulling an all-nighter to make up for weeks or months of slacking.

A much more extreme example of a deadline is Apollo 13's flight to the moon. During this mission, an explosion occurred that damaged the air filtration system. If NASA's ground team couldn't come up with a solution within a few hours, the astronauts would die. With this intense deadline, engineers and scientists desperately tried everything they could think of to repair the filtration system. Only at the last minute did they come up with a crude solution that the cognitively impaired astronauts could implement. It worked and saved the lives of the crew. This is just one of many examples where teams come up with remarkably creative solutions when necessary, even in seemingly impossible situations.

A more common example of how deadlines work in a corporate environment is IDEO, a design firm famous for their innovative designs, including the first Apple mouse. IDEO has earned their reputation by consistently coming up with award-winning designs for robots, medical equipment, consumer electronics, cars, toys, and more. They do this in three months or less and claim the time pressure plays an essential part in fueling their creative juices.

One thing to understand is that for deadlines to work, they must be considered meaningful. In other words, the time pressure needs to be a positive challenge for a good reason. It's imperative that everyone on the team understand why completing the project in a relatively short amount of time is crucial to the project's success. If they feel it's just being foisted upon them for no good reason, the deadline will backfire, becoming a pointless burden instead of a catalyst for creativity.

At IDEO, the deadlines are for clients, who typically aren't willing to wait a year, or even six months, for results. They need to launch their products, and they expect IDEO to deliver results quickly. This positive and necessary challenge helps to inspire the IDEO teams with a clear goal, which leads to increased focus and productivity.

THE PSYCHOLOGY OF DEADLINES

In contrast to hard deadlines, there are soft deadlines. Unfortunately, soft deadlines don't work so well. If you say a task needs to be done sometime within the next three months, most people will ignore the deadline. Unlike a hard deadline that is tied to a date and has repercussions if missed, soft deadlines tend not to have consequences and often aren't tied to any specific time frame, so they lack the power to motivate.

Even more surprising is how deadlines are categorized in the human mind. Yanping Tu and Dilip Soman of the University of Toronto's Rotman School of Management completed a study called "The Categorization of Time and Its Impact on Task Initiation." What they found is that if you set a deadline as Tuesday next week, many people won't bother preparing for the deadline until Monday of that week.

However, if you alter the visual calendar so that weekends are the same color as the weekdays, then it appears like the deadline is in the same contiguous time period. In this case, employees are more likely to start preparing for the deadline in the previous week. The human brain prioritizes by time periods, not the number of days. So grouping deadlines into a single time period inspires people to take action immediately.

"People don't think of future time periods as continuous passages of time," says Soman. "They don't think about the number of days left to make a decision or finish a task, but rather, they tend to categorize future time outcomes—thinking about the deadline coming up next week/

month/year, rather than this one." In other words, deadlines remain soft until the time period arrives. Then they become hard.

So if you want teams to start preparing for a deadline several weeks or months out, you need to either break it down into smaller weekly deadlines or categorize the entire period as a single contiguous block of time. Doing both will achieve the best results.

INNOVATION BREATHERS

Yes, deadlines are powerful, but they are a two-edged sword, and they can have negative consequences. Not all types of creativity flourish under extreme pressure, and not all people respond best to looming deadlines. You need to intermix the creative sprints with downtime, where teams can mull over problems and think deeply. It's a combination of fast and slow thinking that usually comes up with the best results.

Jennifer Mueller of Yale School of Management, along with William Simpson and Lee Fleming of Harvard Business School, completed a study of twenty-two project teams from seven companies. What they found is that creative thinking under extreme time pressure is often difficult, especially when that pressure is maintained over a long period of time.

The results can be:

- Feeling distracted and unable to concentrate
- Experiencing fragmented workdays
- Lack of meaning in their jobs
- Feeling like they are on a never-ending treadmill
- Too many last-minute changes in plans and schedules

My solution is to offer *innovation breathers*, where managers remove all time pressure. This allows their teams to focus on whatever they feel they need to prioritize, engage in exploration, and put together the pieces of the puzzle for the next breakthrough.

I recommend dividing the innovation process up into discrete units punctuated by key decisions. For the sprints, you should set hard deadlines and goals, like testing assumptions, building a prototype, and developing business models. Afterward, you can declare a breather, slow down, analyze what you've done, and give your team plenty of time to explore possibilities. Then you make a decision.

DECISION POINTS

Whenever you gather new data, it's time to step back and make a decision. The decision is usually binary: Either you continue down the current path or you admit it isn't working and go back to the drawing board. The goal is to get the entire process to move along at a rapid pace. Deadlines can be as short as one day, and breathers don't have to last much longer. There are no set rules or prescribed time periods. Your sprints and strolls can vary in length. It all depends on the problem you're trying to solve, your team's capabilities, the available resources, and the personalities involved.

Whatever you do, it pays to limit time, set deadlines, and have clear goals. When you reach a decision point, make sure your decisions are backed up by valid data—not opinions or assumptions. Accepting bad data and moving forward only obscures the truth and increases the likelihood of an even bigger problem down the road. If you manage the process correctly, the sprints and breathers should balance one another out, creating a dynamic working environment where your teams move fast but remain productive and don't become exhausted and stressed out over the long haul.

Chapter 10

Small Scope

I wouldn't touch "visionary" with a 10-foot pole.

—Robert Metcalfe,
coinventor of Ethernet

Many startup founders have a big vision, and along with a big vision typically comes a big project. It's easy for the scope to expand to monumental proportions. While this looks great in a PowerPoint, more startups fail from trying to do too much than too little. Entrepreneurs can latch on to a grand vision but never figure out how to actually make a product customers want. The sad thing is that many investors also fail to understand this. They think bigger is better. They buy into the hype that great startups must change the world from day one.

While many successful startups do wind up changing the world, it's often not the case early on. The startups that tend to succeed are usually tackling relatively small problems at first. It's only later that it becomes apparent how big the original concept can be.

Let's take Twitter. When it began, it wasn't a huge project with a grand vision. In fact, it was the opposite. It was a side project at Odeo, a podcasting company that was failing. The idea was to create the simplest possible microblogging tool. A good engineer could code the original Twitter in a week or so, and that's pretty much how it started. Its scope was limited, and its feature set was bare-bones. No one quite knew what would happen when they released it.

But lo and behold, users loved what they saw, and when it went viral at SXSW, the whole world heard and began jumping on the Twitter bandwagon. I'd argue that the success of Twitter was due primarily to how simple and limited it was. By reducing the scope, they created something that anyone could grasp and use within minutes. That, combined with its unique functionality, allowed it to capture the public's imagination.

Most of the great startups begin like this. Look at Dropbox. It wasn't the first startup to offer cloud storage, but they made it so simple and easy to use that it became an instant hit. The same is true with Google. When their engine launched, it was just a simple search box. There was no Adwords, Gmail, Google Analytics, Google Docs, Google Maps, and so on. Google just set out to build the best darn search engine. Yahoo was way ahead of them, but their engine had a cluttered interface with an entire search directory feature that later had to be scrapped. Google kept it simple and wound up beating out all the competitors.

The most famous example of a company starting small was Amazon. They didn't begin by saying they were going to sell everything on the planet. Instead, they picked one category and focused on it. This category was books, because Jeff Bezos thought it was the easiest thing to sell online. There were millions of books, more than could fit in any physical bookstore; books were nonperishables; books were easy to ship; and people love buying books. It was a smart choice, and it set Amazon on the course it travels today.

In the early stages, the startups that succeed tend to do one thing exceptionally well. Adding a zillion features doesn't help. In fact, it's often the kiss of death. Think of when you go out to eat. You say, "What do I want to eat? Pizza? Okay, what's the best pizza restaurant I know?" A restaurant that tries to make everyone happy by serving pizza, sushi, and Chinese food instantly becomes suspect. Most people choose products exactly like they choose restaurants. They have a need, and they go for the very best one.

When a startup enters Founders Space, I like to ask the question,

"What is the most important thing your product does for your customers?" That one thing is where the team should put 99 percent of its time and energy. All the other features can come later. If the core doesn't work, then nothing else will. It doesn't matter how many new features are layered on top, they won't change the core value of the product or service.

I always advise my founders to begin with the core functionality and build outward from there. Not vice versa. This gives them a clear starting point and goal. The team knows exactly what to focus on. If a feature isn't absolutely necessary for the core mechanic to work, I tell my startups to leave it for later. The art of designing an MVP (minimum viable product) is delivering only the core value and nothing else. To do this the startup must get the product into the hands of the customers as soon as possible, so it can assess their feedback and iterate, until it figures out what customers really want.

This sounds simple, but I see startup teams struggling with this concept all the time. They often launch an MVP only to find out that users aren't engaging. Mistakenly, they believe that if they just add one more feature, it will somehow magically take off. This almost never happens. Instead, the team winds up deluding itself, wasting time and money, and ultimately failing.

Even more common is when teams delay launching their product because they're afraid that if they don't add more features, it won't be a success. Launching a new product is scary. It's the moment of judgment. And no one wants to fail. So they put off the inevitable by continuing to build what they believe to be a better, more robust product, thinking this will increase their chances of success. By the time they launch, they often have a full-blown, feature-rich gizmo with every bell and whistle a user could desire. If it works, that's wonderful. But seldom do truly groundbreaking products come out perfect upon launch. There is usually a lot of iterating to be done. And the more innovative and experimental the product, the more iteration is required.

The real problem is that the more features you add, the more difficult it becomes to make changes. Take a software project. The more lines of code it has, the harder it becomes to make even simple changes. In addition, when it's time to test the product, it can be a cumbersome task.

To make matters worse, the more features you add, the more confusing the analytics data becomes. If your product contains only one feature, you can instantly determine how customers are responding. But if your product has dozens of features, the picture becomes muddy. Are customers engaging for this reason or that reason? What do they really like about this product? What features should we remove?

I've seen teams get completely lost in this mess. They forget what's really important to the customer. Each time they set out to make a change, they start second-guessing themselves. It's a nightmare you want to avoid. Nothing is so painful as removing a feature. Customers may complain, but this may not be valid feedback. They could just be complaining because something they were used to suddenly disappeared. It's far better to have never added the feature than to remove it.

If you look at Twitter, they didn't change much after their initial success. Instead, they focused all their energy on scaling the platform, which wasn't easy. They could barely keep their servers up. And scaling gets even more difficult the more features you add. So keeping it simple pays off when your product takes off.

ADVANTAGES OF KEEPING THE SCOPE SMALL

Easier to build

Easier to find flaws

Easier to fix and improve

Easier to launch in a short time

Easier to use

Easier to get clear feedback

Easier to scale

Easier to market

Innovating is hard, so keeping everything as simple as possible from the outset is essential. Here is the golden rule: Just figure out the one thing that your customers truly want. If that's not enough to build a business, scrap it and start over. Adding more features never changes the equation.

TINY CHANGES

So how do you know what customers truly want? What is that one thing that no one else has figured out? Sometimes the biggest innovations can come from relatively small changes. It's often not a major shift in thinking or a technological breakthrough that produces radical innovation but a tiny change in the way things are done.

Take Procter & Gamble. They've been making diapers since the 1950s under their Pampers brand. You'd think that after over half a century of improvements, they would have thought of everything. How complex can diapers be? But they are just as committed as ever to improving their products and innovating. One of the areas they're innovating on is the "emotional physics" of diapers. In other words, how can they make diapers easier and more emotionally satisfying to use?

After observing how babies squirm during diaper changes, the Pampers team came up with a new idea. They added a simple graphic that helps parents align the diaper correctly. This made an especially big difference for parents struggling to change diapers in the middle of the night. They also created softer-sounding Velcro-like tabs, so it wouldn't wake the baby up. These two changes don't sound like major breakthroughs, but in the world of diapers, they're a big deal.

Upstart competitors, like the Honest Company, have also been innovating on diapers. But their approach has been different. They knew they couldn't beat Pampers in a head-on battle. It was impossible for them to outinnovate Pampers on every aspect of making a great diaper. So they focused on one thing—the growing trend for ecologically friendly, nontoxic products. By using all natural materials, they appealed directly to parents worried about the environment and their children's exposure to harmful chemicals.

The Honest Company created diapers with plant-based inner and outer layers, superabsorbent pulp harvested from certified, sustainably managed forests, no chlorine processing, no harsh chemical bleaches, and naturally derived odor blockers from citrus and chlorophyll. They even touted a bio-based, gluten-free wheat/corn blend in a superabsorbent core. Sounds healthy enough to eat, doesn't it? This was their chief innovation, and it was a huge hit.

Honestly, most parents have no idea if the Honest Company diapers actually function better than Pampers, but they feel they are safer for their babies and better for the environment. By doing this one thing better than anyone else, the Honest Company was able to build their brand and out-flank entrenched competitors. After their diapers were a winner, the Honest Company went on to add more environmentally friendly products, like soaps, detergents, sunscreens, and sanitizers. The key to their success was keeping the scope small at first and expanding only once they understood exactly what their customers wanted.

MYTH: ONLY CREATIVE GENIUSES CAN INNOVATE

Being creative can certainly help you innovate, but you don't have to be a creative genius to recognize a good idea and implement it. There are plenty of examples of ordinary people who have come up with extraordinary discoveries and built thriving businesses on them. In fact, some of the best innovations aren't the ideas of the creator at all; they come from simply analyzing the data.

For example, let's take Instagram. Whether the founders are creative geniuses or not doesn't matter. What's important is that they engaged in a process of analyzing their user data to learn what was working and what wasn't. What they found was that users weren't engaging with most of the features in their cluttered app named

Burbn. It turned out that only two of the features, social sharing and photo filters, were popular. So they stripped out all the other features and launched a new app called Instagram, and it took off. Pinterest, Yelp, and Groupon all came about the same way.

More often than not, innovation is less about the process of coming up with a brilliant idea than it is about identifying correctly what customers need and want from your product or service.

Chapter 11

The Big Opportunity

If opportunity doesn't knock, build a door.

—Milton Berle, comedian

We've been preaching the virtues of small vision, small budget, small time, and small scope. Everything up until now has been about keeping it small, but if you're going to get your big idea off the ground, the opportunity must be *huge*. Think of opportunity as the force that lifts your ten-thousand-pound pachyderm of a world-changing vision into the air.

VENTURE INVESTING

The venture business is now the engine that drives global innovation. Venture firms put the capital into startups, which innovate on everything from gene therapy to virtual reality. Venture capitalists are today's kingmakers, and they often decide which innovations are given a chance to grow and which die on the vine.

For most innovations to get funded, there is one primary criteria: The market needs to be large enough to justify the risk. Even if a project begins with a small idea, by the time it's ready for venture funding, VCs must believe the startup is going to be the next Netflix or Box. No venture capitalist wants to invest in a small or medium-sized business. Their time is valuable, and they have a lot of money to put to work, so anything short of huge doesn't make financial sense.

Let me explain why this is. The venture business is built on exits, meaning companies that either get acquired or go public. Innovation, patents, and technology are all secondary. A breakthrough innovation that can't be monetized isn't an opportunity. It's a waste of the VC's time. Typically one or two investments out of a portfolio of ten or more will pay for an entire fund. These are called fund makers. The return on a startup that goes public is often more than all the other investments in the portfolio combined. This is why large investors go for the home runs over singles or doubles.

The other reason is that large funds have a lot of money to invest. They have investors of their own, who are demanding big returns. These LPs (limited partners) don't want the venture capitalists to sit on their money for ten years. That's not what they're paying hefty management fees for. They want all the money put to work as soon as possible—typically within three years.

What this means for a large fund of half a billion dollars or more is that the venture capitalist literally needs to shovel money into startups, and only companies with enormous growth potential, like Spotify and WeWork, have room to take on tens or hundreds of millions of dollars' worth of capital. This phenomenon has led to the explosion in unicorns—startups valued at over a billion dollars.

These days, even a $50 million acquisition is considered chump change for the larger venture firms. It's not the best use of their precious time. VCs sell themselves as instrumental in the success of their startups, and that means they have to take a board seat on nearly every major investment. Each partner in a firm can sit on only so many boards, so they need large exits to justify their time. Hence, every company in their portfolio must have a chance of being the next blockbuster. It doesn't make sense to allocate a board seat and their time to a startup that is limited to a small or medium-sized exit.

So how does this affect the startup ecosystem? It means that startups who cannot demonstrate rapid growth in a multi-billion-dollar market usually get passed over—even if their prospects for a 10× return are high.

Just do the math: If a venture firm can invest only $1 million over the life of a smaller startup, then even if it's guaranteed a 10× return with a $50 million acquisition, that's just $10 million. For a billion-dollar fund, $10 million is a rounding error.

That presents today's larger venture funds with a conundrum. They need to find potential unicorns, but finding a unicorn is not easy. Unicorns are supposed to be rare—that's how they got their name. So are we creating too many overvalued unicorns to satisfy investor appetites? Suffice to say that the Sand Hill Road venture community needs them to make their business model work. They've simply raised too much capital to have it any other way.

ANGEL AND SEED INVESTORS

On the other end of the spectrum are the angel and seed investors. They don't need a unicorn to make their model work. A smaller exit would be just fine, because they typically don't take board seats and can invest only relatively small amounts of money at an early stage, when valuations are lower. The problem is that by the time an angel-funded startup goes out for a follow-on round, it needs to demonstrate that the startup has potential for a big exit; otherwise, the later-stage venture funds will pass the startup over.

For this reason, smart angel and seed investors avoid startups that don't address a big opportunity. A startup in a small market with limited revenue potential will never be a candidate for an IPO. And the chance of an acquisition drops precipitously if the startup isn't in a sizable market with large growth potential. When startups get repeatedly passed over, it's not a good sign. Startups need money like humans need oxygen. They can go only so long without it. I've seen lots of angel and seed-funded startups die because the anticipated follow-on round fails to materialize.

The fact is that most sizable acquisitions are about buying a growing business in a large market. If a corporation purchases a startup only for its tech or team, not the market potential, the valuation is often less than what investors put into the company. In short, startups focused on small markets usually have small exits or none at all, and the risk-versus-reward ratio just doesn't make sense to most angel and seed investors.

CORPORATE INVESTING

Corporations are the other source of capital. Unlike angels and VCs, they typically don't care as much about the return. Most corporations are more focused on the strategic value. They tend to invest in startups that add significant value to the corporation's core business. That said, corporations are naturally conservative, and some invest only if a respected venture firm is leading the round. This means that the startup needs to meet not only the corporation's requirements but also the VC's, which tends to be a high hurdle that filters out smaller opportunities.

EGO INVESTING

The final reason most startups need big opportunities is pure ego. Whether it's a VC or an angel, investors are human beings, and who wouldn't like to brag about being an early investor in Twitter, Oculus, Facebook, or Fitbit?

Angels tend to be rich, and many of them aren't investing just for the return. They're investing for bragging rights, too. They want to show just how smart they are to all their peers. A startup that no one has heard of is not nearly as much fun as saying, "I was an early investor in Nest." VCs feel the same way, but they have an added incentive: They can use investments in winning companies to raise more money for their venture firms. By loading up their portfolio with brand names like Palantir, Flipkart, Square, and Xioami, it makes them and their fund look like superstars. And every VC I know is out to raise a larger fund. As soon as one fund closes, they're raising another. So having jewels in their portfolio is just smart marketing.

Corporate VCs are no better. They're typically looking for recognition and promotions inside their company. Nothing looks better on their résumés than having picked a few unicorns. Naturally, all this adds to the unicornization of the startup ecosystem, resulting in inflated values and what we call decacorns, a unicorn worth $10 billion or more.

MYTH: GOOD IDEAS ARE RARE

Don't fall for this. Good ideas are everywhere. Look at the explosion of new startups with brilliant innovations. The problem isn't finding a good idea; it's figuring out how to transform those ideas into viable businesses that's the hard part. That's where most startups stumble. They have a compelling idea, but they have trouble finding the right product-market fit.

INSIDE INNOVATION

So what we're left with is the fact that most innovations require big opportunities to get funded by investors, if for no other reason than ego. But is this true for intrapreneurs leading innovation projects inside corporations? The answer is yes and no.

Some large, multinational corporations will kill any project that won't eventually become a billion-dollar business. Management doesn't care about building smaller businesses. It's not their model. If the revenue from a business unit won't make a significant impact on their balance sheet, then it's a waste of time and resources.

The problem is that many of the best ideas and biggest opportunities seem like relatively small businesses at first. Travis Kalanick, the current CEO of Uber, refused to join the company early on because he thought it was a small business! It was only after playing with the idea for a while that he discovered the magic formula: the more drivers on the road, the better the service, which meant Uber could beat taxis at their own game. If Kalanick had walked away from Uber when the company was focused on offering a niche service for those who wanted to order up fancy town cars on their smartphones, he would have missed the big opportunity.

Interval Research Corporation is another example. When it opened its office in 1992 in Silicon Valley, everyone involved was certain that this would be the most innovative company ever created. It had two of the biggest names in innovation behind it: Paul Allen, the cofounder of Microsoft, and David Liddle, the former head of Xerox's new System Development Division, which developed lasting innovations like icons, menus, drawings, windows, and on-screen formatted text. Who can match that?

To top it off, Allen and Liddle weren't going to do this alone. They were determined to build the best team in the industry. They had no trouble recruiting some of the biggest brains in the world, including the first person to make music on a computer, the inventor of the inkjet printer, and the genius behind chaos theory. They even had a parapsychologist on the team. How's that for thinking outside the box?

Their mission was to become the world's innovation powerhouse. Nothing short of revolutionary would be accepted. It was Xerox PARC reborn, with a focus on giving birth to the next generation of multi-billion-dollar businesses. So what happened next?

Believe it or not, Interval Research was a bust. They actually produced a large number of new innovations, but few of these ever saw the light of day. The management team, obsessed with getting it right, killed any project that looked too small to be worth their time. Interval Research needed blockbusters to live up to its bold ambitions and oversized egos. Most of the ideas coming out of their lab seemed like distractions—interesting side projects or hobbies—not the seeds of world-changing companies. Not wanting to waste resources on small innovations, they terminated these types of projects early and often—ultimately to their own detriment.

The pressure to get big results undermined their ability to nurture small ideas. Some of their seedlings might have grown into the big oaks they were looking for, but they uprooted them too soon to tell. This was their downfall. Innovation is a process that takes time to mature. The management team was so anxious to move quickly that they screened out anything that lacked a world-changing vision. And as you know by now, it's thinking big but starting small that leads to successful outcomes—not vice versa.

In the end, Interval Research did launch five startups with grandiose visions and stellar teams, but not a single one lived up to expectations. Lesson learned, or as Buckminster Fuller said, "There is nothing in a caterpillar that tells you it's going to be a butterfly."

CATERPILLARS AND BUTTERFLIES

So how do you spot a big opportunity at an early stage? This is what every investor in Silicon Valley wants to know. It's the holy grail of venture capital.

Unfortunately, despite what you may hear from a few lucky investors, I don't know of anyone who can consistently spot butterflies at a very early stage. Before there's any traction, it's incredibly hard to tell which innovations are going to result in the next global blockbusters. This is because there are too many variables in the equation. Startups are malleable entities, and any one of a thousand things during their perilous journey can derail or radically alter them: a pivot, market shift, conceptual breakthrough, change in the law, stock market crash, new competitor, technology failure, founder dispute, patent issues—and the list goes on. There's almost no way to predict this. Vinod Khosla, a renowned venture capitalist, echoed this in his tweet, "The future is nearly impossible to predict. Caution, debate and discussion necessary."

This isn't to say some investors aren't better than others at identifying promising startups. With good intuition, insight, and data, a talented investor, like Chris Sacca, can consistently weed out the startups with little or no potential and focus in on the ones with higher odds of success.

Experienced investors are fond of saying they bet on teams—not products or markets. That's because a good team will weather the storm and figure things out no matter what happens, while a bad team will fall apart at the first sign of trouble.

Even betting on teams isn't foolproof. The success rate of veteran entrepreneurs isn't dramatically higher than first-timers. Just look at the YouTube cofounders. Their second startup, AVOS, despite having all the money and connections any entrepreneur could dream of, has yet to take off. They've been repeatedly pivoting for several years now trying to figure out what works. In short, picking a good team helps, but it's still only one variable among many.

The same is true for innovation teams inside large corporations. You may think you know which ones are going to be successful, but more often than not, it's the project in the corner that no one is paying attention to that may become the future of the company. Twitter, Gmail, Buffer, Dwolla, and Todoist all started off as side projects.

In their book *The Granularity of Growth*,[1] theorists Patrick Viguerie, Sven Smit, and Mehrdad Baghai argue that most truly big ideas look small in the beginning. Almost all billion-dollar business ideas look like $200 million ideas at the outset. Exponential growth happens only when a lot of little things fall into place—some by design, others by chance. This is why top investors bet on a portfolio of companies, expecting one or two to pay for their losers. VCs who have opted to put all their eggs into a single basket don't last that long. Sequoia Capital, Kleiner Perkins, Greylock, and all the other tier-one venture firms spread out their bets across multiple startups and multiple sectors.

Smart early-stage investors pick their startups carefully. They don't spray and pray. When they find a promising young company, they provide just enough capital to reach a meaningful milestone where they can reevaluate the business and decide whether or not to continue funding it. Short of having a crystal ball, this is the best way to hedge their bets. Then as the startup gains traction, they can help bring in more investors and exercise their pro-rata rights, enabling them to maintain their percentage ownership and put larger amounts of their money to work. In the venture world, this is how small ideas turn into big opportunities.

OPPORTUNITY SPOTTING

So how do smart investors spot potentially big opportunities? I could write an entire book on this, and I will someday, but for now I'll summarize the top five criteria:

- **The Team**—Look for startups with dedicated founders who are passionate about their mission. Don't just look at the CEO but evaluate and interview the entire team, from the interns to the engineers. All of them should be intelligent, competent, and enthusiastic believers. If the CEO cannot inspire and recruit a great team, that CEO will never win.
- **The Customer**—Talk to the customers. Do they love the product? Brian Chesky, the cofounder of Airbnb, likes to say, "Build something one hundred people love, not something one million people kind of like." You want to see customers going crazy over the product. If they aren't gushing over what the startup has, it's not an opportunity. It's a dead end.
- **The Product**—The product should provide an excellent customer experience. This doesn't mean the product must have a lot of features or fancy graphics. It means the product responds to the customer's needs in just the right way. Often extremely simple, plain products can provide the best experience.
- **The Market**—The startup can focus on a niche market to begin with, but its business must have the potential to expand into a market large enough to support a multi-billion-dollar company; otherwise, there's little or no exit potential.
- **The Secret Sauce**—Every great startup has something that separates it from the competition. What is this thing that they do that no one else does? Is it truly different and valuable, or is it just a copycat with some extra features?

There are many other criteria smart investors consider, but these are the most important ones. From my own personal experience investing in startups, you need to look at the details, thoroughly understand the core mechanics of the business, analyze whatever data is available, and then extrapolate to see if the opportunity is truly big enough. There are no shortcuts.

Section Three

STARTUP MIND-SET & METHODOLOGIES

Chapter 12

Challenge Your Beliefs

Progress is impossible without change, and those who cannot change their minds cannot change anything.

—George Bernard Shaw, playwright

How do you come up with small ideas that have big repercussions in your industry? One way is to have your innovation teams challenge their beliefs. All of us believe something. Most of the time, we aren't even conscious of what we believe. We just take our convictions for granted and never question them.

For example, there are many things in people's lives that they accept as true when they're only partially true: the world is spherical (not true); time is constant (not true); what we see is real (not true); Darwin was the first to come up with the theory of natural selection (not true). In reality, the world is an ellipsoid; time is variable; our brains construct what we see; back in the fourth century BCE, the Greek philosopher Epicurus conceptualized the idea of natural selection.

To complicate matters, we are constantly filtering information and placing it into buckets. This is how our minds work. We categorize and oversimplify in order to make sense of a highly complex world with an infinite number of variables. The biggest filter we have is our worldview. This overarching belief system shapes how we view government, religion, and society. Each new piece of information is accepted, molded, or discarded based on our worldview. This has played a pivotal role throughout history, allowing us to believe in everything from Greek gods and mythical monsters to godlike leaders. Society's worldview is so powerful, it can take on a reality of its own.

A good example of this is the Christian Church, which dominated European thinking throughout the Middle Ages and actively suppressed Epicurus's ideas in favor of the Aristotelian view. It took the Enlightenment to open up people's minds to the possibility that the Catholic Church wasn't the sole authority on the nature of things and the scientific method could help explain the world in which we live. Today, we have our own biases, but most of us cannot see them because we're so immersed in our times.

BUSINESS BELIEFS

When it comes to any business, there is an equally strong set of beliefs that guide our thinking. We use our assumptions to filter, shape, and transform all incoming ideas and information. Groupthink is extremely powerful, and the hierarchical structure of most large corporations reinforces this, compelling even the smartest managers to conform or risk losing favor with their peers. Without serious opposing points of view to challenge us, most of us don't bother to question ourselves. We just believe that this is how it works, until suddenly an upstart competitor comes along and proves us wrong. By then, it's usually too late.

Let's take three commonly held beliefs:

- Driving down costs is critical for success in low-margin businesses.
- Offering incentive pay makes employees perform better.
- Holding staff accountable results in fewer screwups.

None of these are true. They are all business myths. Jeffrey Pfeffer,[2] professor of organizational behavior at Stanford University, delves into what we believe and how it affects business. He analyzes the airline industry, where certain airlines are continually losing money and can't compete. "I ask participants to associate various pilots' wages with various airlines,"

Pfeffer says. "People generally assign the highest wages to the airlines that are having the most trouble. Their assumption is that lower wages lead to lower overall costs—and thus greater financial stability and profitability."

In reality, the airlines that pay the highest salaries, like Southwest Airlines, continually outperform those that aggressively cut costs, like United Airlines. Despite popular belief, driving down costs doesn't equate to higher profits or higher customer satisfaction. What happens is that employees are less happy, turnover is higher, and customers receive poorer service.

Whole Foods is another example of going against conventional wisdom. Instead of focusing on driving down costs and prices, like other grocery chains, they went in the opposite direction, increasing costs. Their idea was to provide premium, high-quality foods that customers couldn't get elsewhere. This not only pleased their customers but has allowed for higher margins in a traditionally low-margin business.

When it comes to incentive pay, a similar myth keeps resurfacing. Managers all over the world believe that bonuses motivate employees to perform better. What they don't understand is that giving someone a bonus produces a short-lived increase in productivity, followed by an overall decrease. This is because bonuses focus the employee on what is to be personally gained from doing a good job, instead of the intrinsic reward inherent in doing good work. The people who perform the best don't do it for the money. They do it because it makes them feel good. It's part of their self-worth. Bonuses only undermine this psychological motivator.

"The last one hundred years' worth of research shows that incentive pay does not produce better results in education," argues Pfeffer. Teachers with incentive pay do not outperform. They underperform.

Another busted business myth is that employees must be held accountable for their actions. At Southwest Airlines they found that holding people accountable for mistakes only compelled workers to cover up their blunders. This made errors more likely in the future. What worked better was to not hold anyone accountable, but instead encourage people to openly talk about their mistakes and work together to make changes that would minimize them going forward.

These are just a few examples of commonly held beliefs that when challenged don't hold up to be true.

TEMPORAL ASSUMPTIONS

Even if you don't fall for any commonly held beliefs that are untrue, you still have to challenge all your assumptions, and that's because the business world is in a constant state of flux. New markets are emerging all the time. New business models are replacing old ones. New technologies are upending entire industries. With each advance in technology comes a tsunami of new possibilities. To thrive, and even survive, in today's business landscape, you have to constantly question your assumptions to make sure they are still valid.

Assumptions are only good for a period of time. The fact is that all assumptions are based on past experiences. We need to constantly gather fresh data, retest these assumptions, and make certain the foundation of our business is still solid. The number one reason most businesses fail is because one of the key assumptions is no longer valid.

"Every business leader, no matter the business size or industry, makes assumptions about the organization's business, industry, products, customers, competitors, effectiveness," writes Steve McKinney. "Sometimes, the biggest assumption of all takes the form of: If I build it, they will come. That little sentence, at the heart of so many companies, services, products, is actually hiding potentially thousands of untested assumptions."[3]

CAPTAIN'S METHOD

So how do you go about testing assumptions? When I work with startups, I often ask them to make a list and write down everything they believe to be true about their business, from how they market, distribute, and sell their products to why they choose certain partners and sales channels. Then I ask them to go through this list and systematically challenge each one. They must ask themselves: What if this weren't true? How would that change my business? What if I took a new technology and applied it to this problem—would that enable me to do things differently?

If you try this method, you'll find that it unlocks all sorts of new ideas and opportunities you may have never thought of.

Sample Beauty Products Business

- Teenage girls are our only customers. (What about moms?)
- Teenage girls want to be beautiful. (Not smart?)
- Teenage girls prefer cute designs. (Why not sophisticated?)
- Teenage girls don't care about social issues. (The environment?)
- Teenage girls prefer to pay cash at stores. (Mobile payment?)
- Teenage girls prefer to shop in malls. (Not on smartphones?)
- Teenage girls want less expensive products. (What about organic?)

It's also important to ask the right questions about every aspect of your business.

Sample Questions

- How do customers perceive our products?
- Can our supply chain be improved?
- Are there other ways to approach marketing?
- Do we have the best possible channel partners?
- Are there new business models worth exploring?
- Can we identify new customers for our products?
- Are there markets we're overlooking?
- What strategic relationships could transform our business?
- Are there things we're wasting time and money on?

Another approach is to have your team create a list of available technologies and match them with beliefs, asking: What if we applied these technologies to this problem? How would that change things? Is there a new way to meet the customer's needs?

For example, if you're a security company for manufacturers, you might list out all the technologies available and see how they apply to making factories more secure. This list would include technologies like voice recognition, big data, artificial intelligence, robotics, and biometric sensors. Next try matching these with solutions that satisfy customer needs. You may wind up developing a security robot that patrols the factory floor at night or a security gate that uses biometric data to identify people entering the building and looks up their backgrounds using AI and big data.

At Founders Space, I also often ask startups to go through their business plans line by line and pick out every belief they can find. What data do they have to actually prove these beliefs are true? Is there any supporting evidence? How reliable is the data, and where did it come from? I ask them to do the same for their marketing plans and any other documents that are critical to their business strategy and success.

You shouldn't leave any stone unturned. If you're committed to truly challenging your beliefs, try going back and questioning some of the most important things you've learned throughout your career. What did your former boss tell you? What do business books, like this one, claim to be true? What did your professors and mentors say? Even if some of these were true when you first encountered them, they may no longer be true. In short, you need to become Socrates and question your most sacred assumptions. Only don't go too far, or you may wind up with a goblet full of hemlock.

Also, don't do this alone. You need to make this a team effort. Everyone should be questioning everything, from the admin assistant to the CEO. Nothing is sacrosanct. Nothing is off-limits. You need to give your innovation teams permission to go where no man or woman has gone before. Your innovation teams must be free to question your company's sacred cows, cannibalize existing revenue streams if necessary, and ultimately transform your business.

But don't stop there. You need outside opinions, too. Sometimes your employees and colleagues are too close to the business to ask the right questions. It pays to bring in experts, advisors, and mentors to question your team's assumptions, look for oversights, and come up with unasked questions. When bringing in outsiders, make sure you give them permission to ask the tough questions. Otherwise, most of them will be polite and not question your basic assumptions.

This type of thinking doesn't just apply to startups. Whirlpool, the $14 billion appliance manufacturer, does this by recruiting a network of innovation mentors, called i-mentors, who are trained to help internal business teams question market orthodoxies. It's hard to go against the grain, and these mentors provide advice, analysis, and critical thinking that enables the entrepreneurs to challenge the way things are done. "The most effective mechanism is to institutionalize a procedure of inquiry," writes Seth Elliott. "Seek out second (and third and fourth) opinions about key assumptions for critical decisions."[4]

In short, you must challenge yourself, your peers, and your organization to think critically and deeply about every aspect of what you're doing and will do in the future. This is how you can come up with new insights that contradict commonly held beliefs and clear the path for your elephant to take off.

Chapter 13

Nothing to Lose

Never contend with a man who has nothing to lose.

—Baltasar Gracián, philosopher

Another way to innovate is to think like you have nothing to lose. This is what startups naturally do. An early-stage startup typically has no customers, no revenue, and no constraints. They don't care if they totally disrupt a market. In fact, if a startup can create the same product that larger competitors offer and sell it at a lower price, or even give it away for free, that's a golden opportunity for any entrepreneur. The startup may not make billions in revenue each year, like the entrenched players, but it might be able to figure out how to make tens of millions or even hundreds of millions. And that's a huge amount of money for a startup. It can be enough to take it all the way to an IPO.

Large corporations don't have this option. Most of them are public already, and they are accountable to their shareholders. To have revenue drop by even 10 percent is a disaster. It's enough to tank the share price and get the CEO booted. Few public companies can stomach disrupting their own markets with lower prices. Wall Street keeps them on a short leash, and revenues and profits are expected to go in only one direction, and that's up. In other words, they have everything to lose.

At Founders Space, I like to tell startups there's nothing better than targeting a market where you have nothing to lose and the incumbents have everything to lose. If you're first to enter this market with a disruptive business model, you have everything to gain, while your opponents can only lose. The entrenched players have no way to compete with you except by lowering prices, and most of them would rather die a slow death than slash profits overnight. They've grown fat on the status quo and can't imagine a world where they aren't on top.

Let's look at Skype, a prime example of the "nothing to lose" mentality. When this tiny European startup launched, disrupting the giant telecoms seemed like a long shot. These carriers were entrenched and powerful, and had all the resources in the world at their disposal. They were also making billions from long-distance phone calls. This was their cash cow, and they had no intention of letting anyone disrupt their markets, let alone an unknown startup from Estonia.

But Skype had a secret weapon: VoIP (Voice over Internet Protocol) technology enabled them to offer communications services through the Internet. The telecoms had the same technology long before Skype entered the picture, but the big guys were not about to use it to undercut their own business. Along came Skype's founders, and they did exactly that. They used VoIP to offer free long-distance calls to anyone willing to try their app. They didn't care. Giving it away for free was just the cost of customer acquisition. Skype also had the opportunity to make money by charging for calls outside its network. It was a simple concept, and it worked. Skype wound up beating the carriers at their own game and being acquired for billions of dollars.

Another great example of the "nothing to lose" mentality is E*TRADE. Before E*TRADE was born, traditional stockbrokers charged an obscene amount of money for each stock trade. It could be hundreds of dollars. Sometimes they even took a percentage of the transaction. Using the Internet to eliminate human brokers, E*TRADE was able to offer trades at a fraction of the price and still made good money. Soon consumers expected a flat fee under $15 per transaction. E*TRADE and other online brokers pulled the rug out from under the old guard, flipping the market on its head. Online became the preferred way to trade, and the old business model all but disappeared.

Then along comes Robinhood, the newest disrupter on the block.

Instead of charging for stock trades, they're willing to give away the service for free and make money in other ways. How can they do this? Well, Robinhood has nothing to lose. They're happy to disrupt the disrupters if it means capturing the incumbent's customers and migrating them over to its mobile-first product, where they can monetize them by upselling premium services.

MYTH: THE PERFECT PIPELINE

Many large corporations talk about their "innovation pipelines" as if they've perfected a method of innovation that eliminates failure and ensures success. This type of thinking is fundamentally flawed. You cannot eliminate or even reduce the rate of failure. Failure is an essential part of the innovation process.

As technology advances, it continually creates new opportunities for disruption. So if you work at a big company and want to innovate, you need to start thinking like a startup. You can't worry about cannibalizing your own business, because if you don't do it, someone else will. It's just a matter of time. If the technology exists, some upstart will figure it out and steal your customers by giving away your service. To win, you need to steal your customers from yourself, even if it means taking short-term losses in the process.

Amazon is brilliant at this. They are constantly looking to disrupt their own business. Time and again, Jeff Bezos figures out new ways to use technology to drive down prices and offer more value to customers, even if it means lower margins—all in an effort to stay ahead of the competition. A good example of this is when Amazon allowed competing retailers to sell their products on its website. Why would Amazon, the dominant online store, allow its competitors to sell their products for less right next to Amazon products? Wouldn't this cut into margins? Yes, but it also guaranteed customers would get the lowest possible prices and maximum selection. Bezos knew that Amazon couldn't provide all things to all people by itself, and if he didn't let others sell their products on Amazon's website, those customers would go elsewhere to buy those products.

In the end, Amazon had everything to lose if they didn't disrupt their own market and sacrifice short-term profits. This is the key to innovation. Nothing should be left off the table. If customers want it and technology permits it, give it to them.

Chapter 14

Design Innovation

*My goal is to simplify complexity. I just want to build stuff that
really simplifies our base human interaction.*

—Jack Dorsey, cofounder of
Twitter and Square

I'll tell you something most people don't know about me. I'm a designer at
heart. I love design. My mother was an artist, and I was brought up going
to museums around the world and studying everything from the great masters to abstract expressionists and postmodernism. As a child, I thought I
would be an artist, but my father, an MIT-trained rocket scientist, persuaded
me to study something more practical. After obtaining a bachelor's degree in
electrical computer engineering with near-perfect scores, I rebelled and went
to graduate school in cinema and television at USC. I wanted to be a creative
force in the world. I wanted to design my own reality.

After making dozens of short films and writing scripts, I joined a
Hollywood TV production company and quickly rose up to the level of
development executive. That was where I met the founder of SEGA, the
Japanese game company. He offered me a position in Japan designing
video and arcade games. How could I refuse? Being an avid gamer, this
was a dream come true. So I spent the next several years designing games,
first in Japan and then in Silicon Valley. I developed everything from PC
games to online and mobile games.

Design has always been my passion. I often spend hours leafing
through design magazines or browsing new products on Kickstarter or

simply walking through a city studying the architecture. So when startups come into Founders Space, I can't help but give them feedback on their designs. I often find myself launching into a fervent rant that goes something like this: "Hire a real designer. Don't do this yourself. You're not a designer. You're an engineer, and what you have looks crappy. Nobody is going to put up with a bad user experience. The customer doesn't care about your technology. It's great design that matters."

Everyone thinks of Silicon Valley as a technology-centric ecosystem, when, in fact, design now lies at the heart of the machine. I'd argue that there is more wealth being created now through design innovation than technological innovation. For every piece of technology that is invented, there are thousands of ways to employ that technology in newly designed products, many of which have the potential of opening up and transforming multi-billion-dollar markets.

Design innovation focuses primarily on human factors. All the fields of study shown below impact the design process and how designers approach developing a new product or service:

- **Anthropometrics**—the study of the human body and its movements
- **Physiology**—the functions of living organisms and their parts
- **Psychology**—the way the mind works, including both conscious and unconscious experiences
- **Sociology**—how people relate to one another and interact
- **Anthropology**—how human societies and cultures function
- **Ecology**—the relations of organisms to one another and to their physical surroundings

There was a time when design was relegated to engineers. They tended to design products based on features, functions, and their personal preferences, with little or no regard for human factors. It is only recently that design has come to the forefront. Today product teams often include designers with experience in human factors, interaction design, systems design, and engineering and industrial design. It's not an exaggeration to say that design is at the center of almost every new successful product coming out of Silicon Valley.

Apple didn't become the largest company in the world based on its technology. Steve Jobs wasn't an engineer. He was a designer and creative thinker. If you look at the iPod, which reinvented Apple, it's not a marvel of new technology. There were many MP3 players on the market at the time. It wasn't just about building superior hardware. Apple knew they'd never win the hardware war. Their approach was to rethink the entire experience of playing music on a device. That was why Tony Fadell, who worked for Jobs and helped spearhead the iPod's design, was intensely interested in how to create a better experience for users.

If you take the iPod with its click wheel and compare it to other MP3 players at the time, it was a design marvel. No other MP3 players allowed users to smoothly scroll through long lists of music with one hand, while stopping on a single song with surprising accuracy. Apple created an entire ecosystem that made it a joy to access, play, and purchase music. This included the iTunes online store and the iPod's unique interface, which enabled users to effortlessly browse through numerous songs and playlists.

One innovation that is emblematic of Fadell's attention to detail and insight into the user experience is that he noticed whenever someone purchased a new device, took it home, and opened the box, it wouldn't turn on. This was because the battery needed to be charged. So the customer would have to wait an hour or more before they could use the device. How frustrating was that?

Fadell suggested they make sure every battery was fully charged, so the customer would open the box and instantly be able to use the iPod. It transformed the user experience. Up until this point, no electronics maker had paid much attention to how the product looks coming out of the box—how it feels to unwrap it and use it for the first time. But now most high-end consumer electronics companies ship their products with a charged battery and pay attention to the entire unboxing experience.

This is the essence of design innovation. It's putting yourself inside the head of the customer. How does a person feel when using the product? In the end, it's the experience that counts—not the features. No problem is too small to overlook. If it affects the overall experience, it should be improved. Just look at how carefully Apple designed their packaging. Fadell and his team wanted to delight users every step of the way.

Fadell went on to work on the iPhone. After that, he left Apple to travel the world for eighteen months as he thought about what to do next. "I had to pull back and get out of Silicon Valley to gain perspective and see the world in a different way," he said. So many people forget how important it is to refresh your mind. Working all the time is the death of creativity. Fadell needed to experience life before embarking on his next design journey.

The break apparently paid off, because what he came up with next was the Nest thermostat, a truly groundbreaking product that launched the IoT wave. What Nest did is to rethink the entire experience of bringing smart devices into the home. The Nest thermostat was less an engineering marvel than a design masterpiece. The beauty of Nest is that it's so simple. Instead of programming it, like you do with older digital thermostats, it learns your heating and cooling habits, adjusting itself automatically to provide just the right environment and saving you money in the process.

Nest is also a showpiece. It looks stunning. Instead of having a cheap LCD screen that you have to squint at, it's a beautiful half sphere with temperature displayed boldly in the center and an elegant ring of color around it. It's worthy of showing off to your geeky friends. Early adopters loved it. For them, price doesn't matter if the product's cool factor is off the charts.

Fadell's design philosophy is that it's important to re-create a product category—not just make something incrementally better—and this starts with solving a real problem for the customer. He calls this making painkillers rather than vitamins. Vitamins make you incrementally healthier. You can live without them. But if you're in pain, you need it to stop right away.

How do you know if you have a real problem to solve? Just ask other people. Do they get as frustrated as you do? Can you eliminate their pain points? The greater their suffering and annoyance, the greater the room for innovation. Understanding exactly where existing products stumble is the key. That's how you reinvent a category. With Nest, he wanted to remove the hassle and pain of programming a digital thermostat. No one likes to do that. I personally struggle with it every time I go to a new hotel. Now how does this darn thing work?

MYTH: TO INNOVATE, JUST ASK YOUR CUSTOMERS

Listening to your customers is invaluable, but they won't always tell you how to innovate. In fact, while most customers can tell you how to fix problems and improve existing products, they seldom point you toward an entirely new way of thinking and doing things. If you want to turn an industry on its head, you need to move beyond customer feedback and reimagine your business from the ground up.

In other words, take your customer feedback as the starting point, not the ending point. Ask yourself what insights you can derive from what your customers are saying or doing. It's the insights you gain from this data that become so valuable in innovating.

When Fadell demoed early versions of Nest to his friends and colleagues, many of them wanted additional features. Some wanted a touch screen so they could have greater control. But Fadell refused. He was convinced that the best feature to offer was simplicity itself. The act of adjusting the temperature by simply turning a circular ring was a beautiful experience, and he didn't want to mess it up by adding more complexity.

The reason Google paid billions for Nest was that they wanted Fadell on their team. He understood how to seamlessly weave technology into people's lives. This is an art few people in the world grasp. And it is the future of all products moving forward, whether in the home, workplace or outdoors. Google saw IoT as the next frontier, and Fadell had blazed the trail.

But Fadell isn't alone. There are many other great examples of design innovation. We usually think of Airbnb as a brilliant business model innovation, but it's more than that. Yes, the idea of being able to rent out unused space in your home to travelers visiting your city is a huge leap forward, but what most of us don't realize is how hard this problem was to solve.

Now it seems obvious that people love the idea of making extra money renting out spare rooms, but this wasn't always the case. When Brian Chesky, Joe Gebbia, and Nathan Blecharczyk started Airbnb, all the VCs they talked to thought the idea was crazy. Who would let strangers into their home? How could anyone trust random visitors in their private space? What if the stranger was a thief, or worse, a rapist or murderer? The consensus was that Airbnb would never amount to much. People just didn't want to take that sort of risk.

Luckily, two of the three founders were designers. They had met at the Rhode Island School of Design and understood the principles of design thinking. Their challenge was to make people feel comfortable with the novel idea of sharing space together, even though they had never met.

If you look closely at Airbnb, the site feels both friendly and safe. The descriptions and instructions are warm and inviting. The profiles have large photos, so you can clearly see the person. There's also room for a description with just the right amount of space. The reviews are displayed prominently in the profile. Chesky and Gebbia even thought about how to structure the conversation between the hosts and guests. How large should the text box be when people message one another? Where should the buttons be placed? How should users be prompted?

"If you want to create a great product, just focus on one person. Make that one person have the most amazing experience ever," says Chesky. Even calling the users "hosts" and "guests" was intentional. It's like hosting a party at your home and inviting guests, rather than renting space to some stranger. The idea was that you could become friends. It wasn't just about the money but the experience of meeting new people from all over the world and sharing your home and city with them. That's what makes Airbnb so special. That's why people love it.

Most hotels are impersonal. You don't typically become friends with the desk clerk or concierge, but with Airbnb, you are invited into an intimate space where you have a chance to get to know someone personally and share an experience with them. They designed their service with this in mind.

Chesky and Gebbia also made sure the front page was magical. They featured the most attractive and romantic spaces right on top. It gave users the feeling they were going on an adventure—something they couldn't get from a typical hotel. The home page featured fabulous tree houses, country farms, luxury apartments, jungle retreats, and even castles. With big, bold photographs and alluring descriptions, it was an entry into a magical kingdom.

All this made Airbnb a sensation that swept the world and changed how we all think of travel. And Airbnb isn't alone. Box redefined how we think of file sharing through design. Slack reshaped enterprise communication through design. Xiaomi captured the low-end smartphone market through design. Snapchat and WeChat took messaging to a new level through design. WeWork reenvisioned the office and workspace. Uber and Lyft remade transportation through design. And the list goes on.

Understanding design is essential to innovation. In the coming decade more product categories will be reinvented by design than any other type of innovation. Why? Because design doesn't require a huge amount of capital—just exceptionally talented people who can perceive what customers really want from a product or service. This means any entrepreneur with a laptop has the potential to disrupt an entire multi-billion-dollar industry if they can figure out the customer's pain point and design it out of existence.

My very first entrepreneurial success came out of design. My partner and I created a computer game called Gazillionaire that was meant to teach students and adults how to become entrepreneurs. It was a game where you started your own trading company in the psychedelic Galaxy of Gogg. The game was technically outdated the day it was released. Our publisher only agreed to distribute it because their QA team had fallen in love with it. The animations were crude, the graphics were homemade, and the tech was primitive, but that didn't stop it from becoming a hit. People adored the unique experience it created, and it received glowing reviews from the critics. In fact, our publisher was upset that our little game received better reviews than their multi-million-dollar Star Trek franchise.

Shockingly, Gazillionaire, along with its companion games, Zapitalism and Profitania, are still selling today. Schools and universities around the world are using them to teach business and economics, while adults e-mail us saying things like, "I finally understand why I have to get rid of my credit card debt!" The point is that good design beats big budgets and tech wizardry almost every time.

I tell entrepreneurs that if they want to succeed, they shouldn't get an engineering degree or MBA. There are more than enough engineers and MBAs coming out of college right now. What we need are more designers who can figure out how machines and humans can better work and live together. Human computer symbiosis lies at the center of a massive shift we are now undergoing. This is where the hard problems of the future lie and the potential for massive change exists.

New possibilities for design are unfolding every day with advances in technology. Design thinking extends into how connected devices communicate, the types of data sensors gather, how we interface with augmented reality, and what electronics we strap to our wrists, embed in our bodies, and connect to our brains. Right now, there are thousands of businesses that are waiting to be totally disrupted and new markets created simply through design thinking.

Chapter 15

Business Model Innovation

The same products, services or technologies can fail or succeed depending on the business model you choose.

—Alexander Osterwalder,
author and theorist

Why recycle an existing business model when you can innovate, rewrite the rules, and steal the market out from under the feet of your competitors? This is what Silicon Valley startups do all the time, and it's created a huge amount of value. It comes down to one thing: breaking the rules. Business model innovation is about studying the rules of the game and then systematically cheating by breaking, bending, and twisting them. Only by rewriting the playbook can startups gain an edge by which to take over a multi-billion-dollar market.

One thing I've found is that it's not always the Harvard MBAs who are the best at this. Often it's the untrained rebels, like Jobs, Gates, Zuckerberg, Thiel, and Musk, who come up with the cleverest ways to break the rules. I also don't have an MBA, so I might be biased. I learned by running my own companies, and I can't help but think this might play to my advantage because I naturally "think different." I don't know the rules, so I'm fine with breaking them. I tend to be open to new business models. In my mind, anything is possible. When a startup comes into Founders Space, I ask them to show me the proof that their idea is grounded in reality. If they can present some evidence that customers truly value their offering, that's what's important. No matter how unorthodox the model, it's fine by me as long as the data backs up the vision.

Just think of how Craigslist started giving away free classified ads. This wasn't how the game was supposed to be played according to traditional print media. Newspapers counted on classifieds as their bread and butter. Without them, how could they survive? But Craigslist has done just fine giving them away for free, because their cost structure and model are entirely different.

"It's really hard to run a business against somebody who is not acting as if it were in business," says Bill Gurley, a VC at Benchmark. With radical business model innovation, the startup may not even appear to be a competitor. Their model might be so foreign to the incumbents that it's more like an alien invader hell-bent on destroying their world.

Granted, not all business model innovations are radical, but all of them do share common traits that make them one of the most powerful forms of disruption and worthy of analysis. Below are three examples of recent startups innovating on their business models and lessons we can take away.

UBER AND UBERFICATION

Uber has set the standard for business model innovation. They shrewdly inserted themselves between the customer and the service provider, disrupting the taxi industry.

The beauty of Uber is that people don't become attached to their taxi driver, and even if they do, most wouldn't bother to directly call the same driver next time because this person may be busy, across town, or not working. So there's little leakage, meaning customers don't cut Uber out of the transaction. Also, people use the service frequently, and taxi fares can add up to a lot of money. The lifetime value of every customer is high, which means Uber can justify sizable customer acquisition costs—hence, its massive funding rounds. Uber can also outcompete any taxi company on price, service, and options. All this adds up to an extremely competitive model.

So what can Uber teach us? First of all, the Uber model is powerful because it nails all six criteria:

- **High Margins**—Taxi fares aren't cheap.
- **Valuable Resources**—Anyone with a car can be a driver.
- **Repeat Customers**—People often need transportation.
- **Scalable**—The business can grow fast.
- **Replicable**—The same model works across geographies.
- **Mass Market**—The service appeals to a broad customer base.

Uber also focuses on what the customer wants:

- Faster
- Smarter
- Simpler
- More convenient
- Feels good
- Cool

Lastly, Uber has obsessively worked to make the process frictionless:

- Press a button
- No delays
- No negotiations
- No cancellations
- No negativity

Uber's business model also benefits from the network effect. The more drivers it has on the road, the more passengers benefit by faster service, and the more passengers it has, the more drivers it attracts. It's hard for competitors to match this.

The way Uber disrupted the taxi business has been so successful that it has led to the Uberfication of everything from deliveries to dry cleaning to doctors. The danger is that not all businesses are analogous to the taxi industry. Many companies who claim to be the next "Uber" will fail because their business models simply don't work.

AIRBNB

Airbnb is the other wunderkind of the startup world. It has created the classic disruptive marketplace. Its business model works because they tapped into an extremely valuable untapped resource: people's homes. By allowing everyone to rent out space in their homes, they've been able to offer more locations at a better price with more variety than traditional hotels. Their two-sided marketplace is also highly defensible. The more hosts that offer space, the more guests Airbnb attracts, and the more guests they attract, the more hosts will sign up. Bingo—the network effect in action.

Airbnb's model also has many of the same traits as Uber:

- **High Margins**—Rentals aren't cheap.
- **Valuable Resource**—Unused space in people's homes.
- **Repeat Customers**—Many people travel often.
- **Scalable**—The business can grow fast.
- **Replicable**—The same model works across geographies.
- **Mass Market**—The service appeals to a broad customer base.

More recently, Airbnb added instant booking to remove a friction point, minimizing the time required to coordinate with the host. This was a real pain point for me, so I'm happy. Just press a button, and it's booked. All this makes Airbnb another stellar example of a business model innovation that works. There are other marketplaces that just don't function as well because they lack one or more of the ingredients mentioned above.

SOFI

SoFi doesn't have all the elements of an Uber or Airbnb. Instead, it's taken another approach. SoFi has transformed the student loan industry by focusing on creating a lifelong community. When students take out loans from SoFi, they aren't just being saddled with debts. They are joining a special group that offers to guide and support them over the life of the loan.

SoFi claims their members save more than $18,000 on average. The revolutionary part is that SoFi is turning student loans, commonly thought of as a predatory business, into a positive social activity. SoFi offers their members career counseling and entrepreneurship courses, as well as invitations to community events and happy hours. They make taking out a loan sound like joining a fraternity or sorority. This is not banking as usual. SoFi then goes on to upsell their members on mortgage loans, personal loans, and wealth management.

SoFi also has their own criteria for evaluating members' credit, which is different from the big banks and other lenders. SoFi takes into account the member's education, work experience, and financial history. They charge no origination or application fees and no prepayment penalties. To top it all off, they offer unemployment protection, which means SoFi will suspend a loan if a member is laid off later in life. This may cost SoFi some money, but the strategy pays off when it comes to marketing, allowing them to grow fast and attract college students at a much lower cost. But what they are doing is much more than that. As you can see, SoFi's model entirely changes the playing field. They aren't even in the same league as traditional lenders. It's a whole new way of thinking about the customer, and this is what makes their approach work for millennials.

The lesson here is that business model innovation isn't confined to the financial model. It includes the entire value package. SoFi has redefined what it means to take out a loan. It's no longer a transaction but an entry into a special club, where their customers receive membership benefits the rest of their lives.

MYTH: IMPROVED PERFORMANCE IS THE KEY TO INNOVATION

If only improved performance was all there is to innovation, life would be so simple. But it's not true. Think of Skype. It wasn't more convenient, faster, or higher quality than a traditional phone call when it launched. In fact, it was painful to use most of the time. But it was cheaper! People will put up with a lot when you give it to them for free. Value comes in many forms, and performance is only one of them.

NGCODEC

NGCodec's founders know video compression better than almost anyone in the industry. When I met them, they were developing a next generation codec that could compress and encode video ten times faster and far cheaper than anything on the market. This technology is necessary to deliver video over the Internet. Everyone from YouTube to CNN uses it. NGCodec's founder had been working on this for over a year, they had paying customers, and were on the cusp of making everything on the market obsolete. But they weren't able to raise capital in Silicon Valley, despite the fact that their timing was perfect with 4K video, which made the problem of encoding more acute every day.

The issue was their business model. They were using hardware to encode the video, which they planned to license out to customers. This meant they were stuck with a lengthy integration and deployment process, slow sales cycle, and limited upside. It wasn't scalable. They couldn't grow to a multi-billion-dollar company this way.

After spending a few hours with them, I gave them one piece of advice: "Don't license hardware to your customers. That's the wrong business model. You need to take your service into the cloud and adopt the SaaS [software as a service] model. I know it's not what you envisioned, but this is the future of video encoding. People don't want hardware. They want solutions."

The CEO was receptive and redid his entire business plan, incorporating the new model. Three weeks later, he called me up. They'd closed $3 million in venture funding and were off to the races. The lesson of this story is that if one model doesn't work, try something else. You can't just innovate on your product. You have to think of the product and the business model as two parts of the same machine and innovate across both simultaneously.

TRUE INNOVATION

It's not easy to achieve a truly radical business model innovation that is capable of disrupting an existing market or creating an entirely new one. Most startups only manage to develop a competitive edge for themselves, not entirely rewrite the rules of the game. That's why startups like Uber, Airbnb, and SoFi are worth so much. They are rare beasts. Like them, if you can figure out how to change the rules, you can change the world, defy physics, and make your elephant fly.

Chapter 16

The Builder's Trap

When you're dealing with machines or anything that you build,
it either works or it doesn't, no matter how good of a salesman
you are.

—Marc Andreessen, venture capitalist at
Andreessen Horowitz

I like to tell my startup founders to keep their fingers off the keyboard
at the beginning. "Don't allow your engineers to start coding from day
one," I exhort. "That can send you down the wrong path!" Good engineers
love to code. The first thing they'll want to do is dive into building something cool. The problem is that what's cool to your engineers isn't always
what the customers think is cool. The customers may want something
entirely different.

Starting to build from the outset is often not only a waste of time, it
can be a recipe for failure. The more time your team sinks into developing
a product, the more everyone will want to believe in it. No one wants to
give up and discard their hard work. After months of developing a product, teams become emotionally attached to their creation. Even when evidence appears that what they've built isn't what customers want, teams will
often push forward, adding new features, fixing problems, and searching
for ways to make a failing product succeed. The more time and resources
they sink into the failing product, the harder it becomes to finally face the
truth. This is what I call *the builder's trap*.

In 2011, Michael Norton of Harvard Business School, Daniel Mochon of Yale University, and Dan Ariely of Duke University did a study, and they found that when you make something, you value it much more highly than others do. Their research consisted of different experiments, including one where participants assembled IKEA furniture and another where they created origami figures.

In the IKEA experiment, the subjects were given the task of assembling IKEA furniture. Researchers then asked the subjects to value the furniture they assembled compared to furniture assembled by professionals. What researchers found was that the subjects were willing to pay an average of 63 percent more for the furniture they assembled themselves, even when it was poorer-quality work.

In another experiment, researchers had subjects make origami frogs and cranes. Then they had experts make similar origami frogs and cranes. Even though the experts' work was obviously superior, the subjects valued their own creations equally. At the same time, participants who hadn't been involved in the creative process placed far greater value on the work of the experts.

This is now commonly called the IKEA effect. It's a cognitive bias in which people place a higher value on products they've worked on. In other words, people become emotionally blinded by their own investment of time and creativity. The lesson here is that when your innovation teams begin working on a product or service, they will gradually become more attached to the work, and this attachment can prevent them from seeing reality. Even when evidence suggests their customers don't need the product, it's easier for the creators to think, "How can we fix this?" rather than admit they produced something of little or no value.

Heck, I've fallen into the same trap. Everyone who knows me will attest to the fact that I'm a passionate guy. I put everything I have into whatever I'm doing: work, love, play! So when I came up with the amazing idea of turning the entire world wide web into a virtual world, I couldn't help but fall head over heels for this concept.

Everyone I showed the prototype to was equally enthusiastic. It was a game where players could create an avatar and literally walk across the web. Your avatar could appear on top of Google, Amazon, or Facebook, and you could chat, talk, exchange virtual goods, play games, and set out on adventures to find hidden treasures. You could take your avatar to any online store and go shopping with friends, hang out on a band's site and listen to tunes with fans, or go to any news site to discuss the top stories. The possibilities were limitless.

The only problem was that we had too little proof this actually worked. The evidence came in early that our creative concept wasn't resonating with users. They liked the experience initially, but after several weeks, they stopped coming back. Turning the Internet into a giant virtual space sounds amazing, but in reality, almost none of the big virtual worlds, including Second Life, has lived up to its promise. Users prefer structured gameplay over free-form spaces where they mingle and interact with other people.

Unfortunately, this was not obvious at the time. Virtual worlds were the hot ticket, and I fervently believed we could figure this out if we just had more time. I'd fallen into the builder's trap. My passion for our game only delayed the inevitable pivot. I could have saved time and money if I'd built less and analyzed more. They say love is blind. So please don't fall in love when you're innovating, or you'll end up like me: heartbroken.

Chapter 17

Targeted Prototypes

It's not an experiment if you know it's going to work.
—Jeff Bezos, founder of Amazon

The best way to avoid the builder's trap is to build targeted prototypes. A targeted prototype has several key attributes. The first is that it takes the least amount of time and effort to build, yet it allows your team to test basic assumptions about your business.

Targeted prototypes come in many flavors. There's no single template. Most of your targeted prototypes will not resemble your final product. Their job is just to help you gather data. What you need to do is list out all the assumptions your business makes and concoct a unique experiment to test each one. These experiments usually involve some sort of prototype that is especially designed for testing and validating specific assumptions.

For example, if you want to test whether or not consumers will buy your product, you can build a landing page in half a day using tools like Wix, Squarespace, or Unbounce. Then you can take preorders by simply driving targeted traffic to the site using Google AdWords or Facebook. You can quickly assess whether people will pay for your product or not.

When ShoeSite.com launched with the goal of selling shoes online, the founder, Nick Swinmurn, didn't build out everything. First, he wanted to test his assumptions in as simple a way as possible, so he launched a very basic website and put up images of shoes with prices taken from local shoe stores. He collected orders from his site, then bought the shoes at local stores with his credit card and shipped them to customers. Was he making money? No. But this way he could validate the market without spending a lot of time and capital building out a supply chain, renting warehouses, and stocking inventory. The experiment proved so successful that it attracted Tony Hsieh, who renamed the startup Zappos, raised venture capital, built a huge business, and sold the company to Amazon for $1.2 billion.

MYTH: INNOVATION REQUIRES BIG BETS

Money doesn't always buy you innovation. Some of the most powerful and far-reaching innovations were done on a shoestring budget. Take Airbnb. The cofounders didn't have much money, and so they inflated an air mattress in their living room for their first guests. It was a low-budget way to test their business model. Most startups begin this way.

Here's another story that shows the importance of validating before building. A startup came to Founders Space with an interesting idea: a marketplace for sharing commercial kitchens. The food tech business was exploding. Companies were popping up all across the country that needed to prepare meals for delivery to people's homes. The problem was that there weren't enough commercial kitchens available. In the United States, by law you must prepare the food in a licensed commercial kitchen if it's for sale to the public. So this startup envisioned creating a marketplace that would match companies who needed a commercial kitchen with restaurants that weren't using their kitchens during off-hours.

With the brother being an engineer from Microsoft and the sister leading business development, the founders of this startup made a good team. When we first spoke, they were about to build out the entire platform, which would take them months. I told them to stop. Don't build anything.

First prepare a targeted prototype. They had to know if this business model worked before they spent all the time and energy creating the software.

"Put up a simple landing page," I said. "Have a form that people can fill out, and then do all the matchmaking on the back end manually." Taking my advice, they stopped building and put up the landing page. Then they called restaurant owners and asked if they'd be interested in renting out their space to companies that wanted to prepare food during off-hours. At the same time, they contacted companies that needed to use commercial kitchens and asked if they'd be interested in signing up.

They quickly found out that the market was too small and fraught with problems. Restaurant owners were reluctant to have someone else messing up their kitchens. When they did agree, the hours weren't always suitable to the renters. Then there were issues with what equipment the restaurants had and how things were laid out. Also, how would they manage the supplies and food storage for the companies? Suffice to say this wasn't a business they wanted to be in. Luckily they found this out quickly and with minimal investment in time and money.

The thing to keep in mind is that targeted prototyping is more of a process than a product. The prototype should be constantly morphing as your team learns what works and what doesn't. If the targeted prototype is your landing page, your team should test and tweak everything, from the pricing to types of products, user experience, user interface, designs, product names, and ad copy. This is called A/B testing, where you test one element against another. For example, test design A and see how many users respond positively versus design B. With each iteration of the prototype, your team should go back and incorporate what it has learned into the next version, thereby creating a continuous feedback loop. By making the feedback loop and creation process one and the same, you'll minimize the temptation to fall in love with your product, because your product becomes the process of discovery.

It's important to keep in mind that not all prototypes require coding or technology. Some of the most effective targeted prototypes don't involve any hardware or software. A targeted prototype can be anything from a

FLOW CHART OF FEEDBACK LOOP

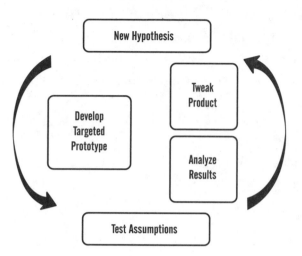

verbal pitch to a pen-and-paper presentation. As long as the prototype allows you to test and gather data, that's enough. Some of the best targeted prototypes can be created with off-the-shelf tools, including the following:

- Pen and paper
- Board games and Monopoly money
- Costumes and role playing
- Whiteboards and markers
- Mind-mapping software
- Computer graphics and drawing tools
- PowerPoint presentations
- Flowcharting software
- 3D animation tools
- Video cameras
- Photographs
- Prototyping software
- Open-source software

There's no single way to prototype a new idea. Try multiple techniques and see what works best. The key is getting your innovation teams to think creatively and engage customers early and often. Have them try something out on a customer and then come back and rework it. Then go back out and try something else. Every time you touch a customer, your team will learn a thing or two and better understand the problem that needs solving.

THE PATH TO RADICAL INNOVATION

Chapter 18

Go to the Core

Know your core competencies and focus on being great at them.
—Mark Cuban, cofounder of
Broadcast.com and TV personality

It can take years to develop your company's core competencies, such as manufacturing processes, proprietary IP, or distribution relationships. These can be your most valuable assets, and some are extremely hard for competitors to copy. So when innovating, it helps to start by asking yourself a few questions. What does your company do better than anyone else? What are the talents of your team? What know-how do you possess that no one else does?

If your company has a worldwide distribution network, exclusive sales channels, powerful brand, trade secrets, mature ecosystem, refined processes, or defensible patents, you'll want your innovation teams to take advantage of them. If you can leverage and build upon your core competencies, your chances of success are far greater than if you try innovating in an area where you have no expertise or advantages.

In other words, you need to focus. You don't want your innovation teams working on whatever strikes their fancy. For instance, if you're in the business of manufacturing auto parts, it would be unwise to have your teams developing 3D food printers or health-tracking wearables. This may sound bizarre, but I've seen it happen. It's often tempting for innovators to jump on the bandwagon and embrace whatever trends they see happening, even though they have little to do with the company's core business.

When Nike decided to create the Nike+ FuelBand, a wearable similar to Fitbit, they spent a small fortune. Not only was the product development costly, but the launch required a marketing blitz, complete with TV commercials featuring LeBron James and Serena Williams wearing the product on court. "You can't have a barrier or restriction to that core competency," said Nike's lead engineer, Aaron Weast. "If we constrain ourselves by a circle of competency, we'll do ourselves a disservice. You need a willingness to punch through it."

Despite the initial fanfare and all the hype, the FuelBand never took off. While Fitbit captured 69 percent of the market and Jawbone grabbed 19 percent, FuelBand never made it past 10 percent. Nike wound up laying off 80 percent of their hardware team and stopped production. Why did this happen? The main reason is that Nike lacked the expertise and competency to launch a competitive product. The FuelBand didn't work that well. Users complained. Replacements had to be sent out, and ultimately Nike agreed to a $2.4 million settlement with customers.

To be fair, FuelBand wasn't totally out of Nike's core competency. It leveraged Nike's strong sports brand and unrivaled marketing machine. The problem was that it had too many areas that didn't overlap with what Nike does best. Nike is a shoe company at heart, and developing hardware and software is not easy—especially when competing against savvy startups whose primary competency is hardware and software. So was FuelBand a mistake? Not entirely. It was a first step in the right direction of building a new connected platform. However, this example illustrates just how difficult it is to succeed outside one's core competency, even with a strong fit like a sports wearable and the world's leading sports shoes, apparel, and equipment company.

This isn't to say Nike can't develop competency in hardware and software. It's just that this doesn't happen overnight. The company needs to stick with failure after failure if it's ever going to get there. To Nike's credit, they switched to developing an app for the Apple Watch, letting someone else take care of the hardware piece. Nike might get it right this time because it's a simpler proposition. They can't just give up every time they hit a wall.

The problem with going outside one's core competency is that most companies aren't able to stomach a continual string of failures in a business that doesn't align 100 percent with their core. They give up when the going gets tough, which results in nothing but a loss. So before you develop outside your core, you need to be sure it's a path you're fully committed to going down—despite repeated failures, time lost, and costly blunders.

Google is an example of this type of company. They are willing to commit vast amounts of money and resources to develop new core competencies, which require new distribution channels, marketing approaches, technology, and ecosystems. Is this the right choice for most companies? I'd argue that it isn't. Google is one of the few companies in the world that can afford to take this type of high-risk gamble.

Even for Google, it's not easy. They have dozens of projects going at once, ranging from ingestible cancer-detecting pills to drone deliveries, energy kites, and Internet balloons, and most of these projects fail. Here are just a few of Google's many flops:

- Google Glass
- Google Lively, a virtual reality space
- Google Answers
- Google Print Ads
- Google Radio Ads
- Dodgeball, a location-specific social networking site
- Jaiku, a Twitter clone
- Google Notebook
- Google Shared Stuff
- Google Buzz
- SearchWiki
- Knol
- SideWiki
- Google Video
- Google Catalogs
- Google Wave

And the list goes on . . .

And this doesn't include Google X, a "moonshot" factory, which has killed over one hundred projects so far, including a hoverboard, a space elevator, buoyant cargo planes, vertical farming, and even a teleportation device! Despite a never-ending string of failures, Google persists in attempting to develop new core competencies, and occasionally it succeeds. Android is one example of this. Android wasn't an overnight success, but with persistence and many iterations, Google was able to develop mobile software as their core competency, and this paid off big-time.

The sheer difficulty of developing a new core competency is why most companies are better off innovating close to the core. It's so much easier, and payoffs are more frequent. Let's go back to Nike. Nike has a long history of innovating on top of their core competency. It started with the waffle trainer, which Phil Knight created using his wife's waffle iron, and now includes over six hundred patents and inventions, such as Air Max cushioning, Flyknit form-fitting fabrics, and HyperAdapt self-lacing technology. This continual stream of core innovations is what made Nike a world juggernaut and keeps it on top. Nike is also constantly pushing into adjacent markets, leveraging their core competencies to offer new types of athletic apparel and equipment, and then reaping the rewards.

Google's biggest successes have also come from innovating out from its core to adjacent areas. AdWords is the monetization engine behind search. Maps is an extension of search into the physical world. Google Earth layers information on top of Maps. Google Books allows users to search more than ten million books. Gmail and Google Docs enable users to communicate, create, share, store, and search their personal content. And Android takes it all to mobile.

The lesson here is that your chances for success go up dramatically when you expand from your company's core outward. Chris Zook and James Allen of Bain & Company did a study of 1,850 companies and found that most profitable, sustained growth comes when companies push out the boundaries of their core business into adjacent spaces. The best results come from developing a formula for expanding those boundaries in repeatable, predictable ways. In other words, you need to develop a plan for continually expanding from your core competencies into related areas.

Nike has done this consistently, expanding from jogging to tennis, basketball, golf, and soccer. Nike's formula is to start with shoes, which they know best, and establish a leading position in the target market. Then it follows up with a clothing line endorsed by the sport's top athletes. In golf it was Tiger Woods, while in basketball it was Michael Jordan. Then it follows up with equipment and accessories. This winning formula has allowed Nike to eclipse their competitors.

Nike's operating profits were $164 million in 1987, while Reebok's were $309 million. By 2002, Nike had grown its profits to $1.1 billion, while Reebok's had declined to $247 million. By 2015, Nike exceeded $30 billion in revenue. Both Nike and Reebok started out in the same market, with Reebok winning, but Nike figured out how to expand into adjacent markets, systematically expanding their core and opening up new opportunities. Amazon, Vodafone, and Dell have all employed this

FLOW CHART OF NIKE'S STRATEGY

strategy. They expanded into adjacent customer segments, introduced new product lines, developed new distribution channels, and then moved into neighboring geographic markets.

According to Zook and Allen, when a company tries to launch a new initiative, it fails 75 percent of the time. However, companies that innovate from the core outward, using a repeatable formula, have double the success rates on average. This is because they can leverage their core competencies, processes, and know-how, benefiting from the learning-curve effect and strategic advantages.

How can you do the same? It starts with discipline and focus. Don't just innovate willy-nilly. You need a plan. To begin with, when you engage your innovation teams, ask them the following questions:

- What are our company's core competencies?
- How can we leverage these effectively?
- What type of products play to our strengths?
- Can we gain an unfair advantage over the competition?
- What adjacent areas can we expand into?
- What is our plan over the next five years?
- How does this sync with our long-term vision and mission?
- What formula can we develop for expanding into new spaces?
- How can we do better each time?

You must take a rigorous approach to succeed. Most successful CEOs won't focus on a new market unless they are certain they can be one of the top three players within a few years. During interviews, Zook and Allen consistently heard the best CEOs say, "Never put the core business at risk." They evaluated lots of opportunities but only focused on one at a time. This ensured they didn't get spread thin or distracted.

Olam is a great example of this. They started out as an intermediary between Nigerian producers of shea nuts and cashews and big food processors like Planters and Mars. Olam figured out how to export commodity products from chaotic developing markets profitably and reliably. This innovation became their competitive advantage. They then began to look for ways to leverage this core competency in other markets, expanding to Burkina Faso, Ivory Coast, Ghana, and Cameroon.

Olam then expanded from its core of shea nuts and cashews to cocoa, coffee, sesame, and other products. Each time, they changed only a single variable, either the product or the location, but everything else remained the same. They are now a $1.9 billion multinational business whose customers include Kraft, General Foods, Nestlé, and Sara Lee. Olam grew revenues at 84 percent and earnings at 28 percent, with a return on capital of 35 percent from 1997 to 2003. This is while most of their competitors just plodded along.

The lesson is clear. Innovate on one thing at a time, learn what works, and then innovate again, gradually expanding your core. With Nike+ FuelBand, they were innovating on too many things at once: hardware, software, new technology, new distribution channels, and so on. This was why they failed.

A. G. Lafley, the CEO of Procter & Gamble, likes to say, "Complexity is the bane of a large organization. It strangles growth." Under Lafley, P&G sold off most of their food and beverage businesses so they could focus on their core competencies—cleaning and personal-care products—and drive innovation in the areas they knew best. This narrower focus enabled Lafley to remake the company, better leveraging P&G's unique talent, processes, and resources, while increasing innovation across all its core businesses.

In the late 1990s, sales of Crest toothpaste were waning, so the company developed two new innovative products that took advantage of existing customers, brand, marketing infrastructure, distribution, and sales channels. The innovations were in adjacent areas: teeth whitening and brushing. Crest Whitestrips and the Spinbrush were the first innovations, and they generated over $200 million each in new sales their first year.

P&G is a master of innovating from the core outward. They are constantly looking at and analyzing adjacent markets, then coming up with ideas for new products that leverage as many of their strengths as possible.

"When I became CEO of Procter & Gamble in 2000," said Lafley, "we were introducing new brands and products with a commercial success rate of 15 percent to 20 percent...Today, our company's success rate runs between 50 percent and 60 percent. About half of our new products succeed. That's as high as we want the success rate to be. If we try to make it any higher, we'll be tempted to err on the side of caution, playing it safe by focusing on innovations with little game-changing potential."

The other benefit of Lafley's approach is that it allows P&G to scale globally. By focusing on the core, they were able to expand geographically at a much faster pace. Today, over 40 percent of P&G's innovations come from outside the United States. Their employees in India, China, Latin America, and Africa are all part of the innovation process.

P&G was able to launch new products with barriers to entry, strong customer loyalty, and established distribution, marketing, and sales channels. This enabled them to move faster, scale bigger, and enter new markets around the globe, all while limiting the risk inherent in innovation.

As we can see, the best innovators build upon the strengths of their core business, taking their companies into adjacent markets with category-defining products and services. If you can do this, you've gone to the core and increased your odds of success.

Chapter 19

Engage Your Customers

What I tell founders is not to sweat the business model too much at first. The most important task at first is to build something people want.

—Paul Graham, cofounder of Y Combinator

When startups enter Founders Space, one of the questions I ask is "Who is your customer?" Another question is "How much time have you spent with them?" Surprisingly, many startups haven't spent much time at all with their customers. This sounds crazy, but it's true of most early-stage startups. They may have had some brief conversations, but the majority of them haven't spent nearly enough time understanding their customer's business. If there's one thing that prevents the majority of startups from ever getting off the ground, it's the lack of customer engagement at the beginning.

I had a startup come to Founders Space with the goal of connecting manufacturers in China with product designers around the world. I thought this was a smart idea, since good design can help a typical electronics gadget to far outsell the competition. A marketplace that matched manufacturers with top design talent could be valuable.

The problem was that the CEO hadn't spent enough time with her customers. She had strong ideas about what she wanted to build, but those ideas weren't rooted in the needs of her primary customers. She was a designer by training, so she clearly understood what designers wanted, but she had only a tenuous grasp on what manufacturers desired. This was impeding her progress. I told her that she needed to spend as much time as possible with the manufacturers in China, find out exactly how they wanted to engage designers, and build her marketplace in a way that delivered exactly that. Only by doing this could she hope to succeed.

Just like this startup, your innovation teams need to get out of the office and into the field. Most engineers and creative types would be happy to be left alone to work on their projects without ever talking to a real customer, but this is a huge mistake. Customers can be their best source of information. They can't design and build anything without first understanding the often unexpressed and unmet needs of the customers.

Let's imagine your customers are retail stores in shopping malls. In this case, your innovation teams should spend as much time as possible in malls talking to the retailers and learning what they do on a day-to-day basis. Nothing beats hands-on experience. In the process, your team can build relationships with retailers, figure out how they operate, and spot areas for improvement. If your team members spend enough time with them, ideas will come up that they may never have thought of. This type of knowledge can't be had from reading a book, taking a meeting, or conducting a survey. It comes only from being there.

Saad Ehsan, whom I worked with at Founders Space, knows something about being there. His startup idea came from his first job. Shortly after graduating college, he landed a coveted position at Nishat, one of Pakistan's largest textile conglomerates. He was in love with his new job until he actually had to do the work, which consisted of the mind-numbing task of scraping data and plugging it into an Excel spreadsheet.

"I would be mindlessly staring into a computer screen till late at night," says Saad. It was torture for him. The sheer tedium of this job, however, motivated Saad to innovate on a solution. He approached his brother, an engineer, and together they began building a system that intelligently automated redundant and repetitive tasks. If done right, his software could replace him.

Saad wound up quitting the textile company just four months after joining. He thought his boss might be upset, but instead Nishat offered him a better job. Saad turned the offer down to launch AItomation, and his old employer wound up being his first customer.

Whenever your team sees one of your customers getting frustrated, this is an opportunity you don't want to pass up. Each annoyance that crops up is fertile ground for innovation. These are what your team needs to be harvesting. You should train your teams to be aware, take notes, and discuss everything. For instance, if you have five innovators in the field, they should get together weekly to compare notes, share what they've learned, and brainstorm on possible solutions and opportunities.

FedEx is a good example of how customer engagement can lead to new innovations. Hospitals, one of FedEx's important customers, wanted living tissue and organs shipped to patients around the world. This precious cargo needed to be in perfect condition. But how could they tell if something happened during transit? Doctors don't want to implant a new kidney if it was damaged during shipping. To solve this problem, FedEx worked closely with surgeons, patients, and medical device suppliers. What FedEx came up with was SenseAware, a technology that tracks the package's location, barometric pressure, temperature, light exposure, and humidity. This innovation has enabled hospitals to know the exact conditions the tissues and organs were exposed to en route, which can make a lifesaving difference. Without engaging with their customers, FedEx would never have come up with this solution.

Starbucks has taken a different approach. They not only encourage customer feedback but they've built a transparent platform. As of writing this book, the "My Starbucks Idea" site had received 11,677 ideas on social responsibility, 24,063 on location and atmosphere, 24,268 around their Starbucks Card, and a whopping 46,368 on their coffee and espresso. All of these suggestions came directly from customers over the Internet. The platform shows which ideas are being reviewed, tested, and considered.

Starbucks puts the best ideas into practice. For example, to be more socially responsible and save energy, they installed LED lighting in stores. At the behest of customers, they partnered with Postmates to deliver drinks and food, they added lunch wraps to their menu, they created Starbucks

Birthday Cake Pops, they rolled out splash sticks, and they introduced a number of new coffee flavors.

This tight integration between customer suggestions and innovation has created a strong community and positive feelings. It has also been important in helping Starbucks solidify and extend its leadership position.

FASTER HORSES

Customers are good at providing ideas for incremental innovations, but when it comes to radical innovations, it's another story. Henry Ford is famous for saying, "If I asked customers what they wanted, they'd have said faster horses." Steve Jobs also preached, "It isn't the customer's job to know what they want." To their point, what customer would have come up with a car when everyone was using horses? Or the iPhone? The fact is that customers usually can't imagine what's possible or what the best solution is.

Kawasaki Motors found this out the hard way. After introducing the Jet Ski, an innovative personal watercraft, Kawasaki asked customers what they wanted, and customers requested extra padding on the Jet Ski's sides to make standing more comfortable. Kawasaki listened, while competitors went ahead and developed similar products but with seats. Guess who won out? Kawasaki lost their dominant market position because customers preferred sitting to standing—even with extra padding.

The problem wasn't that Kawasaki listened to their customers. It was that they didn't ask the right questions. When you ask customers what they want, they tend to describe what they know. They can seldom imagine a product that is radically different. Instead, they focus on incremental improvements on existing solutions—like the padding. To get around this, your innovation teams need to ask what customers want the products to do for them. It's a subtle change in phrasing, but it makes all the difference.

If Kawasaki had asked their customers what outcome they desired, their customers would have probably answered, "A more comfortable way to ride the Jet Ski." This in turn would have opened up all sorts of possibilities. Adding extra padding on the sides would have been just one possible solution, while adding a seat would have been another.

Daina Burnes Linton, CEO of Fashion Metric, learned the same lesson. When she started her company, she thought that when shopping for clothes people would like to take a picture of the outfits and get instant feedback from a personal stylist on the fit and look so they didn't end up buying the wrong thing. When she ran this idea past her friends and family, they loved it. Luckily, she didn't believe them. Instead, she went back to potential customers and asked an open-ended question, "What's the biggest problem that you have when you're shopping for clothes?" To her surprise, not a single person said they had a hard time deciding what to buy. Not one person. If she hadn't asked the question in the right way, she would have built an app nobody wanted. How you ask the question is as important as what you ask.

Cordis, a medical-device maker, has taken this process to the next level. They had their innovation teams design outcome-based customer interviews, where they asked what outcomes customers desired—not what solutions customers wanted. A moderator guided the conversation. The moderator made sure to weed out answers that pointed at solutions. Whenever a customer suggested a solution, the moderator would ask: Why did they want this solution? What would it do for them?

Next Cordis organized the outcomes, removing duplicates and categorizing them. After this, they conducted a survey where participants rated the outcomes in terms of satisfaction and importance. Then they used a mathematical formula to gauge the potential of each opportunity. The result was an extremely valuable data set that their internal innovation teams could use to develop new products and services. Knowing what outcomes the customers wanted enabled Cordis to explore a variety of products and evaluate each on the basis of delivering the desired result. Cordis took what they'd learned and developed the artery stent. This one innovation wound up doubling Cordis's revenue in two years and sent their stock soaring.

WHO IS THE CUSTOMER?

It's not only important how you ask the question; it's critical to whom you ask the question. Many organizations will solicit feedback from their power users or lead users. These are the customers who know everything about the company's products. They are experts. The problem with their feedback is that it's not always relevant to the majority of customers.

U.S. Surgical, a medical instrument manufacturer now owned by Tyco, found this out. After receiving repeated suggestions from an elite group of surgeons, their power users, they developed a set of sophisticated instruments that could move and rotate in multiple directions. They were sure this was going to be a hit. However, it didn't turn out that way. The majority of surgeons found the new instruments too complicated to use, and reorders amounted to less than 5 percent.

The lessons are clear. Engaging your customers is important, but only if you ask the right questions to the right people. Seldom is a good product or service developed in an airtight box. R & D labs cut off from the rest of the world are not the answer. And asking customers what they want usually results only in incremental improvements. To get radical improvements, your innovation team needs to deeply understand what your customers actually need, even if they can't articulate it. The more deeply you engage your customers, get to know their businesses, and gather the data, the clearer the possibilities become.

Chapter 20

Observe

It takes humility to realize that we don't know everything, not to rest on our laurels and know that we must keep learning and observing. If we don't, we can be sure some startup will be there to take our place.

—Cher Wang, cofounder of
HTC Corporation

Let's talk about the power of observation and how it can give your innovation teams insights that they would otherwise overlook. At Founders Space, I remind my startups not to try to impress the customers with how much they know. That's the wrong approach. Instead, they need to shut their mouths.

One of the best ways I've found to observe customers is to watch over their shoulders without saying a word as they use your product or a new feature for the first time. The hard part is being quiet. Even if they ask you a question, you should not answer. Just nod and let them continue talking. All the time, pay close attention to what they're doing with your product, what experience they're having, and where they get frustrated. Make sure to ask them to say out loud everything that comes into their heads as they use the product. Take careful notes, then use those notes as your data.

If you provide software, hardware, or cloud services, this type of observation can be done as part of the market research, presales, setup, or training process. Your team can ostensibly be there to help your customers, but in reality, they can perform a dual role: trainer and observer. This way they can learn from your customer, identify customer needs, and figure out whether your product is delivering on its promise.

P&G operates all over the world, and each market has unique requirements and needs. In India, P&G found that 80 percent of people don't use washing machines. If this is the case, how could they expand their market for washing machine detergent? To figure this out, they sent teams to observe how the majority of Indians hand-washed their clothes. What they found out surprised them. Even though Indians were washing everything by hand, they still used laundry detergents meant for machines. The problem was that these detergents often caused skin irritation, abrasions, and burns. This observation led P&G to develop a special detergent designed for washing by hand. They called it Tide Naturals, and it was a breakthrough.

The power of observation is central to the innovation process. Watching and learning is how you innovate. What you want to avoid is what I call the *seller's syndrome*. This happens when your innovation team stops listening to the customers and instead launches into sales mode. Their mission becomes obtaining affirmation that their solution is right, rather than observing and learning. I've seen this happen time and again. Instead of hearing what the customer is actually saying, startup founders try to convince the customer that their product provides the best possible solution. They will even go so far as to filter out negative feedback and focus only on what confirms their beliefs. This type of behavior is what prevents innovation teams from making progress. They just spin their wheels unable to see what's really going on.

Your innovation teams must understand that innovation is not about coming up with brilliant ideas; it's about being a detective, gathering evidence, interviewing the customers, and piecing together the underlying truth. Epiphanies and divine inspiration seldom lead to innovation. What does work is developing the skills of observation. This includes learning how to listen, asking the right questions, figuring out how to capture the necessary data, and analyzing it correctly.

MYTH: YOU CAN SPOT A WINNER

Most babies come out of the womb looking pretty ugly, and the same is true with new innovations. You usually can't spot a winner until it's cleaned up a bit. Travis Kalanick didn't see the full potential of Uber right away. Andrew Mason dismissed the idea of group couponing (Groupon) even when his investor brought it up repeatedly. Stewart Butterfield overlooked the potential of enterprise messaging (Slack) the first time around; it was only after his second failed game that the lightbulb went off.

More often than not, your team's initial assumptions and ideas will be wrong. This is a fact that your team must face if they are going to succeed on their quest. It's your job to get them to understand the wisdom of admitting their naïveté and commit to a process of continual discovery. Below are some good strategies for how to hone one's powers of observation and questioning.

First, don't be in a hurry. Many of your best, most productive team members are the ones who rush from one task to another, always trying to get things done. This is great for productivity but not so great for learning. Instead, make sure your team members slow down sometimes and observe what's happening around them, ask questions, and engage with colleagues and associates. This can result in a wealth of information that might otherwise have been overlooked.

The next strategy is to have your teams get outside of their own heads. Many of the most intellectually capable people are so captivated by their own thoughts that they refuse to engage with the outside world. You need to help your teams turn off their overactive imaginations and spend time studying the outside world. Have them practice listening instead of talking. Make your team members get into the habit of asking questions instead of coming up with answers. This sounds easy, but for some people it's incredibly difficult.

Passive listening is an art that needs to be cultivated. It's not enough to listen carefully. If your team member is fidgeting or fooling with a phone or interrupting at the wrong times, it can skew results. The best listeners train themselves how to listen without distracting their subject. Psychoanalysts are masters of this technique. Talk show hosts are also experts at passive listening. Simply by nodding at the right time or raising an eyebrow or not speaking, a good listener can encourage the subject to give information they otherwise wouldn't have divulged.

It also helps to recognize one's insecurities. When team members are worried about what others think of them, they stop listening. They may be anxious about their hair or how they're dressed or what they said to someone last week. They may be so insecure that they can't help trying to be the smartest one in the room. All these traits stifle observation. You need to help your team members to abandon their egos at the door and focus on the problem. All that matters is what they learn—not how they're perceived.

Observation is also about stealth. Your teams can't be obvious about what they're looking for. If they are, others will try to perform for them, either consciously or unconsciously. Most people want to be helpful, and if they get a sense that your innovation teams are searching for an answer, they will come up with one, whether it's right or wrong. It's human nature to try to please those around us. You need to be careful not to contaminate the experiment with any unintentional biases. Being observant is not just about asking the right questions and listening; it's about how those questions are phrased and how the observation is conducted.

Asking vital questions in an offhand manner and doing it at a time when it feels natural is one technique for minimizing bias. When observing someone doing a job, your teams shouldn't stare or try to interfere. They need to be like a fly on the wall. The less they are noticed making their observations, the more accurate those observations will be. You may want your teams to take a course or read a book on how ethnographers observe foreign cultures. Everything your teams do throughout the process will have an impact on the data gathered.

Let's look at Procter & Gamble again. When they launched Ariel Ultra in Mexico, they were certain the new laundry detergent would be a smash hit. It had twice the cleaning power, cost half as much, and took up half the space. What wasn't to like? When they asked customers if this is what they wanted, they received an overwhelmingly positive response. That was why they were shocked when the product flopped. How could this happen when they'd done everything right?

Simply asking questions isn't enough. If something sounds good on the surface, most customers will say, "Yes, I love the idea!" But this doesn't mean it's really what they want. After the product flamed out, P&G took another approach. They tried the fly-on-the-wall technique, observing how customers used their product in their daily lives without any input or interference. Their goal was to figure out the psychology of the customer. How did the customer perceive their product? What about the detergent that made the customer feel good or bad? Was the detergent meeting their expectations?

What they learned surprised them. Ariel Ultra's new features actually turned off customers. Most people equated using less soap with less cleaning power. Also, the soap didn't produce as many suds as they were used to, so this confirmed their fear that their clothes weren't getting properly cleaned. In response to this insight, P&G came out with a new product called Downy Single Rinse, which produced more suds with less detergent. This helped their customers save time, money, and space while visually affirming that the detergent was doing its job.

This was not only a big hit but a lesson learned. Customers won't always be able to tell you what they want. You have to observe and probe deeply to understand their psychology, perception, and needs.

WHAT REALLY MATTERS

Your teams need to train themselves to look for what really matters. This means understanding the problems and often orchestrating situations where they can uncover the truth about what's happening inside the customer's head and out of sight. To do this successfully, your teams need to discuss and plan in advance how they will interface with the customers and what type of data they need to gather. It's not enough for them just to be present with the customer. They need to figure out how to become part of your customer's decision-making process, access key information your customer may consider proprietary, and work with your customer to build trust and openness.

Part of creating an open, trusting relationship is becoming friends with your customers. Your team should not focus solely on the results. They need to pay attention to the human side of the equation. Building those bonds can be more important than simply perfecting one's observation techniques. If your innovation teams are going to get access to your customers' true concerns, goals, and desires, they need to be open themselves. Different members of your team may have different skill sets. Some may be excellent at coming up with the right questions, and others may be brilliant at analysis, while a few may have the magic touch of making others feel comfortable talking about anything. This type of tag-team structure can enable each of your team members to leverage their strengths and produce superior results.

Reflection is another part of the process. Taking time to mull over details often reveals the hidden meanings behind what people have said and done. After each observation session, have your innovation team sit quietly by themselves and ponder what they've just experienced. It is not by accident that Sherlock Holmes was portrayed to smoke his pipe and meditate on all the facts he had gathered, looking for clues. I don't recommend smoking because it can kill you, but your team members may want to listen to music or sit in a rocking chair or take a long walk. Many of my best ideas come in the shower. Simple activities that allow your mind to open up and explore thoughts are ideal for connecting the dots and coming up with innovations.

Talking out loud is another mechanism for piecing together lots of seemingly random bits of information. You should have your teams engage in discussions related to what they are learning. Each person may have different facts at their disposal or a unique way of interpreting them. Cultivating an open and friendly dialogue, where no one is trying to dominate or push ideas on the others, is one of the best ways to take raw observations and shape them into meaningful data that your company can act upon.

In the end, what your team hears and sees will be the keys that unlock the next generation of innovation.

Chapter 21

Tap Your Ecosystem

In Israel, a land lacking in natural resources, we learned to appreciate our greatest national advantage: our minds.

—Shimon Peres, ninth
president of Israel

When I consult for both large corporations and startups, I make clear that innovation doesn't happen in just one place in your business. It happens across your entire ecosystem. Sending innovation teams out to your customers is just one piece of the puzzle. In addition, you should be sending your teams out to your strategic partners, channel partners, vendors, suppliers, government agencies, manufacturers, and distributors. Ask yourself: Who are we making richer? Who are we making more innovative? Who is vital to our ecosystem?

Take, for example, a supplier. It may seem like they are just selling you something, but if that something is critical to your business, it may pay to spend time innovating with them. If the supplier produces a part you need for a product you're manufacturing, enabling that supplier to see how you use the product and what you need from it may help them come up with a better design.

You can gain a significant edge over the competition by having your innovation teams work hand in hand with your partners to facilitate communication, exchange knowledge, and plan for the future. New research points to the fact that it's not just exceptional talent and cutting-edge technology that make a company successful, it's the ecosystem effect. When companies collaborate with key partners to deliver more value to their customers, major breakthroughs become more likely.

MYTH: ONLY ENTREPRENEURS CAN INNOVATE

It's widely believed that entrepreneurs have some superpower that big corporations just can't match. This isn't true. There are talented, innovative people in almost every organization—big or small. They just need a way to contribute. Apple, Google, and Amazon are big companies, and they have produced some of the most significant innovations of the century.

One startup I worked with envisioned a product that used optical head-mounted displays, like Google Glass, to optimize the pick-and-pack process at warehouses. It was only at the conceptual stage, but the founders were masters at tapping their ecosystem. They realized that the manufacturers of these devices, like Google and Epson, wanted to sell their hardware, and the best way to sell hardware is to have compelling software. By engaging their partners in the innovation process from the start, they managed to get introductions to huge potential customers, including Toyota, Tesla, Walmart, Pfizer, and SAP, before they'd even built a working prototype. This tiny startup, with nothing but an idea, wound up getting several large corporations to actually pay for developing their prototype. After this, they quickly raised $1.5 million in financing from venture capital and corporate investors. This would never have happened if they hadn't tapped their ecosystem.

Another good example of tapping an ecosystem is Tesla. They've managed to do what many experts thought was impossible: launch a new automobile company that can compete with Ford, Daimler AG, General Motors, Toyota, Volkswagen, and all the other entrenched players. They did this by creating their own innovation ecosystem of auto-parts suppliers, battery experts, software and hardware developers, manufacturers, designers, and so on. It's the ecosystem, not Tesla alone, that has enabled Tesla to take the lead in the electric car market.

For example, Futuris, an Australian company that makes leather seats and other components for the Model S, moved into a facility near Tesla so that they could innovate together. "Supply chain localization, and being ten miles down the road from Tesla, is fantastic," said Sam Coughlin, general manager at Futuris. "We can react quickly, and our engineers are constantly working with Tesla." It's this sort of close collaboration that makes Tesla exceptional.

Eclipse Automation, a Canadian company that tests manufacturing equipment, also opened its engineering offices and a service shop next to Tesla. "We have a number of clients in the Bay Area, but Tesla was a driving factor in the decision to set up operations here," said Jason Bosscher, general manager at Eclipse. Tesla's openness and willingness to collaborate in a way that enriches their ecosystem partners have enabled them to innovate faster, act smarter, and succeed where so many other upstart automakers failed.

BEYOND YOUR ECOSYSTEM

Some companies are taking it a step further. They're going beyond their own ecosystems and reaching out to new talent they've never met or done business with before. "It's not enough to build your innovation ecosystem around your company because there's only so many people you know," Mohanbir Sawhney, professor with Northwestern University's Kellogg School of Management, points out. "With innovation ecosystems, your reach is limited, and companies' fields of view are usually limited. They need to take assistance and help from third parties or intermediaries. They make connections between companies and innovators, and harness their potential."

IBM has done just that with "Innovation Jams," which bring together up to one hundred thousand participants to act on opportunities and work out problems. Many of the participants have never worked with IBM before. The fact is that the people you need most are often outside your company and outside your network. They have the expertise to take your business to the next level, but you have to give them a path to engage and collaborate.

InnoCentive, an innovation market maker, is another one that addresses this need head-on. It has more than 250,000 scientists from two hundred–plus companies who've signed up to help companies solve problems. The scientists not only get recognition for solving big problems but also receive cash rewards. InnoCentive has paid out over $48 million in awards to over 2,400 winning solutions over the last fifteen years.

"Can you imagine having a pool of 250,000 PhDs at your disposal to solve a problem?" asked Sawhney. Many of the participating scientists are retired, come from emerging markets, or work for existing labs around the world. For them, this is an exciting challenge and chance to earn some money. For instance, when Netflix used InnoCentive to improve its recommendation algorithm, guess who responded? AT&T Labs. Their scientists wound up solving the problem and winning the prize money.

Often the problems being posted at InnoCentive are problems that have been given up on. They may be impossible to solve inside a company, but according to InnoCentive, the success rate is around 50 percent. That shows the power of looking outside the walls of one's company. The bottom line is that seemingly intractable problems are being solved because they are being opened up to outsiders with unique experience, points of view, and expertise. "Some really interesting nonobvious connections that are made because you are taking problems outside your domain," Sawhney says.

BRINGING PARTNERS ON BOARD

When companies fail to engage all the necessary partners, no matter how innovative their technology, the result is often a disappointment. Take the television market. In the 1990s, Philips, Sony, and others invested billions of dollars to develop TVs with groundbreaking picture quality. The problem was that their TVs didn't take off in the 1990s because they didn't have the right ecosystem partners on board. The lack of signal compression technologies, broadcasting standards, and studio production equipment led to inferior-looking images, even when the TVs were state-of-the-art. Sometimes having a superior, standalone product is not enough. Companies must bring in partners early on to produce the additional elements necessary to build out the full ecosystem and provide value to customers.

Even competitors may be necessary in the equation. For truly groundbreaking innovations, it often takes the strength and ingenuity of multiple companies to raise consumer awareness, pioneer a new market, and drive demand. With this in mind, don't automatically exclude competitors from your list of potential partners. Sharing ideas and collaborating together may be the key to creating an entirely new market. A common mistake that first movers make is to forgo cooperation on standards and other key pieces of the ecosystem in favor of using proprietary technology and patents to shut out the competition. This alone can kill an emerging product category.

Your goal shouldn't be to prevent anyone from knowing or benefiting from what you're doing. Secrecy is a weak friend. Instead, you should analyze your entire ecosystem, figure out who you need to bring into the process, and work on enlarging the pie together so that all parties benefit. In other words, if you're not making your innovation partners wealthier, you're not building an innovation ecosystem—you're going it alone, which can be much harder.

Here are some questions you may want to ask yourself at the beginning:

- Who are our top partners?
- What type of partners do we need on board?
- What do they gain from working with us?
- How can we help them succeed?
- Can we benefit from collaborating with competitors?
- What does the market look like without these parties involved?
- Where have we had success engaging partners in the past?
- What did we do right and wrong?

- What can we do to foster participatory innovation?
- What are various ways to implement innovation partnerships?
- How do we recognize and reward our innovation partners?

INTERNAL ECOSYSTEMS

In addition to looking outside your company, you should be sending your innovation teams to various divisions and groups deep within your own organization. This includes your marketing department, manufacturing, logistics, R & D, sales, procurement, finance, and accounting. Any corporation that grows large enough tends to operate like many separate entities rather than a cohesive whole. There will be groups separated by geography, language, culture, focus, expertise, and function. You need to treat these groups in the same manner that you'd treat outside partners. You cannot expect them to jump on board when you need them. It takes time, effort, and planning to get them involved.

This is no easy task, especially when you have departments that are used to operating like their own little fiefdoms. They may want nothing to do with your innovation teams, and you'll have to work hard to make the benefits clear. One approach is to treat each department within your organization like you would an external partner or customer. Your innovation teams should listen to their needs, learn from them, and together come up with the answers. The goal should be to embed innovation teams in key departments across your organization and allow them the freedom to identify problems, come up with solutions, and build a culture of innovation company-wide.

Take, for example, your own HR department. Let's say you're having a problem retaining employees. Your best employees tend to jump ship whenever they receive offers from competitors. To address this, you create an innovation team comprised of two to eight key people from HR and other parts of your organization. By embedding this innovation team inside HR, you begin the process of discovery.

Naturally, your innovation team shouldn't spend all their time in the HR department. They should be out engaging employees from across your organization, listening to their issues, observing how they do their jobs, and asking the right questions. Through observation and open-ended discussions, they may be able to figure out why some employees are not happy, why certain employees leave and others stay, and how HR can be more responsive. Through this process, your innovation team can take issues that would have festered and come up with solutions that can be tried and tested. If you see retention and morale increase over time, you'll know the changes are working. If not, you'll need to continue iterating.

The reality is that most of your internal innovation teams will produce small, incremental improvements. They won't transform your entire business. But these small changes can make your company significantly more efficient and productive. Even if all these internal innovations remain small, the sum total can add up to give your company a massive advantage over the competition. The beauty of internal innovations is that they're extremely hard to copy. It's relatively easy for competitors to copy products on the market, but it's difficult, if not impossible, for them to replicate internal, organizational processes.

Sending innovation teams out across your entire ecosystem, internally and externally, is no small effort, so you may want to begin with just a few partners and departments and then expand from there. The investment in time and money will pay off. Remember that it takes only one or two tiny innovations that are just right to unlock a whole new line of business or to completely disrupt or transform your existing business. The more teams you have active across your ecosystem, the greater your chances of uncovering that breakthrough. And it may not be a single innovation but the effect of several different innovations across departments and partners that work in conjunction to get your elephant off the ground.

Chapter 22

Data Doesn't Lie

Without data you're just another person with an opinion.

—W. Edwards Deming, author

Gathering data is essential to innovation. What you need to do is actually prove that an idea, which may seem great on the surface, is great in reality. I listen to startup pitches all the time, and I can tell you that it's often impossible to know if an idea that sounds world changing will actually change anything—let alone the world.

Many of the most promising ideas turn out to be duds when you dive deep. All it takes is one overlooked piece of data, like the tip of a submerged iceberg, to sink the ship. If you want to avoid having your project end in disaster like the *Titanic*, you need your innovation teams to be on the lookout for data from day one. Data is critical. Without data, your teams are just taking wild guesses and will inevitably waste a lot of time and money.

One startup I mentored was making a new type of game, where users created the content themselves. The founders kept telling me all the unique and innovative things about their game, but when I asked for the data, it became clear the retention rates and user engagement metrics were dismal. It didn't matter if they had the most innovative game ever made, users didn't want to play it. Numbers don't lie. Finally, I told them to scrap the project and start over. It wasn't going to work. You can't argue with data.

Another example of data shock is exemplified in Grace Ng's story of her first startup. The concept was to give users a more visual way to learn about the world. Instead of typing queries into Google, they could share visual queries through social networks. Grace comes from an ad agency background, so she believed branding was everything. Before launching, she spent six months building, testing, and polishing her new service. She wanted everything to be perfect and beautiful. However, after the product launched, she couldn't get any users to stick. She couldn't understand why, so she interviewed potential users and quickly figured out that no one cared. She wasn't solving a problem they had. If only she'd known this earlier, she could have saved herself nine months of hard work.

Grace went back to the drawing board and came up with another idea. She would launch a service that helps startup founders obtain feedback on the user experience (UX) and user interface (UI). No one was offering this, and it seemed like a real problem. This time, instead of diving into building the product right away, she went to the customers first and gathered data. Conducting the interviews, she found that 60 percent of her target customers expressed a strong interest in the service. Next she needed data on whether they'd pay for the service or not, so she set up a quick and dirty landing page, described the service, and added a Buy button. After driving traffic to the page, she had ten orders in just a few hours. Bingo! This was real.

The third thing Grace needed to know is whether the supply side worked, so she reached out to experienced UX and UI designers, asking if they'd like new customers. She was sure they'd say, "Yes, absolutely!" Who wouldn't want more customers? To her surprise, experienced UX and UI designers weren't thrilled with the idea. They are picky about the clients they take on. They like to carefully vet each new customer in advance and only choose the best ones. Dead end? Not exactly. During the interviews, she learned that when these designers first began their careers, they were eager to have new customers. That was the key to her two-sided marketplace. She realized that her target was newer UX and UI designers, who weren't as well established and wanted to acquire customers.

Even with all this data, she did not begin building her service. Instead, she simulated her business manually using e-mail, connecting the customers who needed feedback with UX and UI designers. This way she could see exactly how the process worked. She wanted to know what type of feedback the customers needed from the UX and UI designers. Was the feedback visual, written, or oral? How did the designers like to work? And what was the best way to facilitate this type of communication? Grace knew she could use this data when designing the service. Once she could no longer handle the workflow herself, she took the landing page offline, analyzed all her findings, and began building the website. The lesson Grace learned was that gathering specific customer data early and often is the most effective way to develop a product. Grace now teaches lean startup methodology as a cofounder of Lean Startup Machine.

Another way to gather data is by looking at macro trends. When Steve Jobs launched the iPad, he was confident it would be a hit, not only because it was a beautiful product, but because the numbers were on his side. In 2010, Pew Research had come out with a study showing that 40 percent of American adults were using mobile devices to wirelessly connect to the Internet, up from 32 percent in 2009. And if you included laptops, it was 59 percent of American adults. Jobs realized that people wanted a more elegant, natural way to access the Internet than a laptop or netbook, and the iPad was the answer. The data and trends all reinforced his hunch.

Dropbox is another example. They began with a simple three-minute explainer video. It demonstrated Dropbox's intended functionality. The result was 75,000 signups overnight—all before they had an actual product. This little test gave them ample proof that their elephant of an idea had wings.

MYTH: INNOVATING IS ABOUT TECHNOLOGY

Many companies think the way to win is to spend millions on research and development of new technologies. They have extensive labs and file cabinets full of patents, but very few of these ever see the light of day. And even those that do often fail. I have spoken at length with the heads of R & D departments in some of the world's largest corporations, and they admit to me that commercializing their inventions has become increasingly difficult. The world is moving at such a fast pace that by the time they get a new product to market, it's often too late.

HOW TO GATHER DATA

As you can see from the previous examples, there are many different ways to gather useful data for validating a new business concept. Below I describe some of the most effective methods:

Google Keyword Tool

Google's keyword tool is a quick and easy way to get an idea of the demand for your product. Start with a search for keywords related to your product. Google will tell you exactly how many monthly searches are performed for various keywords. If no one is searching for what you plan to offer, there probably isn't any demand.

Google Trends

Google Trends offers more data for you. Do a search for your product idea, and you'll see the volume for each keyword over the past several years. Is the trend going up or down? Is demand seasonal or relatively flat? Are there spikes in demand? What causes these spikes? All of this is telling information you should know before embarking on your business.

Friends and Family

Most people tap their friends and family first. This makes sense, since they are the easiest, most accessible form of feedback. However, be careful. The data from friends and family may be skewed. Ask yourself if your friends and family are really the target market. If they aren't, it can do more harm than good to ask them. The last thing you want is to make decisions based on bad data. In addition, they know you and may not be capable of giving you an unbiased answer. My advice is to skip them and go to the actual customers you want to reach.

Customer Interviews

Steve Blank, coauthor of *The Startup Owner's Manual*, is fond of saying, "In a startup no facts exist inside the building, only opinions." His point is that you have to get out and talk to the customer, and interviews are the best way. Just be careful not to ask leading questions. You need to rigorously analyze each question to make sure it is open-ended. Below are samples of open-ended customer interview questions:

- What is your most pressing problem today?
- What products do you use right now to solve this problem?
- What do you like about your current solution?
- What frustrates you about your current solution?
- What do you wish you could do with your current solution that you can't do today?
- How much would you pay for our product if it was available today?
- Whom would you recommend our product to?
- Why is our product important to you?
- Will you preorder our product so you can get it faster?

Blogs and Social Networks

Blogs and social networks, like Blogger, Facebook, Twitter, and WeChat, are a great way to showcase your ideas, engage customers, and gather feedback and data. In fact, I've used them to get feedback on the title of this book. When using social networks, just make sure to target the right demographic. For example, if you're going after teenage males, Pinterest probably isn't the best network to use. Twitch or Snapchat might work better.

Analyze Competitors

At Founders Space, I'm always urging our startups to spend more time looking at their competitors. You may be surprised at just how much data your competitors can offer. Make sure your innovation teams spend plenty of time on your competitors' sites. These can be a treasure trove of data. First, are your competitors making money? If not, why not? If they're doing everything right but aren't growing like weeds, then how do you expect to succeed?

Next look at how your competitors position their business. How do they describe their products? What do they promise their customers? How do they set prices? All this data and more is available on most websites. But don't just stick with their sites. Go to their Facebook pages, Twitter feeds, and blogs. Read all the posts, tweets, and comments you can find. What are customers saying? Are they happy with the product? Is something frustrating them? Are the customers active at all?

Online stores can also offer insights. Look at how the competitors' products are displayed. Read all the user comments and reviews. If customers are upset about the quality or service, this is an opportunity for you. As much as possible, try to categorize and organize this data into meaningful statistics that you can analyze and compare with other competitors.

Look through public records and mine as much data as possible about your competitors. It can be as simple as going to WHOis.net and seeing when they registered their website or looking up news articles and press releases. Find out when they first launched or released new product. If your competitor is a startup, see if they pivoted or not. Look at where they have placed advertisements. That will tell you who they're targeting and how they're marketing their product.

The more data you can gather early on, the better. Do this before you put up a landing page, build a prototype, or spend a lot of time reaching out to customers. You may find that you don't really want to pursue this particular line of business or this new product after all, or you may confirm that you have a better way of doing things that your competitors haven't figured out yet.

Landing Pages

Landing pages are often used to harvest e-mail addresses while a product is being developed. This is not the best use for a landing page. It's much better to use the page to gather valuable data. You can design landing pages so that they appear to be a full website, where customers can actually place orders, make suggestions, or start discussions—even before the product is fully conceived. This allows you to test out a number of key assumptions and gather data on each one. This includes:

- How deeply do customers engage with the idea?
  Example: Create a video of your product and analyze whether or not customers watch the entire video.

- Do customers want to buy your product?
  Example: Try adding a Buy button to your landing page and see how many users click on it.

- How much are customers willing to pay?
  Example: Experiment with various prices, and see which ones get the highest responses.

- What website designs do customers prefer?
  Example: Try several designs of your landing page and see which ones perform best.

- What product designs do customers prefer?
  Example: If your product is a gadget or other physical good, you can mock up sample product designs and see which ones customers choose.

- Which marketing copy is most effective?
  Example: Write various product descriptions and calls to action, then measure the customer response for each one.

- Is your product concept viral?
  Example: Add a Share button and see if customers click on it.
- What feedback do customers have?
  Example: Add a Feedback button and solicit customer input.

A/B Testing

When A/B testing, you can show one group of customers sample A and another group sample B. With simple analytics, you can measure which one is more effective. Samples A and B can be anything from prices to designs to marketing copy. When used in conjunction with a landing page, this type of testing can produce valuable data. With tools like Unbounce, Optimizely, and Google Analytics, you can measure bounce rates, usage, and conversion.

Ad Campaigns

Even when your product is at the idea stage, you can run a sophisticated advertising campaign and measure the click-through rates. You can also gather data on the cost of advertising and use this to predict your customer acquisition costs. Platforms like Facebook and Google AdWords enable you to drill down on demographics and target specific customers. This data can help you build a more accurate customer profile.

Crowdfunding

Sites like Kickstarter and Indiegogo are one of the best ways to gather data, gauge market demand, and make money in the process. However, you need to be careful. It's nice to raise a lot of money, but you want to make sure the pricing is right. Many crowdfunded projects have underestimated the cost and time necessary to produce the final product and wound up unable to deliver. This can quickly become a nightmare. And just because the folks on a crowdfunding site love your product doesn't mean it's a large, scalable business. A lot of the backers tend to be hobbyists and early adopters, which aren't necessarily representative of the overall market or your target customer. Before you go live on a crowdfunding site, it pays to do as much research and data gathering as possible, so that you are relatively certain who you're targeting and that you can deliver on your promises.

Preorder Pages

Preorder pages are similar to a Kickstarter or Indiegogo campaign, except they are typically on the company's website. They allow users to buy the product in advance, helping the company gauge market demand and gather data.

Explainer Videos

Everyone loves explainer videos because they can bring a product to life by showing exactly what the product does for the customer. The more you can visualize your product and demonstrate how it is used in real-life situations, the better. They say a picture is worth a thousand words. If this is true, an explainer video is worth at least a thousand pictures, which comes out to a million words.

Targeted Prototypes

Targeted prototypes come in many forms, including PowerPoints, digital images, 3D models, pen and paper mockups, role playing scenarios, and minimum viable products (MVP). A good example of the single feature MVP is Foursquare. When they launched, the only feature was the ability to check in at specific locations and earn recognition.

The most common type of targeted prototype is the quick and dirty MVP created entirely from off-the-shelf technology, so it can be rapidly deployed to gather data and test the market. Groupon launched using only WordPress, Apple Mail, and an AppleScript that generated PDFs as orders were received from the website. That was all they needed to test the market.

Fake MVPs

A fake MVP is when you pretend that an online product or service is doing the job, when in actuality the founders are doing all the work manually behind the scenes. When Arram Sabeti started ZeroCater, an online service to match caterers with businesses, he did everything manually, using a giant spreadsheet and e-mail. On the surface, it looked like the site was working, but it was just an empty shell. This allowed him to gather the data necessary to validate his concept.

Concierge MVPs

Concierge MVPs are the same as fake MVPs, except that they don't hide the fact that people are doing the work behind the scenes. In fact, they make this a feature of the product, touting a highly personalized service aimed at a select group of customers. Rent the Runway, a site where women can rent designer clothing, tested its business by offering personalized service to female college students. This gave them enough data to prove out their model.

NEVER STOP MINING

All of the above methods are valuable ways to gather data, but don't stop there. Be creative. Come up with new sources. This is by no means an exhaustive list. It's just a starting point. The more data you gather, the better off you'll be in the long run. And don't fool yourself into thinking you're done gathering data after a month or two. You're never done. Smart innovators are continually gathering data from the day they conceive their idea through launch and forever afterward.

You need to be perpetually gathering data and refining your process and analytical methods. Remember, data is always more valuable than visionary thinking. It should form the basis of your business plan. It's the data that makes it all real. That's what your innovation teams need to focus on. As Jonathan Rosenberg, former senior vice president of products at Google, said, "Back up your position with data. You don't win arguments by saying, 'I think.' You win by saying, 'Let me show you.'"

It doesn't matter how creative anyone's ideas are if they can't back them up with hard proof. At the end of the day, your company will sink or swim based on the facts and nothing else. So having those facts at your fingertips early should be your number one priority.

Chapter 23

Value over Money

Companies that get confused, that think their goal is revenue or stock price or something. You have to focus on the things that lead to those.

—Tim Cook, CEO of Apple

Smart companies focus on value over money. They are willing to sacrifice short-term revenue gains for long-term market dominance. Look at some of the most successful startups in Silicon Valley: Google, Facebook, Twitter, Snapchat, Instagram, and WhatsApp. All of them focused on building value for their users from day one; all of them refused to monetize with ads when they launched; and all have been extremely careful about how to integrate advertising and other forms of monetization so as not to diminish the value to users.

Smart startups, just like smart innovation teams, focus on two things: user satisfaction and growing market share. Anything that harms the user experience or impedes growth is avoided. Startups know that to dominate their market, they must be number one, and that means offering their customers more value than anyone else. Here are a few examples:

BITLY

Bitly, a startup that offers a popular link shortener, used to be something people only used to shorten links. But the company has been relentless about adding value for their customers. They saw an opportunity to gather data about everyone who clicks on a Bitly link, including their motivations, locations, demographics, intent, content preferences, and more. Mark Josephson, Bitly's CEO, says, "We refocused the entire company on helping marketers get the extensive value our product offered that they hadn't realized to date; and it revolutionized our customer experience and value." Bitly's mission is to become an essential tool that provides value to marketers by offering deep customer insights. The result has been more frequent customer engagement for longer periods of time.

ETSY

Etsy is a startup that showcases and sells handcrafted goods to over 20 million buyers. Etsy is always looking for new ways to add value. While most Amazon and eBay users are searching for a product they already have in mind, Etsy's users want to explore and discover unique things to buy. They want to be surprised and delighted by what they stumble across. According to Mike Grishaver, senior vice president of product at Etsy, his team is continually improving how it recommends products, basing their algorithms on factors that go beyond what people have previously viewed or purchased. The result is an adventure that can surprise shoppers with that special item they didn't even know they wanted. Grishaver advises other companies to "look beyond the basic mechanics of what users can do on your site. Find the deeper experience that makes them feel more connected and then infuse that into every part of their experience with you." The results speak for themselves. After each improvement to their discovery algorithms, user engagement increased and satisfaction went up.

AMAZON

Amazon is a master at prioritizing value over money. Jeff Bezos makes sure to always provide his customers with more value than any of his competitors. While selling books, Bezos found customers preferred free shipping. This data led him to launch Amazon Prime, where customers pay a flat annual fee and get unlimited free shipping. Then he found that customers wanted their orders to be delivered as quickly as possible, so Amazon offered Prime members free two-day shipping on all orders.

Amazon also made returns incredibly easy. Unlike competitors that actually make it hard to return a product, at Amazon it's a no-hassle proposition. Just print a label and UPS will pick it up—no questions asked. Does this cost Amazon money? Yes, but it makes the experience painless and keeps customers from hesitating before they buy. They know they can return the product if they don't like it.

Even with these innovations, Bezos kept thinking of how to add value for his customers. He didn't mind deferring short-term profits. Wall Street got the message and gave Amazon more leeway than most public companies. With room to innovate, Amazon added more free services for its Prime members. Next came Amazon Video, where customers received thousands of movies and TV shows at no cost. It was a scaled-down version of Netflix without the monthly subscription fee. Amazon then added free streaming music and free cloud storage for photos for Prime members.

All of these services cost Amazon quite a bit of money, but they lock customers more firmly into the Prime ecosystem, making the switch to a competitor harder and harder to do. I'm an Amazon customer, and I can tell you that I don't even think about switching. Now that I have my e-books, photos, and music on Amazon, I don't want to give them up.

GOOGLE

Google is also a master of this approach. They give away Gmail, Google Maps, Google Docs, and a myriad of other services to their customers. Each time a user subscribes to a new Google service, the ties grow deeper. Giving up Gmail or Google Docs is not easy. And the more you use them, the harder it gets to jump to a competitor like Microsoft. This is what makes Google so powerful. They are always placing value over money. If low price is the only value your company offers, then it's easy for customers to jump ship. Price isn't sticky.

What is sticky are services in which the customer invests time and energy. If I learn how to use a particular piece of software, I'll hesitate to make a change—especially if it took me a long time to master it. That's a lot of work I don't want to repeat. Another sticky value is content. If I upload my content to an app, and that content isn't easy to export, then I'm bound to the app as long as I value the content. The third and most powerful sticky factor is friends. This is why Google tried so hard to lure users away from Facebook to Google+, their own social network. But in the end, even Google couldn't do it. Friends are the stickiest. I may be okay with leaving my content behind, but I'd be loath to leave my friends behind. And friends aren't easy to bring along with you. You may be able to convince a few friends to defect, but try getting all your friends to make the move at once.

YOUR CUSTOMERS

Now let's delve into the three main areas that will determine whether your company succeeds or fails with its customers.

1. Customer Retention

Businesses that bleed customers, only to replace them with fresh faces, ultimately pay the price. Customer acquisition costs are high, and unless you can squeeze enough dollars out of each customer, it's unsustainable. Far better to focus on retaining the customers you have by providing real value. Kissmetrics, a data analytics company, found that acquiring new customers is up to seven times more expensive than retaining existing customers. They also found that 71 percent of customers who ended their relationship with a company did so due to poor service, and 61 percent took their business to a competitor. The average value of a lost customer is $243.

SumAll, another data analytics company, found that 25 to 40 percent of the total revenues of the most stable businesses in its network come from returning customers. Even better, businesses with 40 percent repeat customers generated nearly 50 percent more revenue than those with 10 percent repeat customers. The message is clear: Retain customers by providing value if you want to succeed.

Insightly, a startup that offers a simple-to-use yet powerful customer-relationship-management system for small businesses is a good example of this. They are constantly working to increase their own customer retention. One way they did this was to identify four features of their service that loyal customers used most often and then educated the rest of their customers on these features. The vice president of customer success, Lynn Tsoflias, believes that entrepreneurs need to "guide customers to their goals and help them gain the maximum value from the solution." The result for Insightly has been higher customer retention and satisfaction rates.

2. Types of Value

There are many different types of value you can provide a customer. Price, quality, service, and selection are the most obvious ones. But there are also customer experience, reliability, community, content, functionality, aesthetics, cachet, speed, reputation, brand, security, and so on. Innovators need to understand every element of their business that can provide value and work to improve each of them, until the sum total is the best in its class. Every form of value that can be offered should be identified and maximized throughout the lifetime of a product.

This is what the world's most successful companies do. They never stop looking for ways to increase the value to customers. This winds up being their number one goal, and it's their best defense against competitors stealing their business. Only by thoroughly understanding the value proposition and the customer perception can a company effectively compete in the marketplace.

MYTH: THE MORE FEATURES, THE MORE INNOVATIVE

Adding a lot of features to a product doesn't make it innovative. In fact, more features usually make it less innovative. The most innovative products tend to be simple. They have one key feature that adds value customers can't get from any other product.

3. Customer Loyalty

Have you heard of Net Promoter Score? It's a popular tool for evaluating customer loyalty, and it was introduced by Fred Reichheld in a *Harvard Business Review* article entitled "The One Number You Need to Grow" in 2003. It measures whether or not customers will recommend a company's products or services to friends and colleagues. Many Fortune 500 companies use this data to gauge their performance.

Net Promoter Score works by asking customers a simple question: How likely are you to recommend this company, product, or service to a friend or colleague? The customer gives a score from 0 to 10, where 0 is very unlikely, and 10 is extremely likely. Promoters are those who give a 9 or 10. Passives are those who give a 7 or 8. And Detractors give a 0 to 6. Net Promoter Score is calculated by subtracting the percentage of Detractors from the percentage of Promoters. The higher the score, the more satisfied the customers, and the more likely the company is to outperform the

THE VISUAL FOR NET PROMOTER SCORE

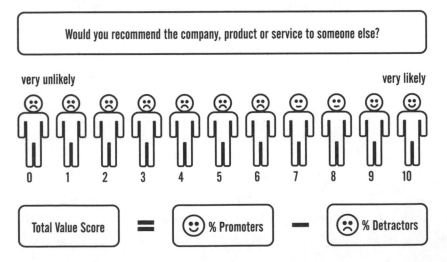

NET PROMOTER SCORE

Would you recommend the company, product or service to someone else?

very unlikely · very likely

0 1 2 3 4 5 6 7 8 9 10

Total Value Score = 😊 % Promoters — ☹ % Detractors

competition. Brands and corporations use this metric religiously to gauge their progress, pumping money and resources into boosting their score.

This all sounds great, but there's a problem. I believe the Net Promoter Score oversimplifies things, leading to false conclusions. *Bloomberg Businessweek* published the article "Proof That It Pays to Be America's Most-Hated Companies" in 2013. The magazine found that customer-service scores have no relevance to stock market returns. In fact, some of the most hated companies perform better than their popular competitors. Spending money making all customers happy isn't the answer. Many of the most profitable businesses in the world have a low Net Promoter Score.

An article in *MIT Sloan Management Review* entitled "The High Price of Customer Satisfaction" goes further, pointing out three main reasons the Net Promoter Score doesn't work. The first is the Groupon syndrome. Groupon famously—or infamously, depending on your perspective—sold many small businesses on the idea of offering deep discounts to their customers. The result was high customer satisfaction but at a steep price. The discounts attracted new customers, but the majority of those customers didn't stick around past the deal. The special offers also made existing customers happy, but that effect was short-lived. Without a new discount, the happiness faded fast. The bottom line is that no merchant can afford to lose money for an extended period of time, even if this dramatically increases the Net Promoter Score. Simply focusing on boosting the score by any means doesn't make sense.

The second issue with Net Promoter Score is that it doesn't work for companies that address a mass market, like Walmart, which has received a low Net Promoter Score. It's hard for Walmart, which sells everything from clothing to groceries, to provide the same level of satisfaction as specialty stores, like Under Armour or Whole Foods. Walmart simply offers too many product categories to be the best in any one of them. In addition, the broader the target customers, the harder it is to appeal to any single group of customers and attend to their specific needs. Net Promoter Score doesn't take these factors into account, so the results are skewed.

Another problem with Net Promoter Score is that companies like Comcast, which have a virtual monopoly, tend to get extremely low ratings; yet they are highly profitable. This is precisely because their customers don't have a choice. In San Francisco, where I live, if you want services like access to high-bandwidth Internet or live sports broadcasts, Comcast is really the only game in town. It doesn't matter if you want to murder your cable guy for crappy service, there's really no one else you can turn to. For this reason, they can charge exorbitant prices and provide mediocre service, while still retaining their customers.

The same is true if you own the only gas station for fifty miles. You can charge substantially more for your gas and provide little or no service. Sure, this may lower customer satisfaction, but if you're the only one with the product and your customers need it, they don't have a choice. Just look at Apple—they get away with charging substantially more for their phones than almost anyone else. That's because they've created a virtual monopoly. You can't buy an iPhone from competitors, while Android manufacturers have to compete on price. Could Apple charge less and increase their Net Promoter Score? Sure they could, but why should they?

Another flaw in the Net Promoter Score lies in the fact that it doesn't take into account the customer's value to the company when gauging customer satisfaction. Under Net Promoter Score, all customers are considered equal, when in reality they are not. Some customers are much more valuable to a company than others. Repeat customers, who spend lots of money, are far more valuable than freeloaders, who cost the company money. To consider their input as equal gives a distorted picture of what really matters to the business.

This is why I'd modify the Net Promoter Score and call it the Total Value Score. Unlike the Net Promoter Score, the Total Value Score emphasizes the total value a company, product, or service provides to the customer in relation to direct competitors. Here's how it works:

1. Ask this question: Would you recommend the company, product, or service to someone else over these competitors: _____
2. If there are no real competitors, the business is a virtual monopoly, and the Total Value Score is not applicable.

3. If the business is not a virtual monopoly, each customer is asked to give a Value Score from 0 to 10 in answer to the above question, where 0 is very unlikely to recommend and 10 is very likely to recommend the company.

4. The customers are then categorized into two groups:
   High Value Customers = profitable or valuable
   Low Value Customers = not profitable or not valuable

5. Here's the formula:
   Detractors = percent of High Value Customers giving a score of 0–6
   Passives = percent of High Value Customers giving a score of 7–8
   Promoters = percent of High Value Customers giving a score of 9–10
   Total Value Score = percent Promoters - percent Detractors

So let's say you have 35 percent Promoters and 10 percent Detractors, then your Total Value Score is 35 - 10 = 25, where the highest possible score is 100 and the lowest is - 100.

The Total Value Score solves several issues I have with the Net Promoter Score. First, the Total Value Score uses only data from high-value customers. Next, it asks customers if they'd recommend the company, product, or service over a competitor. After all, the score only makes sense in comparison to direct competitors, like Walmart versus Target. Walmart shouldn't be compared to specialty retailers.

Despite the fact that the American Customer Satisfaction Index shows that Walmart has the lowest satisfaction levels among all major grocery retailers in the United States, customers continue to flock to Walmart, making it the largest grocery retailer in America. This is because Walmart offers more total value than the competition, even if they fall short in verticals like groceries. Whether you love or hate Walmart, their mega stores with strong buying power, variety of products, and cost-effective supply-chain management enable them to keep prices low and margins healthy, while servicing a mass market.

The same is true when Jeff Bezos creates value for Amazon. It's always the total value that matters at the end of the day. Amazon doesn't have to be the best in every product category they sell online. In fact, they will almost never be able to compete with specialty retailers, but that doesn't matter. There's no point in Amazon spending an enormous amount of time and money trying to win every possible niche. They're not in that business. They're a superstore, and they win by being the best default online shopping destination, just like Walmart does offline.

Comcast is a similar story with a twist. While I love Amazon, I personally think Comcast charges way too much and provides poor service. But in my market, the alternatives are worse. So if you asked me to rank Comcast, their Net Promoter Score would be negative, but their Total Value Score would be N/A (not applicable) since there's no real competition. Yes, I'd be happier if Comcast lowered their prices and improved service, but as long as Comcast has a virtual monopoly, it doesn't matter what I think. In other words, satisfaction matters only in comparison to equivalent competition.

Once there's equivalent competition from other providers, then Comcast will be compelled to improve or lose market share. We're starting to see this happen as more TV programming migrates online and competitors offer better, cheaper broadband service in some markets. It's only a matter of time before Comcast feels the pain. When this day comes, Comcast will either be forced to improve quality, cut prices, or differentiate themselves, or they will lose customers.

In "winner takes all" markets, customers move quickly toward the one company that offers the best overall value. If your innovation teams can't offer customers the most value, they need to rethink their strategy. Cutting price is only a temporary solution. It doesn't change the basic equation. Value always trumps money when it comes to owning the customer. That's why the winners always put value over money.

INNOVATING INSIDE ORGANIZATIONS

Chapter 24

Fear Factor

Failure seldom stops you. What stops you is the fear of failure.

—Jack Lemmon, actor

In this chapter I'm going to explain why fear is the bitter enemy of innovation. Whether you are working in a startup or a large corporation, fear can undermine your best efforts if you let it take hold. This is especially true in large, bureaucratic organizations with hierarchical structures. Fear thrives in this type of host, slowly killing any attempts at innovation, like a deadly parasite.

Let's begin with human nature. Human beings are innately fearful. It's part of our DNA. It's how we survived. We are especially fearful of how others within our group perceive us. This is because we evolved as social creatures where our well-being was dependent on the other members of our tribe.

The prehistoric world was a harsh place filled with ferocious animals, hostile tribes, droughts, famine, and disease. Homo sapiens were more successful than other species, because we learned how to cooperate and work as a group. If we upset our fellow sapiens, they kicked us out of the tribe, and our chances of survival plummeted. Being expelled from the group was a virtual death sentence. Even if a tribal outcast managed to find a way to stay alive, it was nearly impossible to find a mate, so the DNA wouldn't pass on to the next generation. In short, playing it safe and avoiding doing anything that may risk one's standing in the group are traits reinforced through thousands of years of natural selection.

If you are going to innovate as a company, you must overcome this hard-coded fear. This is because innovating is the opposite of playing it safe. It's inherently risky, the stakes are high, and the process involves failure. To make matters worse, corporations are usually structured hierarchically, with inflexible rules, rewards for success, and punishments for screwing up.

All managers want to take credit for good ideas, but nobody wants to be associated with bad ones. So a typical manager would rather not innovate unless she knows it's going to work. But if a project is new and has never been done before, it's impossible to know if it will succeed. As Jeff Bezos, founder of Amazon, likes to say, "It's not an experiment if you know it's going to work."

The result is that managers are hesitant to innovate. They are also loath to kill off a project once it's started, even if it's clearly headed nowhere. It's much safer to keep the project going and pray the team will figure out a way to save it in the eleventh hour. In most companies, this results in a massive waste of time and resources. It ties up the best teams on hopeless endeavors, demoralizes the participants, and produces little of value.

What you must instill in your innovation teams is that their job is to rapidly go through idea after idea after idea, 99 percent of which will die on the vine. And even when they commit to an idea that seems promising, it will probably wind up roadkill. At the end of the day, the majority of venture-funded startups fail, and the same is true with truly innovative projects inside corporations. And the more innovative they are, the higher the failure rate.

In every innovative endeavor there are a great many unknowns, and most people instinctively shy away from taking chances. People don't like uncertainty. Numerous studies have shown that people will almost always choose a certain outcome over an uncertain outcome, even when it is to their disadvantage. For instance, when people are offered an 85 percent chance to win $1,000 (with a 15 percent chance of winning nothing) or simply receiving $800, the large majority will choose the sure thing over the gamble, even after it is explained to them that the gamble is a better deal on average. Just look at the math. If everyone chooses the chance to win $1,000, the average will come out to be: $(0.85 \times \$1,000) + (0.15 \times \$0) = \$850$.

The same logic applies to starting new projects in a company. If you give employees the choice of joining a project that is nearly certain to succeed, although the payoff is small, or taking a risk on an innovative project with a potentially big payoff and a high degree of uncertainty, which do you think people will choose? Small and safe wins almost every time.

We can learn something from how scientists treat failure. They come up with a hypothesis, they run a series of tests, and if it doesn't work, they move on to the next experiment. If scientists threw up their hands and proclaimed themselves a failure the first time they hit a dead end, we'd have no science. Science is about repeatedly trying and failing. There's no stigma attached to experiments that produce results that differ from the hypothesis. This is part of the process. The scientist's job is to continually create new hypotheses, test them out, and record the results as faithfully as possible. When science is done right, it's not about protecting reputations; it's about discovering the truth. There's a truth out there, and it isn't going to change even if the results are faked or ignored. Some scientists have tried this only to be exposed later. Remember cold fusion? What a fiasco.

The problem is that businesspeople are not scientists. They care intensely about their reputations. It's what matters most. Truth is secondary. In the business world, failure is looked down upon. The logic goes that if you're wrong and fail, no one will trust you. To build trust, you have to have an unblemished track record of success. This is how you get promoted; this is how you raise money; this is why you're the boss and someone else isn't. Success is everything in the business world. The result is a toxic elixir that poisons innovation.

These toxins are what keep managers from innovating. Most people are naturally creative. In every sizable company, even the most conservative and stodgy, there are talented, creative people who have ideas and would like to innovate. But they don't, and that's no accident. It's because of how most organizations are structured. Employees tend to be punished for failure far more than they are rewarded for success. Any rational, intelligent person within a structure like this will come to understand that taking a risk on a radically innovative project is not a good career move.

MYTH: IT PAYS TO GET IT RIGHT THE FIRST TIME

Many people think that it pays to get it right the first time. The problem is that teams that try to get it right the first time tend to focus on less risky, less innovative solutions. It makes sense because that's the only way to ensure they'll get it right. So if you don't want to innovate, try to get it right the first time.

In order to have an innovative company at all levels, not just with the scientists in the R & D lab, you need to develop an organization that embraces failure and removes the underlying stigma. At Facebook, they have three tenets that all employees are encouraged to follow: (1) Move fast and break things; (2) What would you do if you weren't afraid? and (3) Put people at the center of things. The first two are designed to give employees both permission to fail and the freedom to take risks. The third is the core of their social network. Combined they form the philosophy that has driven Facebook from a dorm-room project to one of the most powerful and innovative companies in the world.

Only by putting failure at the heart of your innovation efforts and explaining, not covering up, the role failure plays in the process can you move your organization into the future and enable your employees to feel secure taking the type of risks that will lead to the next big breakthroughs. Edward D. Hess, professor of business administration at the Darden School of Business, says, "Failure is a necessary part of the innovation process because from failure comes learning, iteration, adaptation, and the building of new conceptual and physical models through an iterative learning process. Almost all innovations are the result of prior learning from failures."

The mayor's office in Boston has addressed this problem in a unique way. Because cities tend to be even more risk averse and slow moving than most private businesses, getting government employees to innovate has been a challenge. To tackle this issue, the mayor's office established the New Urban Mechanics team, which is made up of individuals who do nothing but innovate for their jobs. In other words, their job is to take risks and fail. These innovators spend all their time helping other departments launch new innovation projects with the goal of solving hard problems.

Susan Nguyen, the program director, explains, "If the project succeeds, the department takes all the credit. If it fails, we take all the credit." This is the key. The innovators give the other departments permission to fail by accepting all responsibility, essentially removing the downside while keeping the upside. By sheltering the departments, they can create an environment of trust and security, which is conducive to experimentation and risk taking.

FAMOUS FUMBLERS

Let's take a quick look at some famous folks who failed:

- Colonel Harland Sanders's secret chicken recipe was rejected over a thousand times. But the colonel never gave up, founding Kentucky Fried Chicken when he was sixty-five years old.
- Mark Cuban failed as a carpenter, cook, and waiter, but he did manage to sell Broadcast.com to Yahoo for billions. Mark likes to say, "I've learned that it doesn't matter how many times you failed. You only have to be right once. I tried to sell powdered milk. I was an idiot lots of times, and I learned from them all."
- Arianna Huffington's second book was rejected by thirty-six publishers. Later she founded the *Huffington Post*, one of the most successful online news websites in America.
- Frank Winfield Woolworth worked at a dry goods store, where his boss refused to let him wait on a customer because "Frank didn't

have enough common sense to serve the customers." Frank went on to found the F. W. Woolworth Company.

- Akio Morita, who cofounded Sony, came up with a rice cooker as his first product. The problem was that it burned the rice. Luckily, he didn't give up there.

- Milton Hershey started three different candy companies, and all of them failed. The fourth time was a charm.

- Bill Gates and Paul Allen founded Traf-O-Data. The product barely worked, and the company failed. Later they started Microsoft.

- When Thomas Edison was a boy, his teacher told him that he was too stupid to learn anything and suggested he go into a field that did not require intelligence. Perhaps Edison's 1,093 patents were a way of proving his teacher wrong. But Edison wasn't an infallible genius. He tried more than nine thousand failed experiments before he created the lightbulb. "I have not failed. I've just found ten thousand ways that won't work," said Edison.

- Fred Smith came up with a business concept at Yale University that nearly earned him a failing grade. This business idea was FedEx.

- Henry Ford's first two car companies failed and left him broke. We all know about the third one.

- Rowland Hussey Macy opened four retail dry goods stores, and all of them failed. He learned from those mistakes, and Macy's was born.

- Richard Branson is famous for Virgin Galactic, Virgin Records, and Virgin Airlines, but nobody talks much about his many failures, including Virgin Cola and Virgin Vodka.

- George Steinbrenner owned a small basketball team called the Cleveland Pipers, which went bankrupt under his leadership. Thirty years later, he led the New York Yankees to an incredible comeback with six World Series entries. It became one of the most profitable teams in Major League Baseball.

- Soichiro Honda applied for a job at Toyota and was rejected. Without work, he began making scooters at home, which he sold to neighbors. These were the first Hondas.

- Walt Disney was fired by an editor because "he lacked imagination and had no original ideas." To add injury to insult, Disney's first animation company went bankrupt. The rest is history.

If you don't remove the fear of failure, your company will be stuck with incremental innovation, where employees improve products and services rather than create entirely new ones. Incremental innovation is safe. There's relatively little risk. It is what corporations naturally do well. But incremental innovation won't stave off disruption or create new markets. It's a defensive move. It enables your company to retain market share, not redefine the market. You will never leapfrog your competitors and produce exponential growth through incremental innovation. For companies to embrace radical innovation, they must first wage war on fear.

Chapter 25

Culture of Innovation

Big companies have trouble with innovation. Innovation is about bad ideas, or ideas that look like bad ideas.

—Ben Horowitz, venture capitalist at
Andreessen Horowitz

Fear of failure is more prevalent in large organizations than startups. Entrepreneurs tend to be risk takers who are psychologically prepared to fail many times on their way to success. In big companies, middle managers thrive on stability and predictability. They joined a large company precisely because it provides a safe, low-risk way to advance their careers and provide for their families.

It's impossible to simply snap your fingers and change your company culture, but there are a number of practical steps you can take. The first is creating a culture of acceptance. You must not only accept failure but also stupid ideas, silly mistakes, contradictory thoughts, and wasted money. No matter how unorthodox or crazy a team member's idea might seem, the person behind it should not be criticized. Not every project has to be approved. There needs to be a rigorous filtering and selection process. But that process should not be overly judgmental toward the individuals behind the ideas. Sometimes what appears to be an outrageous idea on the surface is actually what the company needs most.

Read a little history, and you'll notice a pattern of nutty, unrealistic ideas turning out to be the future. Galileo Galilei was sent to the Inquisition for declaring that the Earth wasn't flat. Charles Babbage died penniless after dreaming up the first programmable computing device. When the UNIVAC was invented, few people could imagine the possibility of a personal computer. It took hippies, hobbyists, and hackers in California to bring about the PC revolution. When Richard Stallman was evangelizing the benefits of open-source software, most corporations thought it was pure madness. What company in their right mind would give away their proprietary code? That was their competitive advantage. When cell phones first came out, who would have thought they'd become music players, cameras, and personal assistants?

So when an employee comes up with an idea that seems ludicrous, you have to remember they may be on to something. It just may be a diamond in the rough. In order not to squash some of your most far-out thinkers, your corporate culture needs to accommodate all sorts of opinions and belief systems. You have to teach your employees not to criticize what's different. You want employees with unconventional and often unspoken views to feel comfortable contributing. Those oddball nonconformists may be the ones you need in the mix if you're going to make big leaps forward.

Peter Thiel, the founder of PayPal and early investor in Facebook, is fond of asking people, "What important truth do very few people agree with you on?" Thiel realizes that the more people who disagree with you, the more potential your idea may have. He makes the point that it's often the freaks who can spot opportunities the rest of us are blind to, precisely because they think differently and look at the world from a unique perspective.

CHANGING THE CULTURE

In an attempt to improve their culture, Google set out to understand exactly what makes teams more innovative and effective. In 2012, they launched Project Aristotle with the goal of determining why some of their groups radically outperformed others. Google's researchers reviewed a half-century of academic papers. One of these studies was conducted by psychologists from Carnegie Mellon, MIT, and Union College. In 2008, they recruited 699 people for a study on what makes teams perform well.

One experiment involved asking participants to brainstorm possible uses for a brick. Some teams came up with dozens of ingenious uses, while others only had a few. Surprisingly, it wasn't the teams with the smartest people who came up with the best results. Some teams scoring only average on an IQ test performed far better than other teams with exceptionally intelligent members. Why was this? What made some teams so much more creative and effective than others, regardless of the individual's abilities?

The answer was how the team members treated one another. Teams that encouraged everyone to participate scored much better. Also, teams with higher social sensitivity, meaning the members could intuit how others felt based on their tone of voice, their expressions, and other nonverbal cues, performed better as a group. These two factors could raise a group's collective intelligence and productivity far above a group with more experienced and accomplished individuals.

To confirm this finding, Google studied 180 internal teams and found that the groups whose members felt the most secure speaking their minds performed best. This is what psychologists call psychological safety. The more open and accepted people feel, the better they cooperate and think together as a single unit. It's the teams who openly debate, interrupt one another, and discuss every aspect of everything that score the highest. Using this data, Google set out to build a culture of acceptance, where everyone could participate without fear of losing status or being criticized. This has been one of their keys to successful innovation.

THE GOD COMPLEX

Tim Harford, an author and journalist for the *Financial Times*, believes that to create a culture of innovation your teams cannot have a God complex. This means no one should believe he or she has all the right answers, no matter how smart or knowledgeable that person is. Everyone should be open to being wrong much of the time. Admitting you just don't know is often the best way to innovate. This opens the team up to unorthodox solutions and new ideas.

Let's look at what Unilever did. They are one of the largest sellers of laundry detergents. When they wanted to innovate on their manufacturing process, they had two choices: (1) they could hire a team of the smartest engineers in the world to design a new nozzle for spraying the detergent onto drying beds; or (2) they could simply build ten random nozzles, try each one, and then select the best design and try ten more variations based on it, until eventually they would come up with the optimal design.

Most companies would choose option number one. Why not just put brainpower behind the problem and come up with the right solution? This problem, however, was so complex that even the smartest minds would have trouble coming up with the perfect design. For situations like this, it's far better to rely on brute-force trial and error than clever thinking. That was what Unilever did, and after forty-five generations, they wound up with the optimal nozzle, which is so unintuitive and complex no person could have possibly foreseen or designed it that way. To innovate, Unilever had to admit their people weren't smarter than simply trying various possibilities until they got it right. This is a big cultural change for most organizations.

OTHER INNOVATION CULTURES

In recent years, different corporations have been taking different approaches to innovation. At Microsoft, the innovation teams are now encouraged to participate not only in product innovation but also business-model and policy innovation. Since making this change, Microsoft's teams have taken the company in a direction that was previously taboo. They've brought free versions of Office to both the Android and iOS platforms. This would have been considered heresy prior to the change in culture. Microsoft is also working to push back against the National Security Agency as well as European Union regulators in the areas of privacy and disclosure. This type of policy innovation was once unthinkable.

Autodesk, a powerhouse in 3D design and engineering software, is also working on building a culture of innovation. They hold a series of innovation workshops, where employees are not trained on how to come up with new ideas. Instead they focus on what to do with the ideas their employees already have. Who should hear the ideas? How should the ideas be presented? What process should be used to evaluate the ideas? The goal is to create a system whereby the employees feel comfortable breaking new ground and understand the steps by which a new idea can become an actual project with the support of the company behind it.

Lou Gerstner, the head of IBM, who helped turn the personal computer into a mainstream product, wrote, "I came to see, in my time at IBM, that culture isn't just one aspect of the game—it *is* the game."

The American Marketing Association looked at 759 organizations across seventeen countries to figure out what made some companies innovate while others didn't. While innovation was influenced by things like government, local attitudes, labor supply, and capital, the most important factor by far was the internal corporate culture. It doesn't matter what industry you are in or how educated your employees are, people will and can innovate if the environment is right.

Jay Rao and Joseph Weintraub published an article[5] that identifies a series of characteristics essential for a culture of innovation. Here's what they suggest you need to pay attention to:

- **Values**—It's not what the leaders say; it's what they do that defines corporate values. Innovative companies invest in promoting creativity, educating their employees, and launching new entrepreneurial projects.
- **Behaviors**—What actions do the leaders exhibit on a daily basis? Are they willing to disrupt their own business, eliminate red tape, overcome roadblocks, and listen to customers? This is what matters.
- **Climate**—Does the organization provide a safe environment that fosters learning, builds trust among employees, and promotes independent thinking?
- **Resources**—What resources can the organization mobilize? This includes systems, projects, capital, and people who can step up and become innovation champions.
- **Process**—Has the organization established an innovation funnel, where good ideas can be submitted, vetted, and put into action?

■ **Success**—What can the organization show for all its work? There are many different types of success, including external validation from customers, enterprise success, and personal success.

Here's how Adobe put the culture of innovation into practice. Mark Randall, vice president of creativity at Adobe, launched a program called Kickbox, where they hand out a red box designed to stimulate corporate innovation. Each box contains a prepaid credit card with $1,000. The employees are free to spend this money in any way they want on their ideas—no questions asked. The Kickbox also contains a six-step guide that takes employees through the process of innovation:

1. Define your motivations.
2. Work out your ideas so they align with corporate objectives.
3. Evaluate your ideas with frameworks, scorecards, and exercises.
4. Validate the problem and the solution.
5. Gather data to back up your hypotheses.
6. Ask for money: Go around and see if anyone buys into your vision!

To sweeten the deal, each red box includes a Starbucks gift card and a candy bar. Adobe distributed one thousand red boxes to employees and held workshops around the world. The results include the following:

■ The acquisition of Fotolia, a stock-photography marketplace
■ Adobe KnowHow, which enables users of Adobe's creative software to publish instructional videos
■ Memory Maker, which has been integrated into Adobe Lightroom as a video syncing feature
■ Project Breathe, an internal program at Adobe for mindfulness and meditation

Adobe has even open-sourced Kickbox so that anyone can download and use it for free. Give it a try, but don't expect the $1,000 prepaid credit card or the candy bar to be included!

MYTH: THE 20 PERCENT RULE

The 20 percent rule is a popular concept that has caught on with many large companies as a panacea for innovation. It's so seductive because it's so simple. It just requires the CEO to say, "Let's give our employees 20 percent of their time to innovate!"

Google's founders didn't invent this concept, but they made it famous. The idea was to give Google employees 20 percent of their time to work on innovative projects that interest them.

The problem is that most managers want their employees to spend 100 percent of their time getting their job done, not dabbling on side projects. Chris Mims, a journalist, wrote that Google's 20 percent rule was "as good as dead" because it became too difficult for employees to take time off from their normal jobs. Ex-Googler Marissa Mayer has gone so far as to say, "I've got to tell you the dirty little secret of Google's 20 percent time. It's really 120 percent time."

Who wants to work nights and weekends without pay? This myth is busted, and that's why you don't hear Google talking about it anymore.

BUILDING TRUST

Central to building a culture of innovation is the concept of trust. Most people are open to change and even risk taking as long as they believe it won't harm them. You can pay lip service to the ideas of valuing failure, but unless you back those up with concrete actions that build trust, employees will still be reluctant to engage.

Trust is not only essential for the employees doing the innovations; it's essential for the entire organization. What if certain innovations make people or entire departments obsolete? What happens to their jobs? Will they be retrained for other positions or let go? Unless management addresses these questions head-on, the trust won't be there. Let's face it: Innovating may be good for the company and shareholders, but it's not always good for all employees.

Here are some questions your company may need to ask when you embark on an innovation project:

- How will this innovation project affect the employees?
- Who will have a say in the process?
- Who will be the final decision makers?
- Will employees be retrained for other jobs if necessary?
- What support is the organization willing to provide?
- Why is this important to each employee?
- What can the organization do to make this a success for everyone?

Answering these honestly is the first step toward building the trust necessary to take big risks and make changes.

FORWARD THINKING

Creating a culture of forward thinking, open debate, and acceptance of the new is the foundation of innovation. Groupthink and the desire to conform are the enemies. The problem again goes back to our prehistoric roots. It was critical for tribes to unite around a single idea and act as a single body for them to survive. Those tribes where everyone went their own way got wiped out. As a result, most humans feel comfortable following those ahead of them. It's far easier to believe what others believe than challenge prevailing truths. History gives us countless examples of this. In the Middle Ages, most people believed that fossils were either nothing but rock, the result of the Great Flood described in the book of Genesis, or grew inside the Earth due to some fertile power. Even in the twenty-first century, most people don't question their belief system. They simply accept a worldview and take all the inherent assumptions as undeniable facts.

In order to change how people think in your organization, you have to challenge orthodoxies. General Electric (GE) launched FastWorks, a program where execs are trained to take risks, learn constantly, and ask questions. Annual reviews have been replaced by continuous daily check-ins and updates. "It's an entire organizational change," says Viv Goldstein, the global director of innovation acceleration. The global titan has even knocked down walls at their headquarters so they can create more collaborative open spaces. Jeffrey Immelt, the CEO, went so far as to turn his dining room at home into an "innovation hangout," with high-top tables, whiteboards, and IKEA couches. "It's about giving people the environment to think in a different way and getting people to take risks," says Goldstein. "I can say this is the most unbelievable experience, and I've been with GE for twenty years."

Having offices painted in bright colors, creating more open space, and adding funky furniture and foosball tables is a nice start, but changing the culture isn't that easy. It involves more than announcing innovation as priority number one and rewarding employees with prizes for coming up with new ideas. It's about changing how people think about themselves and each other, and that starts with acceptance. Many of the most innovative companies are now working to reengineer their culture with this in mind.

"When an idea doesn't work, we're careful not to call anyone into the office," said Sam Ioannidis, hotel manager at Four Seasons New York. In order to change the culture, Four Seasons stopped using words like *failure* and *mistake*; instead they call them glitches. A glitch is something that can be fixed and overcome, while failures and mistakes are more permanent and carry connotations of blame. Changing the vocabulary by which you identify problems may seem silly to some people, but it goes to the core of the issue. Language carries with it a lot of psychological baggage. If you can successfully change how people describe their actions, you can change how they think, and that is a powerful tool in any organization.

Four Seasons launched a company-wide innovation program that provides their thirty-five thousand employees with the tools and behaviors needed to ideate, pilot, and improve guest experiences. These include an innovation handbook and videos. Stacy Oliver, who helps run the program, believes that failure doesn't need to be embraced, but it does need to be accepted as part of business and life.

Google goes a step further. They celebrate failure. Astro Teller, the head of Google X, not only congratulates his teams on each failure, but he'll often give bonuses and extra vacation time to those teams who fail early. "Failures are cheap if you do them first," says Teller. "Failures are expensive if you do them at the end." The goal at Google is to get teams to try to fail as soon as possible. That way they can try something else that may work. This saves time and money, while freeing everyone up to try new things and take big risks.

In a conversation with *Yale Insights*, Tim Brown, the president and CEO of IDEO, said, "Any organization that wants to innovate, wants to be prepared to innovate, I think, has to have a few things in place. One is, and perhaps the most important thing is, methods for having an open mind. A sense of inquiry, of curiosity, is essential for innovation." The second is to "create spaces where trust can happen, where risks can get taken. We tend in our operationally minded view of the world to try and mitigate and design out as much risk as we can, but if you want to innovate, you have to take risks. And to take risks you have to have some level of trust within the organization, because if people get penalized for failure, particularly the kind of failure that's most useful which is where you learn a lot, then they're not going to do it, in which case you're not going to get any innovation."

Eric Berman, a former client partner at Facebook, echoes this sentiment, making clear that at Facebook no one is supposed to be criticized for failing—only for not trying hard enough.

It's more than freedom to fail that makes a culture of innovation. The Hay Group, a global management consulting firm, conducted a study of companies worldwide and found that the top twenty identified as the most innovative shared several key traits. First, 100 percent of the top twenty regularly celebrated innovation, compared to just 49 percent of other companies. Even more important, 90 percent of the top twenty reported that any employee with a great idea had permission to bypass the chain of command with their idea, without any negative consequences. At the other companies, only 63 percent had this permission.

INNOVATION CULTURE #1

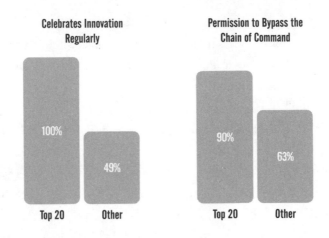

The data also shows that 100 percent of the best companies let all employees behave like leaders. Only 54 percent of peers do this. And 95 percent of best companies see problems as opportunities. In addition, 90 percent of senior leaders at the best companies take time to actively develop their employees. Sadly, only 48 percent of leaders at other companies do this.

INNOVATION CULTURE #2

"Many companies prize innovation," says Rick Lash, director in Hay Group's leadership and talent practice. "But the best companies for leadership approach it in a disciplined way by building agile organizations, promoting collaboration, celebrating successes, learning from setbacks, and fostering a culture that encourages a passion for innovation throughout the organization."

The message is clear. Build a culture of acceptance, openness, and access, where everyone is encouraged to challenge the status quo and come up with new ideas. You need to create an environment that embraces those who think the impossible is possible. Only by harnessing each employee's unique point of view can you open up more opportunities—some of which you may never have known existed. This is how you build a community where radical ideas become actual projects and elephants dream of being eagles.

Chapter 26

What Did You Learn?

I've learnt something from every failure. The products I helped design at the first two companies I worked for were utter failures. But now I know why.

—Tony Fadell, cofounder of Nest

Another way to dispel fear is to focus on learning. Let's say one of your managers spends a year, considerable resources, and buckets of money building a new product that turns out to be a dud; how can you tell this manager that he isn't a failure? The project failed, the company wasted time and money, and worst of all, everyone knows it. Isn't this the definition of failure? How can this be considered even a modest success? What did the company gain from spending its precious money, time, and resources?

Nothing. That is, if you look at it from the traditional "return on investment" perspective. But if you flip the goal from business growth to learning growth, then quite a lot can be gained from failure. Each time a project fails, there is still value to be had, and that value is in what the manager and his team learned during the process. If the innovation team can analyze everything they did and come back to their peers with critical learnings about the customer, the market, the product, and the process, then it isn't a failure. It's actually a step forward.

More often than not, data and insights gained from previous failures lead to the next radical breakthrough. What your teams need to do is to share everything they are learning constantly with the rest of your company. If the customers don't like the new product concept, they need to find out why. If the product can't be manufactured at a reasonable price, they need to understand what needs to change for this to happen. If they spent too much time and money on a poorly conceived idea, they need to review their decision-making process and figure out exactly where they went wrong.

The bigger the failure, the more there is to learn. Every step along the way, you need to remind your team that it's all about what they learn. Great innovations come out of profound insights. They do not mysteriously appear. Epiphanies don't happen in a vacuum. The process of learning is more important than the success or failure of the individual projects. Your teams need to be intensely focused on this process and committed to educating the rest of your company about their discoveries.

A simple way to institute this type of thinking is to ask your teams every week to share their latest failures and explain to others why they think it happened. The focus is then taken off of the failure itself and placed on the process of acquiring knowledge. The team shouldn't be expected to always have answers or even concrete lessons to share. Sometimes just asking the right question is enough. The question itself may spark an idea from someone else in the room that leads to that magic epiphany.

When setting up a structure, all learning should be done as a group, with a focus on questioning every aspect of the business. Here are some questions your groups can ask themselves:

- What did we learn from this?
- What ideas does this lead to?
- What data did we gather?
- How can this data be put to use?
- Can we bring in outside resources to help?
- Who else in the company should be in this room?
- Why did we spend so much time on this?
- What if we changed our process?
- Where does the real value lie?
- Can this learning apply to other groups?

- How can we summarize our key insights?
- How do we communicate these to the rest of the company?
- What if we continue down this path?
- What if we go in another direction entirely?
- How can we improve the process?
- What questions didn't we ask ourselves?

There are many reasons for failure, and most of them aren't the fault of the employees. Seldom do employees intentionally do things wrong, so casting blame doesn't fix the problem. It actually exacerbates it. In these cases, it's far better to identify the problem correctly and then ask the right questions. Let's look at the following situations and explore how innovative companies addressed them:

1. An employee *intentionally* deviates from a prescribed process or practice.

- Why didn't the employee follow the rules?
- What did the employee hope to gain from deviating?
- Can the organization do anything to prevent this from happening again?

According to studies of acute care in hospitals, one in ten patients is killed or injured as a consequence of medical error or institutional short-comings. At Intermountain Healthcare, which has twenty-three hospitals in Utah and Idaho, whenever a doctor deviates from medical protocols, the deviation is analyzed for opportunities to improve the process. Sometimes the deviations produce better results, and this data is collected and shared with all the doctors, leading to changes in the protocol or new protocols. After the implementation of a new protocol, Intermountain Healthcare managed to decrease inpatient mortality from community-acquired pneumonia by 25 percent.

2. An employee *accidentally* deviates from standard protocol.

- Why did the employee deviate from standard protocol?
- Is this a common problem?
- Is there something the organization can do to keep this from happening again?

In 1978, as a United Airlines flight approached its destination, the pilot worried that the landing gear had not come down. Wanting to avoid a rough landing, he postponed landing, as he tried to establish what was the problem. He became so intent on fixing what he perceived as a critical issue with the landing gear that he missed an even bigger problem: the plane was nearly out of fuel. When the tank hit empty, the plane crashed, and there were ten fatalities. It's easy to blame the pilot, but human error was only part of the problem. United realized that casting blame wouldn't fix anything. They had to ask the right questions and rethink their entire system to make sure this type of accident would never happen again.

3. An employee is unable to do the job properly.

- Does this employee have the skills to do the job?
- Was this employee given the proper training?
- How can the organization better pick and train employees?
- Is it a problem with the working conditions?
- Is it a problem communicating or cooperating with other employees?

Back when digital subscriber line Internet service was being rolled out to consumers for the first time, one of the major telcos seriously stumbled when it came to installing the service. They missed 75 percent of their commitments and had over twelve thousand late orders. Customers were furious and reps couldn't keep up with the incoming calls. The company's brand, morale, and reputation suffered. What went wrong? Were their employees improperly trained? Did they lack the skills? Were there problems in the process? The trial program had gone so smoothly.

It turns out that the trial did not reflect reality. It was conducted in a community of well-educated, tech-savvy consumers who had newer computers. The telco also used expert service reps to provide installation and support. In the real world, the conditions were dramatically different, and that led to the breakdown of the process. Only when the telco properly identified the root causes could it begin to address the problems. Along the way it learned a valuable lesson. Any trial program needs to be conducted under realistic, not idealistic, conditions, or the data is useless.

4. A capable employee follows the prescribed process but fails.

- Is the process faulty?
- Is the process incomplete?
- How can the process be improved?

At Pixar, the animation studio, whenever a problem like this occurs, every employee in the company, no matter what their position, is empowered to question the process and suggest changes to how things are done. Additional support can be requested, new tools developed, and requirements updated. Nothing is too big or too small if it can help improve the process and provide superior results in the end.

5. An employee encounters a task too difficult to be completed reliably.

- Why is this task so difficult?
- What expertise is the employee lacking in order to complete the task?
- Can the task be broken down into parts so it is not as difficult?
- Should the task be outsourced to a third party?

When I was helping to run the mobile games group at a public company, the process of QA (quality assurance) testing mobile apps on a variety of phones was complex and convoluted. There were simply too many different types of devices to test and too many elements to the software for a single QA tester to complete reliably. The solution my team came up with was to break the QA job down into parts and assign different tasks to different members of the team. The result was increased speed and fewer errors.

6. The process is too complex even for a capable employee to deal with.

- Can the process be simplified so it is easier to manage?
- What parts of the process are unnecessary?
- Can the process be redesigned so that errors don't occur?
- What parts of the process are causing the most problems?

At Founders Space, we produced lots of events, and this was fine when the events were simple, but as soon as we took on larger, more complex events, no single employee could be expected to keep track of everything. The solution was to break the process down into parts, create detailed checklists for every aspect of the event, and develop a process so that it all came together on time and without a hitch. Nothing is more embarrassing than producing an event where the projector doesn't work or the beer is warm.

7. Uncertainty about what may happen in the future causes employees to make decisions that produce inferior results.

- What is causing this uncertainty?
- Can this uncertainty be reduced or eliminated?
- How can employees be given better insight into what may happen in the future?

- Are there third parties the organization can tap to help solve this issue?

When the 2008 financial crisis hit, Sequoia Capital, one of the best-known venture capital firms in Silicon Valley, put out a now-infamous PowerPoint called "RIP: Good Times." This was intended for the CEOs of their portfolio companies and explained how they should cut staff, reduce expenses, and prepare for the worst. After someone leaked it, this Power-Point spread through the Valley like wildfire. Employees at my startup became worried about their future. Did this mean they would be laid off? Would our company close up shop? Should they be focused on finding a new job instead of completing the project?

Our management team had to go into overdrive to reduce anxiety and eliminate uncertainty. We did our best to explain the situation and calm fears, while continuing to stress the importance of meeting our development goals. Ignoring the issue would have only made it worse.

8. When conducting an experiment to test a hypothesis for a new product or service, it becomes clear that it won't work.

- What can we learn from the experiment?
- What can this tell us about the new product or service?
- Should the new product or service be abandoned or modified?
- Can the product or service be changed to produce positive results?

When Venmo launched in 2009, their goal was to let users text a band they liked and get an MP3 in return. What they learned from this experiment was that it wasn't a big business. Their initial hypothesis had been wrong, so they started to ask hard questions. Should they keep trying or abandon the idea? What other product could they build using the same framework? These questions led to an app that simplified paying your friends. This time it worked. PayPal purchased Venmo in 2012, and now it's one of the fastest growing payment apps in the world, with over $2 billion in payments processed each quarter.

9. An exploratory experiment intended to gain knowledge or data fails.

- Why did the experiment fail?
- Can we design a new, better experiment?
- Is there another way to get the data or knowledge?
- What can we learn from this experiment?

At Eli Lilly, they deal with these types of failures by holding "failure parties" to celebrate the scientific experiments that fail to achieve the desired results. This helps remove the stigma of the failure and focus attention on how intelligently experiments were designed and what knowledge was gained. It also makes it easier to assign the scientists to new projects. Everyone wants to have a party, so failures aren't postponed. They are celebrated as early and often as possible, saving the company money and resources.

Chapter 27

Going Down in Flames

Entrepreneurship is really hard and painful. I'm not sure I'd recommend it for anyone who can't handle the extreme stress.

—Naval Ravikant, cofounder of AngelList

All happy companies are alike; each unhappy company is unhappy in its own way. Was it Leo Tolstoy who said this? Or Donald Trump? Never mind. The point is that we can learn more from failure than from success. And the more spectacular the failure, the more we learn. So I'm going to take the time to go through several case studies of failed startups and see what we can take away from each.

HOMEJOY

Homejoy was the darling of Silicon Valley. On the surface, the idea was tempting. It was Uber for your home. Need someone to clean your home? Homejoy would crowd-source it, guarantee a great experience, and charge less than the industry average. They claimed they could do this all through scaling efficiently.

The global market was estimated at $400 billion, and the plucky startup had no trouble raising $38 million from top venture capitalists, including Google Ventures and PayPal founder Max Levchin. So what went wrong? What could go wrong?

If you look at the business model, it becomes clear. With VC dollars, they were intent on expanding fast, so they offered deals, subsidizing the cost for new users. Want your house cleaned for only $19? Homejoy would do it at that price, because they believed the lifetime value of their customers would more than pay for the promotion.

The cracks started showing up early. Customers weren't sticking around, and the reason was poor quality. The cleaners were subpar, and Homejoy didn't do a good job at vetting them. The thing Homejoy failed to grasp early on was that good housecleaners have no trouble getting work. In fact, they are in high demand. Word of mouth spreads fast, and if they've been in business for a while, they usually have to stop taking new clients. So why would they sign up on Homejoy and share their hard-earned profits?

So that left Homejoy with beginners and slackers: the cleaning people who didn't know what they were doing, or those who did such poor work that they couldn't get referrals. Homejoy was so busy expanding into new markets that they never figured out how to attract better talent. The result was dissatisfied customers. You can't have a two-sided marketplace without both sides adding value.

Meanwhile, Homejoy was growing like a weed. They expanded into thirty cities in six months, including London, Paris, and Berlin. "Every time you launch in a new market, it's like launching a new startup," said Adora Cheung, then CEO of Homejoy. Uber was going global, so why shouldn't Homejoy? The difference was that Homejoy's model was broken.

Housecleaners aren't like taxi drivers. They don't disappear after the job. Good housecleaners tend to stick with the same clients for years. Homejoy was taking 25 percent off the top. Why should any cleaner get down on their knees and take this? Many of the best cleaners used Homejoy to get new clients, then dropped the service, getting paid outside the Homejoy system. They call this platform leakage, and Homejoy's poorly conceived fee structure didn't help.

Former employees claimed that only about 15 to 20 percent of customers booked again within a month. Homejoy claimed it was 30 to 40 percent in some markets. Either way it wasn't enough to stop them from hemorrhaging cash. In the end, the churn, leakage, poor service, and rapid expansion proved a lethal combination. The company burned through tens of millions without ever addressing the flaws in their business model. Let this be a lesson to all innovators: It's fine to experiment with business model innovation, but make sure the numbers add up.

CHERRY

Travis VanderZanden walked away from his executive job at Yammer, where he stood to make roughly seven figures in stock options. That's a lot of moola to leave on the table, but when you have a dream, you have to go for it. His dream was to allow users to press a button on their phone, and their car would be cleaned within an hour. He even developed a proprietary method for cleaning the cars without water, so this could be done anywhere. To top it off, the US car wash market was $19.64 billion.

VanderZanden put in $500,000 of his own money and then raised $4.5 million led by Shasta Ventures, a prominent Sand Hill Road venture capitalist firm. He was off to a good start, but then reality set in. There were too many things VanderZanden didn't consider. First, he was charging $30 per wash, which is pricey, especially when most drive-through car washes charge $10 or less. But he had to charge this much because sending someone to your home or office is expensive. It's not like one of those automated car washes at gas stations, which require minimal human labor.

The second problem was that people don't need their cars washed all that often. Maybe if you're a fanatic about keeping your car clean, you'll get a weekly wash, but most of us can let a month or more go by before considering it again. By the time a month has passed, a typical person has visited at least one gas station with a car wash priced at $10 or less. It's more convenient just to drive through than pulling out the Cherry app and scheduling a wash.

This was enough to pop VanderZanden's soap bubble. Sadly, he wound up shutting down the startup. If only he'd spent more time with the customers up front, we could have told him $30 was too much!

REWINERY

Founded by Brazilians Joana Kollier and Paulo Lerner, Rewinery was on a mission to get you buzzed at home, in a hotel, at the park, or wherever you happened to be! Just press a button, and the wine would show up within an hour. Some of their wines were priced as low as $5 to be competitive with local grocery stores and outlets, while others were premium wines but still sold at a discount. So why did this refreshing startup fail?

I believe it's because most of us don't order wine that often. I know that I don't, and when I do get wine, I usually sample one bottle, and if I like it, I go back and buy a case, which lasts me a while. Then there are the true wine connoisseurs. They always have plenty of wine at home, and seldom, if ever, run short. So they wouldn't need this service. They're also extremely picky about what wines they drink. Price is not their main concern. It's the hunt for the next great wine that matters most.

The rest of us nonconnoisseurs tend to be more price sensitive, and there are plenty of bargains to be had at local retailers like BevMo! The problem with Rewinery is that it's expensive to deliver wines on demand. So if they appeal to the low end of the market, they can't make a profit. And the high end doesn't need their service. That leaves them with no business at all.

Au revoir, Rewinery! This elephant will never fly.

ICECREAM.IO

Icecream.io was the Uber for ice cream. Why did they melt away? Because it's a silly idea. There simply isn't enough profit in delivering ice cream on demand to individuals who press a button on their cell phone whenever they happen to get the craving. Sometimes it pays to get a reality check.

Before you dive into a new project, please ask people you trust to tell you honestly if the idea is a good one.

TURNTABLE.FM

In 2010, Billy Chasen and Seth Goldstein launched Stickybits, a mobile app where brands stick QR codes on products and users can scan them for rewards. The idea was compelling enough that the pair raised seven figures in funding and grabbed the media's attention. But it failed to take off. Users didn't seem to care, so Chasen and Goldstein pivoted into something totally different. Inspired by their love of music, they came up with Turntable.fm, a music discovery service where avatars mingle as virtual DJs spin the tunes.

In the first three months, Turntable.fm attracted more than 360,000 users and raised $7 million from big name VC firms, like First Round Capital, Polaris Venture Partners, and Lowercase Ventures, as well as celebrities like Ashton Kutcher, Jimmy Fallon, Lady Gaga, Kanye West, Troy Carter, and Guy Oseary. The media went gaga over their business concept, calling it "the next big thing" in online music and a real threat to Pandora.

Sadly, what starts out well doesn't always end well. After the initial surge, users got tired and began defecting to other sites. The fundamental flaw was that Turntable.fm didn't provide enough value. It was a novelty. It wasn't something users want to engage with repeatedly.

The utility factor was low, and chatting with other avatars in virtual environment wasn't sticky. It wasn't like a well-crafted game or movie. In addition, people aren't used to listening to music in a virtual space. For most of us, music is a background experience. We listen as we drive, exercise, and work. We don't spend a lot of time discussing and engaging with the music itself. This is a less common social behavior, and it requires the user's full attention. "People would get this burnout after a few weeks," admitted Chasen. "Turntable takes a lot of time. It's almost like a game, so it's harder to do during work."

Nir Eyal, a researcher on habit design, believes that habits form when users have a perceived utility and engage with a product frequently. Spotify and Pandora achieve this because they allow users to easily access an enormous selection of music wherever we happen to be, while Turntable.fm had minimal utility and entertainment value.

The moral of the story is that even if both Lady Gaga and Chris Sacca adore you, that doesn't mean you're on to something. If you can't keep your customers coming back for more, all the love, money, and initial success in the world won't save you. Novelties often spike in the first few months, then quickly fade away because they fail to provide any lasting value to the users. Some elephants can jump, but staying in the air is the hard part.

THERANOS

It may be tempting, but don't make the mistake of announcing that your technology works before it actually does. That's what Theranos's inexperienced founder did. A Stanford grad, she founded the company at nineteen with the attractive idea that her startup could bring the world cheap and painless diagnostic tests taken from a single drop of blood.

Many of Silicon Valley's top VCs fell for her story and drove the valuation of the immature startup all the way to $9 billion. The dirty little secret was that Theranos was outsourcing most of their testing to third parties, and the results were far from stellar. Sadly, Walgreens reportedly failed to verify Theranos's proprietary Edison finger prick testing technology worked as claimed before deploying it in forty-one Wellness Centers in Arizona and California.

It wasn't until the Food and Drug Administration cracked down, calling the nanotainer an "uncleared medical device," that people started to take notice. Having lawsuits swirling and facing the potential for criminal charges wasn't a pretty picture for the shareholders or the founders. Remember, there's no crime in pivoting, especially in Silicon Valley, but there is a crime in misleading investors and the public. That can put you in jail, or at the very least, ruin your reputation. If your technology doesn't do as promised, just own up to the fact, delay the release, and look for other options. Don't do what Theranos did.

EZUBAO

In China, they've had even worse problems with their peer-to-peer lending startups. Ezubao, one of the darlings of financial technology, perpetrated what appeared to be a $7.6 billion Ponzi scheme. They offered mostly fake investment products to their nearly one million investors, then spent lavishly on gifts and salaries while burying the evidence.

This led the Chinese authorities to arrest twenty-one people and put in place new laws regulating the industry. The lesson here is that no matter how tempting, don't innovate on the truth. Creative products are one thing, creative accounting another. Keep your visions of the future grounded in some form of reality, and as soon as things are not working, stop what you're doing and come clean. That's not only the right thing to do, it's the smart thing to do.

QUIRKY

I'll continue this tragedy of errors with Quirky, a startup near and dear to my heart. When I first heard of this spunky little company, I fell in love with the concept. It was something I wish I'd come up with. They were empowering individual inventors to dream up new ideas and helping them bring their inventions to market through a collaborative effort. The beauty was that anyone could join in, contribute their talent, and vote on the best ideas, while Quirky would do the heavy lifting and provide royalties to key participants.

Quirky captured the imagination of makers and hobbyists around the world. VCs also went nuts over them, funding the startup to the tune of $185 million. Their investors included all-stars, like Andreessen Horowitz, Kleiner Perkins, Lowercase Capital, RRE Ventures, and GE Ventures. And the press hopped on the bandwagon. Ben Kaufman, Quirky's founder, appeared on *The Tonight Show*, in a Sundance short documentary, and in nearly every tech and business publication in America.

In came an avalanche of ideas from wannabe inventors, like the step-on drinking fountain for dogs, decorative muffin-top molds, and a smart piggy bank complete with app. The community voted on the best ideas, while Quirky took care of everything from patents to marketing and distribution. Quirky enjoyed initial success with its simple but ingenious inventions, including its Aros smart air conditioner, Pivot Power bendable power strip, Nimbus smart alarm clock, and Cordies cable separator.

In just six years, Quirky brought more than four hundred products to market. With its capital and connections, Quirky managed to get their products into major retailers across the country, as well as online. With so much going for it and so many products, how could Quirky fail?

The reason was simple: It tried to do too much. If you look at most successful companies, especially startups, they keep their focus narrow. Apple didn't launch a hundred products when it reinvented itself. It started with the iPod, and only when that was successful did it launch the iPhone. GoPro just had its Hero camera. Nest focused on its thermostat. Fitbit pushed its activity tracker.

Quirky, on the other hand, was so busy launching products that it couldn't focus on making any one of them truly great. Its Aros smart air conditioner had potential, but the company never fully worked out the bugs and polished it. Developing breakthrough products requires iteration and attention to detail. Also, many of Quirky's products were never intended to be home runs. They were more like solid singles and doubles. A rubber band with hooks is a nice idea, but it's not going to become the next billion-dollar business.

Startups that win tend to focus on the big opportunities, not a lot of little ones. The smaller wins seldom add up to as much as a single large one, yet each of them sucks up a lot of time and resources. Quirky got caught in a cycle of burning cash without having any blockbusters to cover the escalating costs. Adding more products to the mix didn't help; it actually hurt. And so this one strategic mistake snowballed, killing the company in its infancy.

In other words, more elephants doesn't mean more success. Pick one and make sure it has everything it needs to take flight. Getting something large, heavy, and cumbersome off the ground requires focus.

USERACTIVE

I'll conclude this section with another story close to my heart. Scott Gray, a serial entrepreneur and one of Founders Space's most colorful instructors, has learned all of his startup lessons the hard way—by making mistakes. Scott's most excruciating mistakes were made with his first startup.

At the time, Scott was at the University of Illinois at Urbana-Champaign. The university has an illustrious history as a major driver of educational technology and the Internet. PLATO, the world's first attempt at computerized education, along with Telnet, the first way to control servers through the Internet, and Mosaic, the first web browser, were developed there.

Useractive was a spin off of the Calculus & Mathematica teacher link program. Scott and Tricia, his wife, designed and built a system that allowed students to create computer programs through a web browser. They also developed online programming courses and a custom learning management system.

Once spun off, Useractive began making money and was growing steadily. This was when Scott made his hellish mistake. He saw competitors receiving large investments to scale their businesses. Worried that he wouldn't be able to compete, he went after venture capital funding. Not long after, a local VC came through with a solid offer. The only catch was that they had the right to place an experienced CEO at the helm.

This seemed reasonable to the founders, none of whom had extensive experience growing a company. The honeymoon period didn't last long. According to Scott, the CEO spent most of his time modeling sales projections but didn't actually sell anything. At the same time, he increased the staff by a factor of four.

Tensions rose as the company's burn rate escalated. To make matters worse, just as Useractive was about to close a $2 million deal with Accenture, the CEO made a misstep, and the deal imploded.

With expenses outpacing sales, Useractive had to go back to the VCs for more money. Scott tried to convince the investors to fire the CEO, but they refused. The only other option was to reject the investment and kick out the CEO. The founders still had the power to do this, and Scott and Trish felt passionately that it was their best option. Unfortunately, it meant laying off 75 percent of their staff, which the other cofounders couldn't stomach. So they took the VC's money and kept the CEO.

A year later they'd burned through their second round of financing and were back in the same position. This time Scott wasn't going to sit still. He'd formed a special relationship with O'Reilly Media, a publisher and educational course provider. O'Reilly now accounted for the majority of Useractive's revenue. Scott managed to get O'Reilly to make an acquisition offer for Useractive. He took this straight to the investors, but with one condition: the CEO be removed. Seeing no choice, the VCs agreed. Scott had finally gotten Useractive back!

But even this didn't go as planned. According to Scott, the corporate attorney was best friends with the CEO and kept dragging his feet. In the end, the acquisition went through and everything finally looked up. Scott and his team had kept the dream alive: Useractive was part of O'Reilly Media and had a bright future. Only there was one more problem. During the six months it took to close the deal, O'Reilly had a corporate reorganization, and the newly acquired Useractive was left on its own without a budget. But that's another story!

The takeaway is that it doesn't matter how innovative you are if your team is broken. Taking on investment is like getting married. Make sure you can live with the spouse, because divorce is never easy.

Chapter 28

Unblock the Path

A good plan violently executed now *is better than a perfect plan next week.*

—Gen. George S. Patton, American
military commander

Whenever you have innovation teams within your organization, they are going to hit roadblocks. They are going to encounter obstacles they simply can't find a way around. Maybe it's the marketing department that says, "Look, we'd love to help, but we're in the middle of our most important marketing campaign of the year. Come back later." When your innovation team comes back, the marketing department may refuse to commit enough resources, or they may drag their feet. At this point, your innovation team is stuck. They can't move forward. How do you deal with this?

There are a number of possible solutions. You could take someone from marketing and assign them to the innovation team. Or you could allow your innovation team to hire an outside consultant or marketing firm. The problem is that this type of approach can upset your marketing department. Your marketing managers may not want the company's brand compromised by a third party. They may want to keep control of the process. However, if they aren't willing to commit adequate resources to your innovation team, they need to give up their control. It's not easy, and it won't be pretty. There will be politics involved. Managers will get upset when they see their domain infringed upon and power eroded.

In the large public company where I worked, I saw firsthand the role that politics played. The marketing department was obsessed with protecting and controlling the corporation's brand and all communications with the media. My group, however, wanted to move fast. We were a satellite office, and we were developing mobile apps, including games and media apps. It was a highly competitive, fast-moving space, and we had to get our products out the door quickly and market them aggressively—just like our competitors were doing. To that end, we needed marketing's support. This created unavoidable tensions.

To be fair, the marketing department had a point. We were cowboys. All of us were startup guys before joining this company, and we were used to doing things our own way. Naturally, some of the execs were worried we might say something to the press, and that something could affect the share price or upset the plans of the CEO. There were also the legal issues to be considered since it was a public company. What we said could form the basis of a shareholder lawsuit. There's a reason corporations have marketing and PR departments that keep tight control.

Keeping us on a short leash is understandable, but it still made it difficult for our group. We were required to ask for approval on everything from the app names to marketing materials, the use of the company logo, every single press release, and what we were allowed to say to journalists. With so many constraints, how could we compete with the thousand and one startups nipping at our heels? How could we take risks on innovative products? How could we hope to push the limits of what's possible on mobile? We felt that we were trying to run a hundred-meter dash with an iron ball and chain around our ankles.

In the end, our biggest, most innovative project, a social dating app, was never released. They killed it because they didn't like the app's name and thought it was too sexual. It was similar to Tinder but pre-iPhone; this was back in the days of flip phones. We'll never know if it would have been a success or not, but it would have been nice to find out. It would have taught us a lot and led to other innovative products. As a result of the politics, several key executives and I left the company and launched our own startups. My former company not only lost out on our innovative projects, but it lost some of its most driven, hard-charging employees.

So how can you avoid making this mistake? First, you must make clear to every department and every person in the company that your innovation teams are different. They do not have to play by the same rules. If a department cannot help them, they are free to go elsewhere. They can hire outside talent, engage third-party firms, and even collaborate with competitors. In short, they should be allowed to do whatever it takes.

Innovation teams need to be treated as autonomous startups within the organization. If they need a computer tomorrow, they shouldn't have to go through a lengthy procurement process. They should be able to whip out their credit card and buy it online. If they need prototypes ready by next month, they should be able to circumvent the design engineering department. If the company's factories aren't ready to handle small batches, they should be able to hire whomever can deliver the goods on time and at the best price.

EIGHT RULES TO LIVE OR DIE BY

Here are eight simple rules that will help you unblock the path. These include some thoughts and ideas I've shared in the previous chapters:

1. Make Innovation a Priority

Create a sense of urgency around the mission, so that everyone knows it's important and jumps on the innovation train or gets out of the way.

2. Form a Coalition

Create partnership between the managers of the existing business units and the innovators. Having the innovators siloed doesn't work if you want to reap the benefits across your company. Everyone must be on board. You can do this by sharing ownership and credit with all the key players.

3. Have a Vision

Without a vision of a new future, there's nothing for your team to get behind. The vision must be clear and compelling, then you can build your mission around this and launch whatever strategic initiatives are necessary.

4. Recruit Volunteers

You'll be surprised what someone will do when they aren't getting paid for it. Often volunteers can contribute as much as the core innovation team. The best volunteers will come from within your company. They will be doing it because they believe in the vision and mission. It's the future of the company, and they want to be a part of making it happen. Give them a way to work with your team, helping your innovators get around roadblocks, find additional resources, and solve problems.

5. Create New Paths

There's a reason big businesses have strict protocols and clear reporting lines. Their job is to optimize performance in the core business units, and they aren't about to jeopardize millions or billions in revenue for a tiny, unproven project. Hence, they'll always push the innovation teams to conform with established processes. You have to empower your innovators to find other avenues to reach their goals. They need to be able to blaze new trails, take shortcuts, and cross forbidden boundaries, otherwise the corporate gears will crush them.

6. Set Realistic Goals

Innovation can be a long, meandering, and painful journey. To make it work, have your teams break it up into smaller milestones, which can be used to measure progress and share learnings. Have your team run in short sprints, establishing hypotheses and testing them. After each one of these, your teams should share their findings with all the key players in the company. Each success and failure should be taken as a group learning opportunity and celebrated.

7. Don't Give Up

Some initiatives start off with a bang, but after a few months they run out of steam, as most of the key players go back to doing business as usual. Those innovators may keep chugging along, but without the support of management behind them, they may get pushed to the side and forgotten or pulled back into existing projects. Don't let this happen. From the CEO downward, everyone must be on board for the entire ride.

8. Embrace Change

All of the above require radical changes in your business. If you want to get your elephants airborne, you'll need to be prepared to overturn long-standing traditions, rewrite established protocols, and upset a lot of people in the process. That's just the nature of the innovation game.

INTRAPRENEURSHIP

A number of the big guys are putting the eight rules into practice. At Mastercard, which has more than ten thousand employees and $9.5 billion in annual revenues, they've launched Mastercard Labs, where they've incubated startup initiatives like ShopThis!, a platform that lets consumers shop for products directly from a digital magazine page. ShopThis! began as a nine-person team and was told to fail fast. "It feels just like a startup," said Phillip Honovich, a twenty-five-year-old who joined Mastercard right out of school. ShopThis! is just one of dozens of minicompanies Mastercard has launched to help reimagine the future of commerce and payments.

Mastercard also teamed up with Whirlpool to produce a smartphone app that lets users pay for and monitor their laundry remotely at self-service laundries. No more sitting around waiting for the load to get done. Normally, it would have taken weeks just to get approval for a new project like this. However, by unblocking the path, the app was conceived and approved in less than a week.

Mastercard doesn't stop with Mastercard Labs. They take it up a notch by awarding prizes of up to $250,000 to top intrapreneurship teams in the form of a company-wide competition. "It's more than financial incentives," says Garry Lyons, Mastercard's chief innovation officer. "It's the motivation to do something interesting and get access to brand credibility and our network. It's like their own business inside our walls."

Mastercard and Whirlpool aren't alone: American Express, Coca-Cola, General Electric, MetLife, Mondelēz International, Tyco, IBM, and Cisco are all unclogging their product pipelines and giving intrapreneurship a try. Unlike previous attempts, they are not looking to simply spin off new entities. Their goal is to instill the spirit of intrapreneurship throughout their entire organization, infecting not only the twenty-somethings but also the seasoned managers and old guard.

For example, GE has funded more than five hundred employee-initiated projects and has enabled teams to develop them in ninety-day sprints. When projects failed, the managers would learn from the experience and reboot. Johanna Wellington, a research leader at GE, came up with one such project. It sought to commercialize solid-oxide fuel cells, which can convert natural gas into electricity. "We have the same agility of a startup," said Wellington, "and it could have a huge impact on the bottom line long-term."

Chip Blankenship, CEO of GE Appliances, issued this challenge to his internal teams: "You're going to change every part the customer sees. You won't have a lot of money. There will be a very small team. There will be a working product in three months. And you will have a production product in eleven or twelve months." The goal has been to act like a lean startup inside the giant. So far, the results have been impressive. The product development costs dropped by 50 percent, the teams moved twice as fast, and their sales doubled. GE also recruited more than five thousand coaches to train their executives on how to take risks, embrace failure, and think like a startup. They even sent key employees to work inside startups to see how the other half lives. Tyco also made education a priority. They invited well-known entrepreneurs and venture capitalists to give talks to their internal teams.

Coca-Cola partnered with external entrepreneurs to develop new products and services. One of them is Wonolo, an Uber for temp workers who can restock Coca-Cola brands at stores on demand. "It's the new way of working that eventually every large company will embrace," says David Butler, Coca-Cola's vice president of innovation.

If the big guys want to recruit and retain the best talent, they have to change. When asked, the vast majority of millennials say they'd prefer to work for a startup. They crave the freedom, challenge, and responsibility that comes with starting something new and building it from the ground up. Mastercard has picked up the gauntlet, hiring millennials at a dizzying pace. Younger workers now make up 38 percent of their employees, up from just 10 percent in 2010.

The one thing most big corporations can't match is equity. No one is going to wind up a billionaire from running a purely internal startup. That's why companies like Cisco Systems are experimenting with the "spin in" model. This is where they take the best ideas, fund them like a VC firm, and send them out on their own. Only there's a catch: They have the right to buy them back in the future. This can transform the intrapreneurs into entrepreneurs, while giving them the freedom and structure of a true startup. However, it does risk stirring up a hornet's nest of jealousy from those employees not allowed to participate.

DON'T ACCEPT NEGATIVITY

Beware, my friend. Having a bunch of recent grads running around acting like independent startup founders inside a large, established organization sounds good on paper. However, a wave of negativity can well up whenever someone is trying to change the status quo—especially a cocky, twenty-something with an MBA. You have to be careful, because those most likely to be annoyed and jealous may be some of your top managers.

People are naturally territorial creatures and like to have control over their domains. The last thing most of us want is someone from the outside, especially a junior, making changes, demanding things, and messing up our carefully laid plans. But this is exactly what your innovation teams will do, because that's what startups do.

The resistance to change in many organizations is so strong that they become paralyzed. This is why 70 percent of new, large-scale strategic initiatives fall short of their goals, according to Kotter International. Innovation initiatives are the most threatening of all, because they typically propose radical changes. If given half a chance, the natural antibodies within your company will swoop in and kill off these invaders, as if they're an infection that must be wiped out before it spreads.

There are many ways to prevent this, which we will describe in detail, but let's start with the most basic one: negativity. You have to begin with how people think about change itself. Change can be viewed as positive or negative. It's the half-full versus half-empty cup of milk. There should be no room for half-empty cuppers in your organization. Everyone must know that pessimism kills innovation and it won't be tolerated.

Negative attitudes more than anything else can squeeze the life out of innovation teams. Start by making your entire company aware of expressions that stifle progress, and challenge them to become mindful of how they speak. Here's a list of phrases to avoid, but you can go much further:

- That's impossible.
- We can't do it.
- What a stupid idea.
- Our hands are tied.
- We don't have the time.
- It's against our policy.
- You've got to be kidding.
- This is ridiculous.
- We don't have the budget.
- It's not in the rules.
- That's not what they're looking for.
- You'll never get it approved.
- You've got your head in the clouds.
- It's not our responsibility.
- We'll never make a profit.
- That's not how things are done here.

History is rife with examples of naysayers, many of whom were brilliant people but couldn't see the future. It's easy to let past experience and commonly held beliefs blind you to new information and possibilities. No matter how smart you think you are, don't ever believe you own the crystal ball. If these guys can miss seeing the next tsunami, you can, too:

- Thomas Edison famously said, "The phonograph has no commercial value at all."
- Robert Milliken, Nobel Prize winner in physics, said, "There is no likelihood man can ever tap into the power of the atom."
- William Orton, president of Western Union, said, "This 'telephone' has too many shortcomings to be seriously considered as a means of communication."
- Harry Warner, founder of Warner Bros. Pictures, exclaimed, "Who the hell wants to hear actors talk?"
- Darryl Zanuck, who cofounded 20th Century Fox, said, "Television won't be able to hold on to any market it captures after the first six months. People will soon get tired of staring at a plywood box every night."
- Thomas Watson, chairman of IBM, commented, "I think there is a world market for about five computers."
- Ken Olsen, president of Digital Equipment Company, said "There is no reason for an individual to have a computer in their home."
- Robert Metcalfe, coinventor of the Ethernet, said, "I predict the Internet will soon go spectacularly supernova and in 1996 catastrophically collapse."
- Clifford Stoll, author and computer geek, said "The truth is no online database will replace your daily newspaper, no CD-ROM can take the place of a competent teacher, and no computer network will change the way government works."
- Steve Ballmer, Microsoft's CEO, said, "There's no chance that the iPhone is going to get any significant market share."
- Steve Chen, cofounder of YouTube, was concerned about his company's long-term viability when he said, "There's just not that many videos I want to watch."

So how do you keep very smart people from blocking the path? First, don't listen to them. Everyone is blinded by their own prejudices. That's part of being human. And the smarter you are, the more reason you have to believe you are right and the other guy is wrong. Smart people aren't always the best at seeing what's really happening around them. The only way to battle the naysayers is to make sure your innovation teams are led by positive thinkers. Studies have shown that optimists succeed far more often. They rise to a challenge. When the odds are against them, they want more than ever to win.

MYTH: INNOVATION CAN BE PLANNED

They say life is what happens while you're making other plans, and innovation is what happens when you throw out the plans and start looking for something new. Innovation can't be planned. By its very nature, innovation is discovering the unknown. You often don't even know what it is you're looking for. Most great innovations are stumbled upon. They occur during the exploration process, and you seldom know when, how long, or what resources are required. All you know is that you have hypotheses that need to be tested, tweaked, changed, and retested, until you figure out what actually works.

JUDGING PROGRESS

Often innovation teams are judged by the standards of a mature business. They get barraged with questions like . . .

- Why are you late?
- How come you're over budget?
- When are we going to see a profit?
- Why do you need this resource?

- Can't you do it the way we do?
- What process are you following?

These are fine questions for an existing product line, but for a new, untested business, they make no sense. Innovation means experimentation, and that requires a different set of criteria and questions. Their progress should be measured by their ability to run effective experiments, which prove or disprove their hypotheses. If you fail to set up a parallel structure and unique evaluation process for innovation teams, then you are dooming them to failure. Their path is blocked from the start.

The legal department can also be a roadblock. Talk about a deal killer. Corporate lawyers alone can squash the chances of an innovation team ever getting to market. I've seen it happen more than once. This is a tricky situation because even the CEO is often reluctant to override corporate counsel. It's not uncommon for legal to hold up a deal for months, negotiating terms that may be a big deal if you're mass-producing a product but don't really matter for an experimental project. In startup time, months are like years. Yes, there will be issues around liability, indemnification, trademarks, patents, government restrictions, existing regulations, and a host of other things, but these seldom matter. Most startups live with the risks. After all, their biggest risk is running out of time and money. It's not getting sued—at least not when they are just starting out.

YouTube, FanDuel, and Airbnb would have never existed if typical corporate lawyers were involved. There are just too many legal issues. But the fringes of the law are often the most fertile grounds for innovation. If you refuse to let your startup teams venture into this territory, you may be missing out on the next frontier, where all the growth lies.

To solve this thorny issue, your innovation teams need to be able to avoid in-house counsel, whose primary motivation is to protect the mother company and not get fired. Instead, allow your teams to engage a trusted third-party law firm that is used to working with startups. Getting the right lawyers involved from day one is imperative. The most experienced startup law firms are located in Silicon Valley, but even inside these institutions you still need to identify a lawyer that isn't afraid to make judgment calls. The lawyer has to be the type that can cut through the legal mumbo jumbo and say, "This risk is worth taking. This risk is not." Those type of lawyers are all too rare, but they are what enable startups to push the legal limits of our society, thereby opening up new markets.

Now what about press or branding issues? For talking to the press, you may want to lay out rules in advance. Have your marketing department train individuals within each innovation team, coaching them on what to say, how to say it, and what not to say. Then let them go do their jobs. For branding, you can have the innovation teams come up with their own subbrands, websites, and other materials that are separate from the company's main services and products. With some creative thinking and cooperation, you can solve most of the issues in a manner that's satisfactory to all parties.

Radical innovation requires radical changes in your corporation. You may want to make the innovation groups part of a subsidiary that services the parent company. This subsidiary can be structured like an incubator, bringing in team members and supporting them in whatever way works best. The subsidiary's mission should be to unblock all paths and help the innovation teams work harmoniously with all departments across the organization. The fact is that you have to be prepared to compete with startups, and the only way to do that is to put in place the structural changes that allow your innovation teams to act more like startups.

Startups don't have any constraints on them. They are constantly swerving around hazards, making U-turns at dead ends, climbing over and tunneling under fences. If you give your innovation teams this same freedom, they will thrive and things will start to get done. If you don't, they will become frustrated and lose momentum.

Chapter 29

Align Motivations

Talent wins games, but teamwork and intelligence win champion-ships.

—Michael Jordan, basketball star

I have spent a lot of time with the executives of multinational corporations talking about their strategies, and I often hear that they've made innovation their number one priority: Everyone in the company is on board; every manager has been instructed on innovation and is committed to making the change. After hearing this, I usually ask if the managers are still required to hit their revenue targets. "Absolutely!" they respond. "They must hit their revenue targets. That hasn't changed."

The problem is that these two instructions contradict each other. If I'm a manager, and you tell me that I must hit my revenue goal, but I must also innovate, what am I going to do? I'm always going to make sure to hit the revenue goal because that's a clear target. It's well-defined. My bonuses and future promotions are probably tied to this goal. I've done it before, and I know exactly what I need to do. Innovation, on the other hand, is vague. What does *innovation* mean? I may not even know. What's the chance of success? I can't even gauge that. How will that be valued? I have no idea, but I know if I miss my revenue targets, my bonus will be less, and I may even be passed up for future promotions.

If I'm a savvy manager, I'll pay lip service to innovation to keep the upper management happy, while continuing to put the bulk of my resources toward hitting my revenue goals. I may divert a token amount to innovative projects, but I'd make sure none of those projects do anything to jeopardize my revenue target. The result is that the upper management can believe innovation is happening and everyone is on board, while nothing of substance ever changes.

The problem becomes more acute when you have innovation teams demanding resources from different departments within your organization. What's the win for the managers? Why should they take their valuable team members and allocate them to a project that isn't even officially part of their department? Shouldn't they focus on their own issues? What about the core business? They only have limited capacity. And who are these innovators? They aren't top executives. They are just some young project managers with a crazy idea that probably won't work.

If that's not enough, ego also comes into play. Why should these upstart innovators be allowed to make demands? And what if they get lucky and succeed? They will make the rest of the company look like dinosaurs. They may even wind up getting promoted over everyone else. What's to be gained by helping them? They'll just steal all the glory!

The list of possible grievances goes on ad infinitum. The only way to deal with this is to build it into the structure. First, the managers of existing business units need to be shown exactly why it benefits them to foster innovation. They must understand that their jobs are on the line. This is the future of the company. There's no other option. This isn't a pet project. It's how business must be done moving forward.

Just like what the mayor's office in Boston did, department managers should be given credit for the success of any innovation that involves their department. In fact, the innovation teams should not be the superstars. They should be considered facilitators who bring about innovation throughout the company as a whole. The credit should be shared equally among all participants. No one individual or group should claim the project as their own. Otherwise, it will create jealousy and territorialism—the enemies of innovation. In short, you need to align the motivations of the innovation leaders, the innovation department, and the other business units.

One way to accomplish this is to create an innovation board for each project, defining whose job it is to oversee and guide the innovation team so that the project is on track. The board should be composed of members of the key business units whose cooperation is essential for the success of the innovation project. The board members and their departments are allowed to take the credit if the innovation succeeds, and if it fails, the innovation team takes responsibility. After all, the job of the innovation department is to learn from failures. So they will analyze any failures and come up with key learnings they can share with the rest of the organization, while any success will be a group effort, with credit going to all the business units involved.

Another name for the innovation board is a cross-functional team or guiding team. It doesn't matter what you call it, the goal should be to accomplish the following seven objectives:

- Share ownership of the innovation teams across the organization
- Promote horizontal collaboration and cooperation
- Include all levels and functions of employees—not just senior execs
- Create a guiding strategy team that can oversee execution
- Knock down interdepartmental barriers that stand in the way
- Obtain resources and support from all essential stakeholders
- Share credit for any success with existing business units

MYTH: YOU CAN SCHEDULE INNOVATION

This just isn't true when innovating. It's not like driving to work. Innovation isn't a linear path. You can't set a schedule and stick to it. It's more like prospecting for gold. You can finish a project quickly and wind up with fool's gold. The project may be done, but there's no breakthrough innovation. The schedule is less important than the process. If you get the process right, your chances of figuring out what works goes up and the time it takes goes down.

REDEFINING METRICS

Another key factor in aligning motivations is to redefine your metrics. You cannot rely on the same metrics used to evaluate your core businesses. These metrics don't apply to new projects. New initiatives can't compete at the same level as mature products and services, and it creates a disincentive for everyone involved to try to impose inappropriate metrics on them. If you use a Balanced Score Card or an equivalent strategy performance management tool, you need to recalibrate it to take into account metrics that are designed specifically for innovation projects. These include substituting metrics like revenue for learning, market share for project milestones, and so on. Your innovation metrics should map directly to the innovation process shown below:

INNOVATION PROCESS

The innovation teams should be judged on criteria such as:

- Were the appropriate milestones established?
- What was the progress against these milestones?
- Did the team come up with meaningful hypotheses?
- Did the team run smart experiments to test these hypotheses?
- Did the team learn from both successes and failures?
- Did the team effectively share the learning with the rest of the company?

You can adjust and tweak these to whatever is appropriate for your business. The key thing is that revenue and efficiency are typically not included. This is because most innovation projects are not at the stage where they have meaningful revenue or a need to worry about efficiency.

That comes later when they are ready to scale. At the innovation stage, the focus should be on conducting the right experiments and learning every step of the way. It would be nice if these could be summed up as simple numbers like revenue and cost savings, but that's not possible in most cases. Instead, innovation teams require a more subjective metric, where experienced innovators, perhaps even outside consultants, can evaluate the progress and provide feedback to keep the projects on track.

After the metrics have been established, you will need to address personal incentives. These include how individuals are reviewed on their performance, how bonuses are awarded, and how raises and promotions are considered. Giving the innovation teams inflated compensation is a mistake. The overall compensation should be equivalent to the rest of the organization. Otherwise, you'll wind up breeding resentment, which can lead to conscious or unconscious sabotage and opposition to the innovation projects. This is another form of misalignment that needs to be avoided. Everyone needs to feel like they are on the same team and being treated in an equivalent manner, or their motivations become conflicted.

It's basic group psychology, but you'd be surprised at how many companies make the mistake of thinking they need to give the innovation teams oversized bonuses or credit for their achievements. If you're going to do this, make sure equal rewards go to existing business units who cooperate and help facilitate the innovations. That's the only way to get everyone on the same bus heading the same direction.

In short, you will need to adjust your entire evaluation system in order to reflect the introduction of innovation projects into the process. To accomplish this, you will need to ask yourself the following questions:

- How do the innovation projects affect existing business units?
- What is the impact on both short-term and long-term goals?
- What resources will the innovation projects require?
- How will these projects affect revenue/efficiency of key business units?
- What impact will the projects have on other departments?

- How do we adjust the performance metrics to accurately account for this?
- What effect will this have on the current incentives and rewards?
- How can we mitigate this impact and align motivations?

Finally, you need to hit the following four points. You cannot afford to miss any of them:

1. Innovation starts at the top. The CEO and upper management must be fully on board. You will need to put in place innovation KPIs (Key Performance Indicators) for the management team that will drive significant commitment to long-term innovation. A good example of this is a KPI that measures the rate of experimentation. In other words, how many experiments can a team run to validate or invalidate various hypotheses in a given period of time?

2. Your top executives should be spending between 25 percent and 50 percent of their time on planning and implementing what comes next for the company. That's their number one job, while the managers that report to them run the day-to-day operations.

3. Everyone in the company must understand the cost of not innovating. If the company doesn't innovate, its competitors will. What does this mean to the company's existing markets and revenue? Where will that leave the company in five or ten years?

4. Innovation investment must be directly linked to the growth gap that innovation is intended to close.

As you can see, it's not as simple as saying, "Innovation is priority number one." Those are just words. The hard part is reimagining your organizational structures and then coming up with a new system that works for all the stakeholders. This is where most innovation efforts succeed or fail.

The best way to plan for success is to get everyone on board from the start. Only by rethinking your entire system and fully aligning motivations can you do this. You cannot rely on the enthusiasm and goodwill of everyone involved. You must make careful and well-considered structural changes to every part of your business. This way you can ensure that everyone's motivations are aligned and your innovation initiatives thrive and ultimately reshape the company.

Section Six

BREAKING THROUGH BARRIERS

Chapter 30

Velocity and Organization

Move fast. Speed is one of your main advantages over large competitors.

—Sam Altman, president of Y Combinator

Velocity is a big problem for any innovator. If you're going to get an elephant off the ground on a short runway, you've got to run fast. In today's world of rapidly evolving technologies, every six months the startup landscape changes. What's valid today isn't necessarily going to be true tomorrow. I've seen startups made obsolete in a matter of months. For large corporations, it's even worse. If your innovation teams have to jump through so many hoops that it takes them half a year to test a single prototype, the entire market will have shifted beneath their feet. What they were building may not even be relevant anymore.

High-velocity startups don't have this issue. They run fast. They can go from idea to launch within months, not years. Your team needs to do the same thing. They need to be scrappy, unencumbered, and untethered. They can't be bogged down waiting for permissions or wading through mounds of paperwork. You have to clear the bureaucracy from their path if they are going to reach a velocity where they can get off the runway and into the air.

Don't fool yourself into thinking that speed is a luxury only lean startups can afford. Velocity matters for all companies. It's no longer enough to have established distribution channels, marketing muscle, and dominant market share. In the new world of disruptive technologies, your innovation teams are in a race for their lives. Whatever they're working on, you can be sure half a dozen other companies are working on the same idea at the same time—and some of these are optimized for speed.

"We don't belabor, we don't debate, we move," said Eric Berman, a former client partner at Facebook. Rollin Ford, CIO of Walmart, echoes this when he says, "There are very few secrets out there anymore. The only competitive advantage becomes the speed aspect. Organizations need to keep embracing innovation and new technology models. At the end of the day, it's about getting from point A to point B quicker than everybody else."

Remember, time affects all aspects of your business. Technology never stands still. It's always evolving. A single new technology can radically alter your industry overnight. At the same time, the life cycle of products is shrinking. A product used to be viable for years; now it's often only months before a newer, better version appears. In software, it can be days. Aggressive startups push new builds daily just to keep ahead of the competition. Neville Roberts, enterprise CIO of Best Buy, sums up what most executives feel: "A lot of our revenues come from innovation, but it gets copied quickly. We have to get innovation out there quickly."

A company that consistently comes to market with new products and services before anyone is viewed as a leader—not a follower. The impact on the brand can be enormous. People want to buy from innovators—not copycats. For a company to stand out in a crowded market, building an image as an innovator is invaluable. Ask any marketing professional, and he will tell you that the public wants authenticity. They want to buy the real thing. That means whoever is perceived as the originator receives a significant marketing advantage, while everyone else is looked on as imitators. Winning over customers is critical, and being first gives your company a psychological edge. As my relative, Mark Rosenthal, who was part of the original team that created MTV, Nickelodeon, VH1, and Comedy Central, liked to say, "Name it and claim it!"

"You have to wake up every day and say, 'What are we missing?' Every day you have to get up and run faster than the next guy," says Rollin Ford.

So how can you get your innovation teams to move as fast as startups? Big companies have a handicap. Most employees don't want to work too hard or risk too much. That's why they choose a stable corporate job over joining a startup or striking out on their own. Startups are different. Their culture is one of do or die. Everyone has to be on board, from the lowliest assistant to the CEO.

It's not easy for big companies to instill the type of urgency and motivation found in startups, where even the regular employees can become millionaires overnight. Just look at Google. When it first launched, the administrative assistant, chef, and graffiti artist all received stock options. Now they're rich! At an established company, it's much harder to get the employees to drink the Kool-Aid. Just compare these two stories: Join a startup—everyone gets wealthy; join a large corporation—make the top execs wealthy. That's what we see in the media every day.

Startups also have the advantage of the founding team. They are hyper-motivated, have a large equity stake, and won't get the payoff if they don't succeed. Everything is on the line for them. They often don't even have a steady paycheck, so they are motivated to run as fast as they can to get their product to market and raise capital. Corporate managers, on the other hand, aren't under the same type of pressure. They get paid as long as they don't screw up, so caution is preferred over speed.

What can you do if you're a manager in a large corporation? How can you possibly move as fast as a startup? The first thing you need to do is recognize the problem, then start designing solutions. Let's begin with the basics. Put on the innovation teams only people who are highly motivated by the challenge, not by a paycheck or bonus. No slackers. No freeloaders. They must be the type of people who feel compelled to get stuff done—no matter what the obstacles. You don't want debaters or procrastinators. You need self-motivated doers.

Once you have a team with the right DNA, you need to create a fast lane in your company, where there are no speed bumps or speed limits. Get everyone out of their way. They shouldn't be waiting on approvals longer than a few days. If it hasn't been approved or denied within a reasonable amount of time, then it's an automatic green light. All the routine paper-work that most departments have to process should be waived for innova-tion teams. Your team leaders should be authorized to buy whatever they need with their own credit cards and know that they'll be reimbursed later without being second-guessed. Having leaders you trust is essential.

The innovation teams should also be given diplomatic immunity for treading on toes and breaking rules. If they need to cut a deal with a com-petitor, they should be empowered to do it. If they need to hire an outside design firm at twice the price, that's their choice. If they say something to the press that ruffles feathers, they won't be fired. In other words, it's the autobahn. They can drive as fast and hard as they like without worrying about getting a ticket.

FAST ORGANIZATIONS

Fast lanes are important, but you don't want to completely silo off innova-tion from the rest of the company. This creates psychological segregation, where the rest of the organization feels like they don't have to move fast or participate. You need to speed up your entire business, not just the inno-vation teams. So you must make clear that everyone has to innovate and accelerate their operations, while at the same time giving the innovation teams freedom to maneuver around obstructions.

Outsourcing is another way to turbocharge your business. If you aren't the fastest and best at something, whether it's design, marketing, or manufac-turing, find someone who is. Shed your slower, less competent departments and focus on what you're best at. The "not invented here" syndrome is like having a traffic light on a freeway. It can bring everything to a halt and create jams. In today's world, it doesn't matter where something is invented. Only your core IP areas should be kept in-house. Everything else is fair game. To effectively outsource, you need to build a strong supporting ecosystem, with partners you can trust. This may take time, but it will pay off in the long run.

By taking these measures you can increase your velocity, leveling the playing field between your internal teams and startups. It may not be easy, but changing your corporate culture and processes is a must if you're going to compete in the twenty-first century.

KNOW THY MARKET

It pays to know your market. IEEE did a study of 692 new products in development and found that a time-based strategy that emphasizes speed is critical in unfamiliar, emerging and fast-changing markets, while in familiar, existing, and stable markets speed matters less. This isn't to say if you're in a stable market, you can move slowly. You should never rest on your laurels. The point is that if you're in a fast-changing market, you must move quickly, while in existing markets you can spend more time perfecting products, increasing quality, reducing cost, and so on.

In a market where there's a network effect, being first is even more important. Take Facebook, eBay, and Airbnb. They all rely on the network effect, which means that the more users they attract, the more valuable they become, and the harder it is for competitors to overtake them. Once a startup gains dominance and the network effect kicks in, the early mover quickly becomes a monopoly. Look how hard Google, with all its talent and muscle, has been trying to develop its own social network and yet hasn't managed to catch up to Facebook. Who can challenge Airbnb, Snapchat, or eBay in their markets? Only a radically new and superior product has a chance of displacing them, and those don't come often. Once the network effect takes hold, it's usually game over.

MYTH: TECH ALWAYS WINS

Sadly, superior tech doesn't always win. Technology is only one piece of a complex equation that includes marketing, distribution, public relations, user experience, customer feedback, and more. Even if you have the best technology in the world, you may still wind up losing market share to savvy competitors who excel in other areas. Just look at Microsoft versus Apple in the early days, when Windows PCs were far inferior to the Macintosh. Even Steve Jobs, the undisputed wunderkind of innovation, couldn't turn the tide and wound up being booted as CEO from his own company.

BEING FIRST ISN'T EVERYTHING

Let's step back for a moment and admit that being first to market isn't a guarantee of success. You still have to do things right, or someone else will come along and steal your cheese. History has shown us that many markets are dominated by companies that came late to the party. Below are some hard lessons learned on what not to do.

Old-timers will remember Betamax, Sony's proprietary video tape. It's a classic example of a superior technology that was first to market and still failed. How was this possible? Betamax had better picture quality than its competitor, VHS, and the backing of Sony, a powerhouse in consumer electronics. But it had an Achilles' heel. Betamax video tapes were limited to only one hour, while VHS allowed for longer tapes. Since everyone wanted to watch Hollywood movies on video, VHS won. Who would've thought? Betamax eventually offered longer tapes, but it was too late.

Atari is another high flyer that crashed and burned. They invented the video game industry with the release of Pong. They were six years ahead of Nintendo and dominated the market with the Atari 2600 console. How could Nintendo, a Johnny-come-lately with a me-too product, topple them? It didn't. Atari committed hara-kiri. They screwed up the launch of Atari 5200 with an overpriced and poorly designed product. Then came the video game crash of 1983, a nasty recession that caused Atari to bleed cash. When Nintendo came along with the NES, Atari was in turmoil. The market was wide open, and Nintendo jumped in.

Netscape was another superstar that didn't survive. In the midnineties, Netscape had 90 percent of the browser market. How incredible is that?

But its fame didn't last long. By 1998 its market share had fallen to 70 percent and was dropping like a stone, so the management sold the company to America Online, where Netscape disappeared into a black hole. Why did Netscape die? Part of the blame falls on Microsoft's aggressive tactics of bundling Internet Explorer with the Windows operating system, which commanded over 80 percent of the market share. People tended to opt for the default browser. The problem was that Netscape failed to alter its strategy and innovate further, so they got outflanked.

Another early casualty was the first wave of search engines, including WebCrawler, Lycos, Excite, Infoseek, and a dozen others. All of these launched well before Google but none of them made it. The reason was simple: Google was better. It actually produced meaningful search results—not just a collection of sites that happened to contain the search terms.

There were numerous MP3 players before the iPod. All of them worked just fine until Steve Jobs rewrote the rules of the game. Apple's iPod created an entire ecosystem, from the hardware to browsing and buying music. It was beautifully designed, easy to use, and supercool. Apple innovated everyone else out of the market.

Long before World of Warcraft or other big online games, there was EverQuest. It was the king of the hill, with more than 450,000 subscribers. Why did it go the way of the dinosaur? If you played it, you'd know. It was amazing but too frickin hard. Players had to invest vast amounts of time to move up to the highest levels. The further you got, the more painful it became. You could have a life or play EverQuest. There was no in-between. This frustrated many players, and when simpler, more rewarding alternatives like World of Warcraft came out, players abandoned EverQuest. The moral of this story is to know thy customer.

TiVo was first to market with the DVR, a radical invention that enabled everyone to easily time-shift, freeing them from the tyranny of scheduled TV programming. TiVo succeeded in capturing the world's imagination and enjoyed explosive growth. However, the big cable operators didn't sit still. They added the same functionality into their cable boxes and gave it away for free. It wasn't long before no one needed TiVo. The lesson: It's hard to compete when a competitor can afford to give away your product.

Another sad story is Palm. Remember Palm? They were the iPhone before the iPhone existed. The Palm Pilot started off as a revolutionary personal digital assistant, which won over the hearts and minds of Americans. But they made a number of critical mistakes. Just as smartphones were emerging, Palm screwed up. It launched Treo, one of the first smartphones with a color touch screen and web browser, but it was clunky compared to the competition. People didn't want to lug around a brick. Consumers gravitated toward slimmer, sleeker phones. Then along came Apple with the iPhone, and the Treo was yesterday's act. Now no one under twenty remembers the Palm. The lesson: You can't be second-best.

Friendster is the story of a company that could have owned the world. They were the first big social networking site, attracting over three million users in a matter of months. They were live a full year before MySpace and two years before Facebook. With the network effect on their side, how could Friendster fail? Despite bucketloads of venture capitalist money and a new management team, the site remained painfully slow and kept crashing. The company wasn't prepared to scale, so as soon as users had another choice, they jumped ship. The lesson: Customers have a low threshold for pain.

MySpace boomed for a while, as users defected from Friendster in droves, but MySpace failed to innovate. MySpace pages quickly went from entrancing to eyesores. The user interface was awful. Most pages were cluttered with flashing, blinking text and graphics. It felt cheap and schlocky. When people saw that Facebook actually understood how to build a feed and create a community, they dropped MySpace. The rest is history. The lesson being that you can't win with a significantly inferior product even if you're first to market.

These are just a few examples of how innovators and market leaders dropped the ball and let others steal their markets. Speed is essential, but it isn't the only ingredient in a successful startup.

DON'T BET ON LATECOMERS

Despite the high profile cases of latecomers stealing the market, speed still plays a pivotal role in the success of startups in Silicon Valley. As you can see from the above examples, the first-to-market innovators each grabbed market share and enjoyed initial successes, but they either failed to continue innovating or had a fatal flaw in their business strategy or product. If they hadn't had these shortcomings, they would have been hard to beat. If you're going to place a bet, it still pays to pick the horse in the lead.

Speed is so important that when I look at startups, I make a mental calculation of how long the window will be open for them. If they don't gain traction in that time, it's typically game over. One example of this is Survios, a virtual reality startup I worked with. They came out of the University of Southern California—my alma mater. USC is also where Oculus obtained its open-source VR software, and the Survios founders worked alongside Oculus cofounder Palmer Luckey back in the day. They were well positioned to take virtual reality to the next level with their advanced VR device.

They came up from Los Angeles to meet with me. I reviewed their business plan, made a number of introductions, and within a month, they'd raised millions from top-tier Sand Hill Road VCs. It was a good start, but the VR race was already heating up. Over the next year, Sony, Samsung, Microsoft, HTC, and others announced their own VR devices.

Soon it became clear to the founders that they couldn't win. Even though they had superior tech, time to market and distribution muscle were critical. With the window closing fast on new VR devices, they pivoted, focusing all their energy on creating VR apps. The founders were smart. They realized that if they couldn't win the VR hardware wars, there was no point in competing. Better to focus on a race they could lead.

They made a number of early games, including *Zombies on the Holodeck*, and learned a huge amount with each project. James Iliff, the cofounder, has told me on several occasions that they're not just developing games;

they are intent on creating a new language for VR. They believe virtual reality is fundamentally different from any other medium, and it's not enough to translate existing games into VR. All their hard work paid off when they released *Raw Data*, which instantly became the top-grossing virtual reality game in the United States. The game transports you into another world where an evil corporation is secretly stealing human brains, putting them into cyborgs, and selling them for profit. Unlike most VR games, this one doesn't feel like a demo. It's totally immersive and harrowingly intense.

Another example of why it's important to lead the market, rather than follow, is Sidecar, a ride-sharing startup. Richard Branson, a smart guy by anyone's measure, invested in the company, boldly declaring that it was the "early days and, like a lot of other commodity businesses, there is room for innovators on great customer experiences." The problem was that Uber and Lyft were way ahead of Sidecar. They'd captured the public's imagination and taken the lead. In the world of tech startups, there usually isn't room for a number three or four in a market. Branson was wrong. Only fifteen months later, Sidecar's cofounder and CEO, Sunil Paul, announced that the company had lost the race and was shutting down. It was not a "commodity business" like Branson claimed.

Sidecar's story is much more common than that of an upstart coming from behind to overtake the market leader. Whenever a new innovation takes hold of Silicon Valley, we see dozens of copycats jump into the arena. They all claim to have something superior, but at the end of the day, most of them don't have enough to overtake the leader. Within a year or two, they're all gone, and it's usually those who were first that are left standing. So if all else is equal, velocity is everything!

Chapter 31

Iteration Cycles

The real measure of success is the number of experiments that can be crowded into twenty-four hours.

—Thomas Edison

The goal of all this speed is to increase the number of iteration cycles. Only through iterating on your product, making changes, and testing those changes is progress actually made. Getting a product to market quickly doesn't mean it will succeed. Most new products fail and fail miserably. In Silicon Valley, 70 percent of startups that are lucky enough to get angel and seed funding die before they make it to the next round of funding, and even those that do raise additional capital don't necessarily turn into profitable businesses. It's not about getting your product to market that matters. It's the speed at which you learn that counts. It's only by learning what the market truly needs that you can come up with a successful product.

A good example of iterating fast is my second startup. Together with three amazing cofounders, we formed a company called Spiderdance, which came from the wild dance we would do when spinning our web of ideas. One of our ideas was to take a nearly completed massively multiplayer gaming engine and launch a new business. Keep in mind that this was in the dot-com days, a time when nearly all games and apps were single-player experiences. Competing with friends in real time online wasn't common, but we saw it as the future.

I convinced my partners it would be a good idea for me to run around Silicon Valley and talk to every game developer I could find to see if they wanted to build on top of our platform. I believed that game developers would flock to our platform and share revenue. Why wouldn't they? It made no sense for a developer to spend a year or more building out their own massively multiplayer gaming engine when they could simply use ours.

I was sorely mistaken. This was long before Steam and similar platforms became popular. Most game developers at the time had a bad case of "not invented here" syndrome. They were used to building everything themselves and didn't want to rely on anyone else's code. The ones who did agree to use our platform would agree only to a small revenue share. This rude awakening taught me a lesson. Just because something makes sense doesn't mean it's true.

After six weeks, I'd learned what I needed to know. It was time to try something new. Fortunately my partners, one a master coder and the other a brilliant designer, had finished off the engine. Together we launched our own app called Jabberchat, which combined chatting and casual gaming, a new concept at the time.

Jabberchat was an instant hit. Dozens of websites picked it up and embedded it into their pages, while SXSW awarded it Best Online Game. We were thrilled. We'd figured it out, and it had taken us only a couple months. Doing our spider dance, we celebrated sweet success.

However, before the champagne could start flowing, reality intervened. We didn't charge websites for using Jabberchat, so we had no revenue. We had no funding. We were young, inexperienced, and had to feed ourselves. This meant we needed a business model, and unfortunately, nobody would pay for a chat-based game. So we began to look around. We'd heard that companies were creating online advertising networks for the first time. We determined this was the business model we needed.

We contacted one of these early ad networks and had banner ads inserted into our app within weeks, then sat back and waited for the money to pour in. When the first check arrived at our door a month later, our hopes were dashed. Our entire ad revenue amounted to less than $25. That wouldn't even cover one night of pizza and beer, let alone grow a company. The fact was that Internet advertising hadn't arrived yet. We were too early.

It was time to press the Reset button again. The first two pivots were fine, but by the third pivot, we were feeling the pinch. Every day that went by meant less money in our bank accounts. We asked ourselves who would pay us for what we had? That's when we heard through the grapevine that MTV was looking to do an interactive TV show, but they didn't have a platform. This was a match made in heaven. My partners had created NetWits, one of the first online TV game shows, and they'd envisioned Spiderdance becoming an interactive TV platform. Being born hustlers, we found out the phone number of the vice president of MTV Interactive and kept leaving messages on his voice mail. We were sure he'd call us back. He had to call us. They were Viacom, the largest media company in the world, and we were Spiderdance! You know what happened? Nothing. He never called. No one called.

Around this time, my cofounder, Tracy Fullerton, got invited to speak on a panel at the Consumer Electronics Show. She's a gifted speaker, and she began spider dancing on the panel about how we were building the future of interactive television. Sure enough, immediately after her panel, someone came running up from the audience. "I have to talk with you," he said, catching his breath. "You have exactly what we need. It's exactly what we've been looking for!" It was Rick Holzman, the VP of MTV Interactive.

"I know," replied Tracy. "We've been leaving messages on your voice mail."

This was the ticket we'd been looking for. We'd found our first customer, and they were willing to cut a large six-figure deal. To add icing to our cake, MTV was building the biggest interactive TV show ever conceived to date. Up until this time, nearly every interactive TV show was a tiny experiment with a few thousand users. Most of them were limited to set-top boxes and never had a prayer of going mainstream. MTV was creating a new show designed from the ground up to be interactive. It was called *WebRIOT,* and it was a music game show where the audience could play along in real time online using any PC and web browser. The highest scoring players would win prizes and have their names fed back live into the TV broadcast.

We were in business! We'd innovated ourselves into a new market by experimenting with multiple ideas, testing each in rapid succession, and determining a product-market fit. This is what I see my startups doing at Founders Space. Most of them never know if they're on the right track until it magically happens. Many of them stumble upon it by accident while exploring or observing something special happening with their users or customers, while others leap at an opportunity, like we did.

The story of Spiderdance doesn't end here, but this lesson does. This is the innovation process startups go through everyday. To accelerate the learning and discovery process, you need to focus on the rate of iteration. Each iteration cycle is a chance for your team to test their assumptions and discover what works and what doesn't. By compressing these cycles, you can figure out the right solution before any of your competitors do. So when we're talking about speed, we're not talking about how fast your teams reach some arbitrary milestones, like prototype, alpha, beta, etc. Those are meaningless if you haven't gained any deep insights into the business. It's unlocking the secrets of your business and understanding exactly what your customers want from your product that lead to exponential returns.

Reid Hoffman, cofounder of LinkedIn, famously said, "If you are not embarrassed by the first version of your product, you've launched too late." What Hoffman means by this is that it's far more important to put out an ugly product and begin the learning process as soon as possible, than to take the time to develop a beautiful product. This is because your product probably doesn't even do what the customer wants, so you're wasting your time making it pretty. It's speed of iteration that matters, and you can't truly start iterating before you get the product into the hands of your customers.

Surveys, demos, and prototypes can only give you an approximation of what the customer wants. Anyone can say anything, but when you see what customers actually do with your product, the real learning begins. A lead designer at Netflix puts it this way: "We make a lot of this stuff up as we go along, I'm serious. We don't assume anything works, and we don't like to make predictions without real-world tests. Predictions color our thinking. So, we continually make this up as we go along, keeping what works and throwing away what doesn't. We've found that about 90 percent of it doesn't work." This is why Netflix is one of the most innovative companies in the world. They know how to iterate, and that's what took them from a DVD rental company to one of the world's leading media companies, with their own distribution channels and content.

When Marissa Mayer was Google's vice president for search products and user experience, she said, "In the case of the Toolbar Beta, several of the key features (custom buttons, shared bookmarks) were prototyped in less than a week. In fact, during the brainstorming phase, we tried out about five times as many key features—many of which we discarded after a week of prototyping. Since only one in every five to ten ideas work out, the strategy of constraining how quickly ideas must be proven allows us to try out more ideas faster, increasing our odds of success."

You may think iterating this fast will frustrate your team, but the opposite is true. It's much more frustrating to spend months perfecting a feature, only to find out it doesn't do much for the customer. When you compress iteration cycles, it actually frees up the team to experiment. The psychology changes. Your team will be much more open to try things they normally wouldn't. They can just toss something out there and see if it sticks. This makes for a more flexible and adaptive development process, where the team cares more about what they learn than what they built.

Failing fast in Silicon Valley has become the accepted norm. I like to tell startups in our program, "Push for a fail!" That means try to make something fail. Get it out there, rigorously test it, and try to expose its faults. If you can break it, you learn something. If you can't break it, keep trying!

This attitude is meant to combat slow iteration. When a team tries to get it right the first time, they will take more time and try to think through everything. The sad truth is that they fail just as often as those who simply toss it out and see what happens. All their work at trying to polish something seldom makes it right. Most things either work or they don't. And there's only one person who can tell you this, and that's the customer.

MYTH: INNOVATION IS ABOUT SOLUTIONS

Innovation is less about coming up with a new solution and more about clearly understanding the real problem. A common trap many innovators make is to come up with a solution to a problem that nobody cares about. I see startups all the time that begin with an intriguing concept and wind up spending all their time searching for customers that don't exist. Einstein had it right when he said, "If I had an hour to solve a problem, I'd spend fifty-five minutes thinking about the problem and five minutes thinking about solutions."

Anti-iterators love to have meetings, where they debate the pros and cons of product features. Everyone has an opinion but no real data, and it's often those who argue the longest and loudest who wind up driving the decision. The result is that many good ideas are buried without even being tested. People's feelings get hurt. Some team members may even stop contributing because the dominant personalities are shutting them out. Instead of debating, if anyone on the team has a worthy idea, you should assign a team to test it out on customers. Design a quick experiment at a low cost and put it in front of customers, so you can gather as much data as possible. As Sean Rad, founder of Adly, puts it, "Data beats emotions."

Iterating fast has an additional benefit. It makes your customers partners in design. By making changes, soliciting feedback, and incorporating their feedback into the development process, you can turn your most dedicated customers into collaborators in the development of your product. This not only leads to better products but changes how your customers view their role. They contribute their ideas, point out flaws, and take ownership. Before you know it, your customers will become your best evangelists and promoters.

It also reduces the overall risk. Risk gets compounded the longer the company works on something without testing. Every day that passes, more development dollars and resources are spent on an idea with little or no proof that it will produce anything beneficial. By compressing iteration cycles, you are in essence squeezing the risk out of the equation.

Each iteration cycle is a chance to get at the underlying truth that no one else in your business understands yet. These new truths are constantly coming into being. They are born through advances in technology, changes in the way business is done, emergent social trends, and new regulations that remake the landscape. The world is not static. You and your competitors may not realize it, but the entire market may be heading in another direction. If you are slow to find out, you will wind up without a business.

Chapter 32

Lost in the Woods

Never give up. Today is hard, tomorrow will be worse, but the day after tomorrow will be sunshine.

—Jack Ma, founder of Alibaba

If you are trying enough things, experimenting with ideas, and killing off most of them, at a certain point you'll notice that suddenly something is happening. You don't know how or why, but this new thing you came up with is really working and in a way you never anticipated. True innovation seldom follows a straight line. It's a zigzag, roundabout, "lost in the woods" roller-coaster ride. The point being, you never know where you're headed until you suddenly wind up there.

HERE COMES THE SUN

Let me begin with Sun Basket, a startup close to my heart. It's founded by my friends and former business partners, Adam Zbar and Braxton Woodham. They are both extremely smart and resilient. When they began their latest startup, it was a location-based shopping app that matched online buyers with local stores. On the surface, it seemed like a great idea, and they were able to raise seed funding, but it never took off. Customers and store owners just didn't need it.

Like any good entrepreneurs, they scrapped the idea and pivoted. This time they launched Lasso, an on-demand wine and cheese delivery service. The timing was right, so they easily raised more seed funding. But they struggled to get this business off the ground. The on-demand space grew steadily more crowded, and they found themselves squeezed. They were a niche player without the power of companies like Instacart, Amazon, and GrubHub.

If there's anything Zbar learned in his previous startups, it's that if your core business model isn't working, forget it. There's nothing you can do to save it. No matter how hard you try, it's over. So after many months of struggling, they called it quits and rebooted. Third time's a charm, right?

With the same startup and what little money they had left, they came up with a new idea. This time it was called Sun Basket, a service that delivered meals ready to cook. The catch was that they targeted specific diets, like Paleo, vegetarian, and gluten free. Instead of having to search the aisles of your local supermarket for specific products that fit the diet, like gluten free, customers could just subscribe to their meal service and have all the ingredients delivered to their doorstep.

Sun Basket not only tapped into a growing trend for specialty diets, it addressed a real pain point for many grocery shoppers. Like magic, their new idea blossomed into a rapidly growing business. Zbar, being a business development maniac, closed deal after deal, while bringing in over $28 million in venture funding. As of this writing, it's clear they're on the right track. Their annual recurring revenue is $140 million and growing. Are they out of the woods yet? You never know, but it looks like they may make an initial public offering in the not-too-distant future. The point of this story being that when you're lost in the woods, it's important to give up on ideas that aren't working, but never give up trying. You have to keep blazing new paths, even if it feels like you're going backward, until you find your way out.

LEVELING UP

When Stewart Butterfield, Caterina Fake, and their team of Vancouver developers at Glitch were working on their online game, they came up with the idea of allowing players to share photos. You've probably never heard of their game because it didn't do much. It was called *Game Never-ending*, and although the game only appealed to a niche audience, they noticed that the photo-sharing feature had potential, so they spun it off as its own product. Their approach of combining community and photo sharing created a sensation. They called it Flickr, and it wasn't long before Yahoo gobbled them up.

"People sometimes forget how early Flickr came," Butterfield says. "Facebook didn't add photo sharing till a year after Flickr was acquired by Yahoo." In 2008, Butterfield quit Yahoo and went back to making games. This time the game was called *Glitch*. It was a nonviolent massively multiplayer online game where players competed against rival religious factions for converts. This bizarrely creative game was another dud. Instead, users gravitated toward games like Zynga's *FarmVille*. Glitch shut down at the end of 2012, and Butterfield wasn't happy. After letting most of the team go, he and what remained of his team put their minds together. They had to save the company. But what could they do?

That's when they remembered how they'd used Internet Relay Chat (IRC), an old-school chat tool, while developing Flickr to communicate with one another. Back in the Flickr days, they had become so obsessed with IRC that they'd added a lot of features to make it work better for collaborating. Butterfield and his cohorts went back to developing this tool, ditching the antiquated IRC and building a new communications platform from the ground up that did exactly what they wanted it to do. That was how Slack was conceived, and it's now one of the hottest unicorns in Silicon Valley. I can't wait to see what game Butterfield makes next!

NO TIME TO EAT

Rob Rhinehart was thrilled when his startup was accepted into the accelerator Y Combinator with the mission of building wireless networks for developing countries. However, this project went nowhere fast, and the startup quickly ran out of cash. With his cofounders jumping ship, Rob and two of his roommates dabbled in various projects. Rob, who hated to waste time eating, began mixing together supplements purchased on Amazon in a pitcher of water and drinking it whenever he was hungry. Soon he began living off the stuff.

After thirty days, Rob looked and felt great, so he posted his experience on his blog, and Soylent went viral. Rob is now leading a nutritional startup. It just goes to show you that you never know where your next big idea will come from!

STRANGE BREW

Paul Sciarra and Ben Silbermann agreed to quit their jobs to form a startup called Cold Brew Labs. Paul left Radius Capital and Ben quit Google. This was the start of their road to riches! The product was called Tote, and it was an iPhone app that pulled data from online catalogs to create a supercatalog for shoppers on the move. They soon secured funding from FirstMark Capital and were off to the races. Only their horse never left the gate.

Tote went nowhere fast. It was a total flop. In 2009, most people weren't using apps for shopping, and their app was slow and clunky, due to issues with the App Store. What Silbermann noticed was that some users were sending images from the catalog to themselves and saving them. This wasn't a behavior they'd expected, so they dug deeper.

Choosing to develop a new product built around this behavior, they launched a website, iterating on Tote's platform to see if they could engage more users. The new product enabled users to put their images in buckets and organize them. Silbermann didn't call this a shopping service or catalog or anything else. He purposefully kept it vague so that people could use it for whatever they wanted.

Silbermann told the board this wasn't a pivot. It was more of an iteration on the original concept. There was no grand vision or plan. They were just fine tuning the platform to what users wanted. Whatever it was, users seemed to love it. Tote was put to bed and Pinterest took its place. As the growth curve turned into a hockey stick, Pinterest raised loads of capital and became one of the hottest social networks since Facebook. The lesson here is that it pays to observe your customers carefully.

MYTH: INNOVATIONS COME FROM EPIPHANIES

We love stories of epiphanies. We all know the story of how the apple dropped on Sir Isaac Newton's head, and *pop*, the lightbulb went on and he came up with the idea for gravity. That sounds wonderful, but Newton's ideas developed over a longer period of time and involved a deep understanding of physics. The apple was simply a good metaphor for explaining how his ideas work in the real world, and it sparked the public's imagination.

Most scientists and inventors will tell you that their best ideas evolved gradually, and only after repeated testing and experimentation did they actually believe them to be true. Seldom does an idea appear fully formed as an epiphany. If only life was so magical.

WHAT'S THE POINT?

While getting his college degree in public policy at the University of Chicago, Andrew Mason ran a political site called Policy Tree. As a side job, he built databases for Eric Lefkofsky, a successful entrepreneur. Mason was essentially squatting in Eric's offices. Ever the social activist, Mason turned his attention toward developing a new site called the Point, which enabled groups of people to solve problems together. There was no vision of making millions. There was no business plan. This was a site focused solely on the public good.

Lefkofsky, who liked Mason, would provide advice and guidance. At one point, Lefkofsky noticed that while most people used the site to organize a social cause, a group of users decided their cause would be to save money; so they used the platform to try and get group discounts from merchants. Lefkofsky suggested they set up a separate page around group buying.

Mason and others felt this wasn't core to their mission. The idea had surfaced before, and they didn't want to go that direction. But Lefkofsky wouldn't let it go. Then the perfect storm hit. In September of 2008, Lehman Brothers filed for bankruptcy and Silicon Valley hit the brakes on venture capital. Mason and Lefkofsky decided they needed to lay off some of their staff.

At this point, Mason opened up to the idea of testing group buying as a way to generate much-needed revenue. He decided to focus on local businesses and enable them to offer deals to groups of online buyers. The concept was an instant hit. The press and public loved it. The Point went away and Groupon took its place, sprinting all the way to an IPO. The moral of this story is to surround yourself with smart people and listen to them. If Lefkofsky hadn't spotted the golden opportunity and kept hammering at it, there's a chance Mason would never have gotten his elephant off the ground.

HELP! HELP!

Jeremy Stoppelman was personally frustrated about how hard it was to find a good recommendation for a doctor online. Wouldn't it be easier to just ask friends? Together with Russell Simmons, he created an automated system that would e-mail recommendation requests to friends. They then raised $1 million from PayPal cofounder Max Levchin.

Despite the influx of cash, their startup failed to gain traction. Users didn't like to ask friends for recommendations. However, what surprised Stoppelman was that a number of users began writing reviews on local businesses just for the heck of it. This was the key they'd been looking for. They called the service Yelp, and the site now has over 150 million users per month and 100 million online reviews. The moral of this story is that users are often better at elephant spotting than you are. Let them show you where the value lies!

SNOWBOARDING?

Shopify is a great example of a company born out of solving an internal problem. In 2004, Tobias Lütke and Scott Lake desperately needed an online shopping cart for their new snowboard business. However, when they couldn't find the perfect one, Lütke decided to build it himself. The pair was so pleased with the results that they decided to make it available to other small businesses. Shopify now has over 275,000 merchants in 150 countries on their platform, racking up $17 billion in total sales. The lesson here is that nothing beats solving a problem you understand well. Many of the most successful innovators start by eating their own dog food.

MORNING MUD

Howard Schultz fell in love with European coffee and began selling high-quality espresso makers and coffee beans in the United States in 1971. In 1983, when visiting Italy, he became inspired to start a European-style coffeehouse in America. He called it Starbucks, and it was the beginning of America's infatuation with premium coffee. No more crummy cups of joe. His vision has led to Starbucks on every street corner in practically every country. The lesson here is to follow your gut. If you love something, chances are other people will too.

LOVE HOTELS

Long before Super Mario and Donkey Kong, Nintendo made everything from playing cards to vacuum cleaners. It even ran a taxi company and love hotel chain. Only in 1966 did Nintendo dive into electronic game consoles. Sometimes you have to try a lot of things before you hit it right.

DOOR-TO-DOOR

David H. McConnell was a traveling book salesman who liked to give away free samples of perfume to his customers who bought his books. After knocking on a lot of doors, he realized that the perfume was more popular than his books. So he began his own line of perfume, recruited a bunch of women to sell it, and called the company Avon. Ah, the sweet smell of success! Today Avon has over 6 million reps and $10 billion in sales. McConnell learned that what you're giving away for free may be the real product.

GOOFY IS GOOD

Justin Kan and Emmett Shear were childhood friends and Yale classmates. They started out having no idea what they were doing. They just had a lot of crazy ideas. One of them was turning Kan's life into a reality show, where he'd live with a camera strapped to his head 24/7. I remember seeing him walking around San Francisco with the goofy-looking camera. It wasn't much of a business, but Paul Graham, cofounder of Y Combinator, liked the team and decided to invest $50,000.

"We had no idea what we were doing," says Kan. "This much was obvious to anyone who watched." That didn't stop the press from loving it. They made Justin a star, and soon livestreams became the latest fad. Justin.tv transformed into a network, where anyone could lifecast. By 2010, they had 31 million unique viewers per month. Around the same time, they noticed that gamers were using Justin.tv to broadcast their games and tournaments. This was the "Aha" moment. As game streaming grew, they spun off a dedicated site, which they later called Twitch. By 2014, Twitch had 50 million viewers, and Amazon swooped in to buy it for $970 million.

Justin.tv was shut down, but the founders walked away wealthy, and Twitch lives on in the Amazon universe.

How's that for a spectacular series of iterations? The moral of this story is to never stop innovating. Keep it up until someone offers you so much money you can't refuse!

Chapter 33

People Power

The world is not limited by IQ. We are all limited by bravery and creativity.

—Astro Teller, scientist and author

If you want people that think different, you need to get people who are different. It's those people, who have ideas and opinions that few agree with, that can ignite change. They are your catalysts. They can challenge your teams to step beyond their comfort zone. You may be tempted to staff your innovation teams with only superstars—your top scientists, star salespeople, savvy marketers, and most brilliant strategists. But some of them may not turn out to be the best innovators. They may be locked into conventional thinking and miss out on what's possible. In other words, don't limit your innovation teams to top performers. Mix it up. Get your best talent working with others in your organization.

Frank, who sits in the corner with his headphones on and never talks to anyone, may have insights into your business or a way of looking at things that no one else possesses. The same goes for Mary Jane, the kooky person with the outlandish wardrobe and far-out ideas. She may just be the catalyst that inspires the other team members to let their guard down, loosen up, and be creative. When you're building these innovation teams, it's wise to open up the process to the entire company—not just an exclusive group. Have a contest where everyone from the CFO to the janitor can submit ideas and compete for the chance to be an innovator. You may also want to democratize the ideation process, where everyone votes on the best ideas.

This will set the right tone, energize your organization, and make clear that the entire company needs to be involved.

You may be surprised at who transforms your business. Ken Kutaragi was a relatively junior employee at Sony, who spent hours on end tinkering with his daughter's Nintendo. He wanted to make it more user-friendly and powerful. A number of senior managers at Sony were annoyed when his project started to get attention. They felt that gaming was a waste of time and resources. There was no future in it for Sony. Despite the opposition, Kutaragi's side project turned into The Sony PlayStation, one of the world's most successful consumer electronic products ever.

MYTH: PEOPLE LOVE NEW IDEAS

Unfortunately, all people don't love new ideas—especially those in power. Throughout history, those with new ideas that upended established thinking have been imprisoned, burned at the stake, crucified, and persecuted in countless ways. Human beings are, by their very nature, conservative. We like what we know. We trust what worked in the past. Most people desire security and predictability above all else and so will cling to the status quo, even to their own detriment.

The problem is that radical, new ideas tend to threaten the existing power structure. You can't have a breakthrough idea without challenging entrenched interests, and as we know, self-interest trumps innovation every time. People will resist any call for change that threatens their positions and pocketbooks. Because of this, the best ideas don't always win out at first. Even ideas as beneficial as sterilizing your instruments before surgery took years to overcome resistance from well-educated doctors, despite ample evidence that it saved lives.

The key to getting new ideas accepted is to frame them in a way that minimizes threats to the establishment while emphasizing the benefits to all the stakeholders. It's not enough to have a great idea. You have to sell that idea and rally support for it. It's the game of politics. Unfortunately, many creative thinkers and inventors aren't the ones best suited for politics in the office or the government. Just take Galileo Galilei. He annoyed the Pope so much that despite being close friends, the Pope sent him to the Inquisition. Just because you're a genius doesn't mean you're brilliant at everything.

THE RIGHT INGREDIENTS

In chapter 7, we talked about the ideal startup team's DNA. There we said the perfect combination consisted of a Hustler, Hacker, Hipster, and Hotshot. I also touched upon the need for adding a Politician and an Organizer to corporate innovation teams. Let's expand our view on the types of personalities you may need in a larger organization to innovate.

There are specific things you should look for when choosing your innovators, especially when it comes to colleagues and coworkers. More than training, IQ, or motivation, personality characteristics indicate whether or not someone is capable of piercing the wall of conformity. Curious people tend to make the best explorers. When you combine curiosity with a driving passion for creating things, an openness to new experiences, and a nonconformist bent, you're getting close to the ideal innovator.

But don't just choose one type of person. You don't want a homogenous team of people who all think and act alike. You want people with different perspectives, ideas, and backgrounds. That's how you create a dynamic group. Below are the types of traits you should be looking for on any team, and you may find individuals who possess two or more of these traits.

THE OPPORTUNIST

Opportunists are always on the lookout for something that will pay off in a big way. They tend to spot openings in the market early and aren't afraid to jump in. They love new challenges, especially if it means they stand a chance to leap ahead of everyone else. You can have the smartest person in the world, but they can be blind to an opportunity right in front of their face. Opportunists, on the other hand, are always alert for a lucky break and won't hesitate to capitalize on it.

THE DOMAIN EXPERT

Despite all the mythology around innovators who dropped out of high school and changed the world, most innovators are highly educated people with the knowledge and training to connect the dots and realize the possibilities. Innovations are built on deep insights into how the world works, including complex business processes, technologies, and societal trends. For an innovator to understand what's actually happening and recognize what needs to change, they must have the right depth of knowledge in key areas. It doesn't matter if they have a degree from an Ivy League or are self-taught, as long as they know their stuff.

THE FACILITATOR

Having at least one team member with a high EQ (emotional intelligence) is essential. Someone needs to be your face to the rest of the organization. Innovation requires cooperation, and your innovation team will need to get others involved. Someone who has built a strong people network is a good candidate. Innovation is never done alone. Having access to the right people at the right time can make all the difference. Jon Katzenbach, a management guru, sums it up when he says, "In an innovation team, there is no way to divorce the individual innovator from his network." Often the success of a project may hinge on a personal relationship. Having someone able to pull a few strings within the organization can change the equation.

THE STORYTELLER

If the team is doing something truly innovative, someone needs to be able to communicate this to the rest of the organization. Storytelling is the most powerful and effective mechanism to get buy in. Venture capitalists often fund startups based on their story. Make sure someone on the team can talk the talk and sell the vision!

THE DRIVER

There needs to be a relentless driver on the team—the type of personality who doesn't take no for an answer. When things go wrong, which they inevitably will, this person will figure out how to solve the problem come hell or high water. When everything appears hopeless, the driver will double down and try even harder, charging ahead—because that's what drivers do. There's really no substitute for this personality trait. It's what separates true entrepreneurs from office drones.

THE ORGANIZER

Someone must be detail oriented. Disorganized teams don't make progress. Everything turns out to be a mess. You need to have one person on the team that picks up all the pieces and makes sure they fit together. This is typically a project manager, who is an expert at making sure a plan is in place, everyone knows what to do, and nothing falls between the cracks.

THE OUTSIDER

Don't think that everyone on the team must come from inside your organization. Often, adding someone from the outside is just what the team needs. An external consultant, who isn't imbued with the company culture and immersed in office politics, can often push the team to go places they might not otherwise have thought possible. Having a provocateur who isn't shy about prodding the team to take chances can lead the team in new directions. Try to find someone with experience and knowledge that other team members lack. Corporate consultants, veteran entrepreneurs, and researchers with deep domain expertise are often good candidates. Who you choose depends on what the team needs most.

THE COMMITMENT

Most important, you don't want any of your core team members to be halfway committed. It's fine to have part-time members, but the core team needs to be 100 percent dedicated. Most experienced VCs don't fund start-ups unless the founders are fully on board and have quit their day jobs. Carter Griffin, a venture capitalist at Updata Partners, says that entrepreneurs "have to put their entire being behind this initiative, as the ones who try to hedge fail. The ones who don't pour their soul into it typically don't make it." The same is true for innovation teams inside large organizations. Everyone must be focused and devoted to making the project a success. There's no going back!

When you discover teams that work incredibly well together and produce outstanding results, that's when to back off. If you've figured out the winning formula, you don't want to make arbitrary changes. Let them remain a team as long as they like. It's hard to create magic, and when you do, protect and nurture it. These types of combinations are rare and nearly impossible to replicate. One thing I can tell you is that when you see the sparks fly, you'll know it. If you aren't seeing it, shuffle the deck once more!

Chapter 34

Think Different

First they ignore you, then they laugh at you, then they fight you, then you win.

—Mahatma Mohandas Gandhi, leader of the
Indian independence movement

Innovating is not about doing what everybody else does. It's about doing something different. You have to free up the people on your innovation teams. You need to tell them that their job is not to do what's expected. It's not to do what they're used to. It's not even to do what they're good at. It's pushing the limits, making mistakes, going out on the fringes, and transforming the impossible into the possible.

It's hard to break from the herd and go another direction. It's hard to be different. It's hard to innovate. You need to completely change the way you and your team view the world, and that starts with yourself. Take a moment and write down everything you do in a typical day. You'll probably notice a pattern. You do the same things over and over. You go to the same office, talk to the same people, eat the same foods, read the same type of books, watch the same shows, and so on. You need to stop this, shake up your life, and do something different!

The goal shouldn't be to incrementally improve things but to learn how to radically reshape the way you experience the world. If there's one thing I've learned in life, it's that people who achieve greatness are constantly reinventing not only the world but themselves. They don't allow themselves to stagnate. They don't accept who they are as permanent and immutable. They believe they can do and become more when they set their minds to it. They are constantly challenging themselves to look at the world anew. And they are intensely curious about everything.

If you want to know what I'm talking about, just read Teddy Roosevelt's life story. By sheer force of will, he remade himself time and time again, and in the process remade America. He was a weak and sickly child, but he became a fearless war hero, an eloquent public speaker, a master politician, a social crusader, and a world adventurer—not to mention president of the United States. His accomplishments include writing more than thirty books, breaking up the all-powerful trusts, regulating the railroads, protecting workers on the job, passing food and drug safety acts, securing the Panama Canal, creating the national park system, and much more.

Teddy Roosevelt was an innovator who wasn't afraid of any new idea. He was constantly challenging authority and commonly held beliefs. He wasn't content with the status quo. He believed in a better world, envisioned it, and brought it to life. This quote of his sums it all up: "It is not the critic who counts; not the man who points out how the strong man stumbles, or where the doer of deeds could have done them better. The credit belongs to the man who is actually in the arena, whose face is marred by dust and sweat and blood; who strives valiantly; who errs, and comes short again and again, because there is no effort without error and shortcoming; but who does actually strive to do the deeds; who knows great enthusiasms, the great devotions; who spends himself in a worthy cause; who at the best knows in the end the triumph of high achievement, and who at the worst, if he fails, at least fails while daring greatly, so that his place shall never be with those cold and timid souls who know neither victory nor defeat."

My challenge to you is to dare greatly. Look at your strengths and weaknesses, then ask yourself to do better every step of the way—no matter how difficult or impossible it may seem. Don't be afraid to fail. I know many people who were incredibly shy and anxious when they were younger, but they overcame their crippling shyness by putting themselves into situations where they were forced to perform onstage. Some of them are now politicians, public speakers, and CEOs. It is possible for you to rewire your cerebral matter. Studies have shown the brain is incredibly malleable. Humans have the ability to transform not just their thoughts but their physical reactions, psychology, and personality. We can alter fundamental traits, like the propensity for shyness or violence, and reprogram how we respond to the world around us.

So how does this tie into innovation? The fact is that innovation starts with our minds. We need to expand how we think in order to truly be creative. Innovating means coming up with something the world has never seen or tried before. This is no easy task. To think beyond the scope of what normal people can imagine is a gift few possess from birth. It is something that needs to be nurtured. Just as athletes train for marathons or the Olympics, you can train your mind to become a world-class innovation machine.

To begin training yourself, you need to recognize that new ideas don't materialize out of thin air. They come from everything you've learned and experienced brought together through association and manipulated by your conscious mind. Einstein called it combinatorial play. It's the process of taking existing ideas and combining them in new ways, then imagining the results. You can practice this by thinking deeply on a topic while freely associating and testing new concepts in thought experiments. This is how many of the world's greatest thinkers make their breakthroughs.

Here are a few examples of business-oriented thought experiments. Instead of imagining how to make your idea successful, try as hard as you can to kill your idea. Great innovators often start by thinking of every way they can possibly destroy their dream. What would it take to poke a hole in your balloon and have it come crashing down to Earth? Your goal should be to make your company fail as quickly as possible. If you're going to fail, it's far better to do it now, in your head, than later in reality.

Next imagine that a supercompetitor emerges and its goal is to totally crush your business. How would it do this? What would it do to create a better product, disrupt your business model, steal your customers, undermine your ability to compete, and outperform you in every category possible?

Next picture how you would grow and expand your market. How could you double, triple, or quadruple your growth rate? Would you develop new products? Target another demographic? Expand geographically? Is there a path for your customers to upgrade to premium services? What other growth levers can you pull?

Finally, picture your company ten years from now. Would it even be relevant? Would there be any point? What would you need to do to remain in business?

You don't have to be Einstein to benefit from thought experiments. The majority of innovations are the result of taking old ideas from one business and simply applying them to another. Successful entrepreneurs are often the first to spot these ideas and imagine how they can be repurposed. For instance, LinkedIn took the idea of a paper résumé and combined it with a social network; eBay took traditional auctions and reimagined them for the Internet. Groupon combined coupons with group purchasing. Craigslist copied newspaper classified ads. E-mail came from the concept of leaving someone a note on their desk. If you look at any major innovation, you can find its roots in what people are already doing and thinking.

There's a name for this process: knowledge brokering. It's when you take an idea that works in one area and envision it in a new context. Many companies have systematized this process and are constantly mining old ideas and applying them to new problems. IDEO, the Silicon Valley design and consulting firm, has used this method to create some of the world's most iconic products. It encourages its designers to continuously explore and play with usual products and materials, even when they have no immediate applications. IDEO realizes that this knowledge is essential to innovation. It's the raw material for inspiring design thinking. They've even created a system of boxes for storing all the gadgets, electronics, toys, and oddities that employees manage to collect.

Thomas Edison once said, "To invent, you need a good imagination and a pile of junk." This is why it's critical to expand your horizons. You need to fill your mind with lots of useful junk. Elon Musk uses this strategy all the time. He is constantly reading. As a boy he read the entire *Encyclopedia*

Britannica because he ran out of books to read at home. When he dives into a new project, like sending humans to Mars, he reads every possible book on the subject. He will literally bury himself in information, building up a foundation of ideas so that he can begin constructing his road map to the future.

As an entrepreneur, you shouldn't read just business books. I love business books, but I make sure to read everything from scientific journals to classic literature, fantasy, poetry, history, and philosophy. Why do I do this? Because discovering and learning new things from diverse sources compels me to look at the world from multiple perspectives. Is reading something like Sumerian love poems or the history of ornithology a waste of time? Absolutely not. It is the ideas that are outside our normal sphere of engagement that tend to be the most valuable—precisely because we haven't been exposed to them. They force open our minds, spark new thoughts, and serve as the building blocks for creativity.

When I read about how a cognitive musicologist analyzes and understands music, it impacts how I think about business. I can't help but apply the music theories to business problems I am looking to solve. The same is true when I delve into astronomy, quantum biology, religious studies, nutrigenomics, medieval history, and countless other topics that on the surface are unrelated to my job. I'm always on the lookout for new books on subjects where I have little or no knowledge, because that is the most fertile ground for innovation.

When academics analyzed the most innovative research papers, they found that the majority of them contained very few new ideas. Instead, what they did was appropriate older ideas and bring them into new fields. Ideas from psychology were brought into business management to form industrial and organizational psychology. Computational social science combines the use of statistics, big data, computer science, and sociology to understand social phenomena and trends over time. Recombinant memetics borrows from the idea of recombinant DNA to study how memes can be used to address social issues. Cognitive economics combines cognitive science and computational economics, along with theories about rationality and decision making, to devise new models of large-scale economic behaviors.

This type of borrowing ideas from one field and applying them to another is how we innovate. Throughout our history, from before the scientific revolution onward, human beings have been doing this to advance our knowledge and expand our thinking. If you want to innovate, there is no better approach.

I travel a lot, and one of the great joys of traveling is seeing how people all over the world communicate, collaborate, and problem-solve. These experiences give me new ways of thinking about my own role in society, my business, and myself. My best experiences happen when I don't just go to business meetings. It's when I give myself the time and freedom to explore: wander the streets, talk to ordinary people, and learn about the culture. That's when my intellectual understanding and intuitive sense for the culture merge, and new ideas and ways of doing business become clearer.

The world's greatest thinkers often took their best ideas from other cultures, and then adapted them to their own. The Greek philosopher Pythagoras borrowed from ancient Egypt. Monet and van Gogh were inspired by Japanese art. Dante's *Divine Comedy* incorporated ideas from the spiritual writings of Islamic scholars, like Ibn Arabi.

When we're immersed in our own culture, we often don't see things. We take everything for granted. However, when we step into another culture, there is a chance to look at life through fresh eyes. Just think of how different the world would have been without Marco Polo, Ferdinand Magellan, Lewis and Clark, Thomas Cook, Xuanzang, and Ibn Battuta—just to name a few. Moving beyond how we do things in our own culture can help us make new connections and see things that otherwise would have remained overlooked.

Studying history is another valuable source of ideas. Did you know that one of the greatest innovators of all time was Genghis Khan? In the West, we think of him as a brutish barbarian who pillaged and burned his way across Asia, the Middle East, and Europe. But that's only half the story. He was a brilliant man who was constantly experimenting with new ideas and constructed a lasting empire that reshaped the world. He started life as a low-ranking outcast, and the only way to get ahead was to unite the Mongol people. To accomplish this, he did away with class distinctions and built a meritocracy. By taking his weakness and turning it into his strength, he laid the foundation for a global empire.

Khan went on to innovate on the art of war. He perfected lightning-fast strikes, feigned retreats, and siege warfare. He even developed psychological warfare to frighten and demoralize his enemies. In addition, he absorbed all the artisans, scholars, religions, and inventions he came across, folding them into the Mongol social structure. Using the knowledge and talent he acquired, he was able to grow and administer his expanding empire. The Mongols wound up ruling not only China but huge swathes of Central Asia, Russia, the Middle East, India, and parts of Europe. That's not the work of a barbarian. It's the legacy of an innovative genius.

Like Khan, you need to move beyond your comfort zone and embrace the unknown. Push your limits. Go skydiving—even if you are afraid. Just do it, so you know what it feels like. If you've never been to the opera, buy a ticket and experience it live. Find a track where you can rent a race car and take it for a spin. If you haven't participated in a hack-a-thon, do it now! The team building experience is incredible. It's surprising how you can meet total strangers and wind up becoming close friends and collaborators in a matter of hours. This can teach you more than any management book, because you are actually living it.

If you normally go to bed at 11:00 p.m. every night, try pulling a caffeine-fueled all-nighter where you sit and write down whatever comes into your head. You may be shocked at what you come up with. Go backpacking in the wilderness for two weeks. Write a poem. Go to a Zen retreat where you can meditate for days in silence and see how that alters your mind. Seek out opinions that contradict your own. Hang out with local artists, visit their shows, and pull them into your projects. Or simply read a book that you would never have picked up before.

There are countless ways to open up your mind to new experiences, and all of them are good. You just need to get out of your rut and do something totally different. That's how you can be different and think different. It's not enough to have a diverse team, you need to diversify your mind. What you want is as many new and different ideas bouncing around inside your skull as possible. How these ideas coalesce to form new thoughts is the key to innovation. Our brains are combinatorial machines that draw from all of our experiences and piece them together in new ways, until we come up with something that works.

Question everything. Ask yourself why things are the way they are. Be open to opposing points of view. In fact, seek out and embrace what you intuitively know is untrue. See if you can find any truth in it. We all know people who believe things we feel are obviously false. Maybe they have a point we've overlooked or filtered out. The world is constructed inside our heads. All we know is what we believe. But there are many truths out there that we cannot see. People once thought computers would be used only for scientific research, vacuum tubes were the solution, and keyboards were unnecessary. How the world has changed.

Without looking inside and challenging yourself, it will be difficult to lead your team toward a vision of the future that you cannot see. How can you inspire, nurture, and guide your team to new frontiers if you haven't been there yourself? To be a truly great innovator, you need to begin by innovating on yourself.

Chapter 35

One Winner

Don't worry about failure; you only have to be right once.
—Drew Houston, cofounder
of Dropbox

We all know that it's a "winner takes all" world, and we all want to be winners. So we need to ask ourselves what determines a winner from a loser? We've talked a lot about how to innovate, but innovation doesn't matter if you can't reap the rewards. This book is about radical innovation with the intent of creating new multi-billion-dollar businesses. The goal is to have the next Twitter, Google, or Alibaba. But how can you tell if your little idea will grow up into a giant?

Let's start with making money. There are only two real business models out there: Either a customer pays you or an advertiser pays you. That's it. There are no other ways to make money. If the customer pays, you need either a lot of small transactions over each customer's lifetime or a few big ones. The top mobile games induce players to spend tiny amounts of money repeatedly over their lifetimes. Aircraft and auto manufacturers have customers pay large amounts of money but far less often. Either way, the money these companies bring in from customers over their lifetimes must be greater than the cost of customer acquisition and operations, or the business will not succeed in the long run. It's that simple.

The second model is advertising. Yes, there are other ways to get revenue, including online rev share, sponsorship, affiliate programs, and so on. But these are really just another form of advertising. You can't skirt the rules by changing the name. For advertising to work, you usually need a massive number of users to engage with your product—the more frequently and the longer, the better. If your network has too few users or the users fail to engage often enough, you will never be able to sell enough ads to make a profit. Most ad-based services begin to make money only when they have a critical mass of viewers or active users—typically a million or more. If your product can't achieve this, advertising is out.

That's the first litmus test for any new business. Everyone thinks business models are complex, but they aren't. I don't know of a single company that makes money any other way, and if you can't make a lot of money, you can't build a billion-dollar business, so it's back to the drawing board.

The next thing you need to consider is defensibility. For a new business to grow exponentially, it needs a way to fend off competitors. In other words, it needs barriers to entry that enable it to become the dominant player. All great businesses have an unfair advantage that allows them to attract, retain, and monetize customers significantly better than any competitors. Without a substantial unfair advantage, you'll have to compete in a low-margin business, which typically means slow growth and limited profit potential. Clearly, this is not the type of business most innovators are looking for.

So how do you know if your innovation has potential to be a dominant player? Here are *Captain Hoff's Seven Unfair Advantages*:

1. EXPONENTIALLY BETTER

Develop a product that is exponentially better than any of your competitors. If it's not an order of magnitude better, customers will simply go for the cheapest product on the market, and you'll never build a huge business. You need to offer significantly more value to capture and keep customers. As we mentioned earlier, a good example of this is Google. There were dozens of search engines before Google launched, but Google was so much better, it gobbled up all the market share. The same is true with

Facebook. It wasn't the first social network, but it was exponentially better than the competition.

2. NEW MARKET

Create an entirely new market. If your product is so unique and compelling that it's able to define a whole new category, then you are the winner by default. This isn't easy to do, but companies do it all the time. Just look at Nest, the smart thermostat startup that led the IoT wave, and Oculus Rift, the company that put virtual reality on the map. They sold for billions even before their market was proven, because they defined a new market. Other examples include: CrossFit for fitness; Chipotle for fast food; Lululemon for clothing; and IKEA for furniture.

3. FIRST TO DISRUPT

Be the first to disrupt an existing market using new technology or business-model innovations. If you can offer an equivalent product or service at a much lower price than entrenched competitors, you can steal their customers away from them. This is classic disruption. Examples include Netflix for movies and TV; Craigslist for classifieds; E*TRADE for stock brokers; Redfin for real estate; and Simple for banking.

4. NETWORK EFFECT

Tap into the network effect. The network effect is where the value of your business increases the more users you have on your network. Social networks and two-sided marketplaces are perfect examples of this. Nextdoor grows in value every time more neighbors join. Homeaway.com grows in value every time a new renter or host joins. Nearly all the top Internet companies take advantage of the network effect: Google AdWords has advertisers and publishers; Amazon Marketplace has sellers and consumers; Lyft has passengers and drivers; Snapchat has friends; LinkedIn has colleagues; eBay has buyers and sellers, and the list goes on.

5. EXCLUSIVITY

Establish exclusivity with whatever methods and relationships you can use, including patents, exclusive distribution channels, government support, legal barriers, and so on. For instance, ABC, NBC, and CBS had a government-sanctioned monopoly on the broadcast market for years, until new technologies enabled competition from the cable networks. Qualcomm is big on using its patents. Didi Chuxing in China has strong government support.

6. LOCK IN CUSTOMERS

Lock in your customers. Billion-dollar businesses are seldom about a single transaction with the customer. They're about building long-term relationships, where the longer the customers use the product, the harder it is for them to leave. Just look at Microsoft's and Apple's ecosystems. It's hard to give up their products once you start using them. Google Docs and Gmail work the same way. Salesforce has built one of the strongest ecosystems in the world. Great companies tend to build great ecosystems in which customers invest time, money, trust, and emotions. This raises the switching cost, thereby creating a massive unfair advantage.

7. BUILD A BRAND

If you can spot a new trend, societal change, market shift, or pent-up need before anyone else, you can enter the market and build a brand. The brand itself has the power to differentiate your product from everyone else's. Why do people pay more for brand-name drugs, food, and clothing versus their identical generic counterparts? Advil, Prozac, Coca-Cola, Nestle, Cartier, and Prada all have an unfair advantage due to their strong brands. Building brands is costly and difficult. The best way to do it is by identifying an unfilled need in the market and being the first mover.

Don't delude yourself. Just because you have a brand doesn't make it valuable. Just because you filed a patent doesn't mean it's worth anything. Just because you're first to market doesn't guarantee success. Just because you've come up with new technology doesn't mean it will make money. You have to analyze each innovation with a critical eye to see if it truly has the potential you believe it has. The above seven rules apply only when the case is extremely strong. If you have a weak position, then no matter what you do or how many resources you throw at it, it will never become a big business. That's when it's time to press the Reset button.

THE LAST HURRAH

Remember, through all the ugliness, all the failed experiments, all the canceled projects, you only need *one winner* to transform your business. Most great, new businesses are built on a single breakthrough idea: Coca-Cola's soft drink, Gillette's safety razor, Clorox's bleach, Bell's telephone, Ford's assembly line, Intel's 4004 processor, Cisco's router, Facebook's social network, Google's search, and the list goes on.

If your innovation teams work on hundreds of ideas and all but one of them fail, that's enough. One pivotal insight can reshape your entire industry. Keep this in mind, because it's not going to be easy. When there's failure upon failure upon failure, it's easy to throw in the towel and admit defeat. But you need to stick with it. Just remember, the truth is ugly. Most of these projects you're innovating on—most of what you're doing—will wind up in the trash bin. They won't generate any revenue, acclaim, press, or discernible progress. At the end of the day, everyone will wonder if it was really worth it. But don't fear the carnage. Look deeper.

Underneath it all lies the true value. Innovation is not about whether any individual project succeeds or fails; it's about what your teams learn and do. Even if your innovation teams fail to deliver a single groundbreaking product to market or generate any revenue directly linked to their efforts, they are still accumulating valuable knowledge and experience that they can share with the rest of your company. This can help to improve your existing products, customer service, manufacturing, marketing, and sales, making all your departments more innovative and profitable.

In addition, if you're involving employees from every department, as well as from different geographic locations, and putting them together in tight-knit teams, they're forming bonds, building relationships, and developing new internal networks that will make your organization stronger and smarter. Your innovation teams may be together for only a few months, but when they go back to their old jobs, they will bring back with them new approaches, processes, and tools. They will also have established new channels of communication with key people throughout the company. Just like the human brain, the more of these connections you make, the smarter your organization will become. This bridge building alone can be worth the cost.

If you try long and hard enough, if you perfect the process, and if you train your teams in how to innovate, you will eventually make the big breakthrough. It's only a matter of time. Innovation is a brutal process. Most startups fail, and you never hear about them again. We hear only about the handful of big winners and big losers. The tens of thousands of small losers get buried in unmarked graves. Without those failures, however, we would not have the Googles and Facebooks of the world.

Only by daring greatly can you achieve greatness. Only by taking enormous risks can you invent something the world has never seen before. Only by radically altering the processes of your company can you hope to succeed in the future. Only by doing all of this can your organization become healthier, more vibrant, and more creative than it ever was before. Now go out there and make your elephant fly!

Yours truly,
Captain Hoff

Appendix

Types and Areas of Innovation

There are many types and areas of innovation, but I'll spare you an extremely long list and instead briefly summarize some of the most popular ones. Keep in mind that these are not mutually exclusive. Many overlap. A company can practice disruptive innovation, technical innovation, radical innovation, and business-model innovation at the same time on the same project.

Incremental Innovation

Incremental innovation is not about dramatic, sweeping changes, like releasing a revolutionary, new product. Instead, it's about improving existing products or services bit by bit. Good examples of this are cost-cutting innovations, adding new features, and improving quality.

Big corporations love incremental innovation. It's something they know how to do. They can put a process in place, tap into their considerable human capital and core competencies, and gradually improve upon what they have. The goal is simple: make something better, faster, and cheaper.

Incremental innovation isn't just confined to existing products. Companies also use it to develop new products. Google, for example, developed Gmail through incremental innovation. The first version of Gmail wasn't exceptionally innovative or impressive. It was a bare-bones online e-mail solution—like many others out there. But the small team kept working on it for years, gradually improving it, until it was finally taken out of beta and became a hit with the public.

Today, incremental innovation is the dominant form. It's what most large companies rely upon. They spend years refining their processes, streamlining manufacturing, reducing costs, increasing quality, and adding new features so that they can keep ahead of their competitors.

Radical Innovation

A radical innovation doesn't improve upon an existing product but creates an entirely new product category or market. Companies seldom come up with something entirely new and groundbreaking on their first try, so radical innovation has a high failure rate. It usually takes a while and requires repeated attempts.

This is why large corporations with an aversion to failure have trouble pursuing radical innovation. They tend to be conservative, preferring lots of small successes with minimal risk. A manager never got fired for incremental innovations, but more than one manager has lost her job trying something radical that failed.

That's not to say big companies cannot practice radical innovation: Sony did it when it came up with the Walkman, Hewlett Packard did it with the inkjet printer, and Boeing did it with the 747. All of these were huge leaps forward. But the fact is that these breakthroughs don't come often in massive companies. And now that the pace of innovation is accelerating, these corporations can't sit and wait a decade for the next radical innovation to emerge. By then, they may be out of business.

Disruptive Innovation

My definition of *disruptive innovation* is slightly different from that of Clayton Christensen, who wrote the best-selling book *The Innovator's Dilemma*. I define *disruptive innovation* as applying new technology or processes to existing markets in order to fundamentally change the economics, displacing market leaders and overturning alliances. Most established businesses with huge market share have discovered that tiny startups can use new technologies and processes to fundamentally alter the equation, undercutting prices and creating new market footholds.

A classic example of this is Pandora, which disrupted the music industry with its version of online radio. Others include Prosper, which disrupted personal loans; Zenefits, which disrupted HR services; and Robinhood, which disrupted online stock trading. Startups are really good at disruptive innovation, while larger corporations have difficulty rethinking their business models, especially when it involves cannibalizing existing revenue streams.

Architectural Innovation

Architectural innovation is about taking the technology, know-how, and talent from one industry and applying it to another. The risks and costs are lower because the technology is proven. It's only the market that needs to be developed.

A great example of this is when Fagerdala World Foams, a Swedish company, took the memory foam that NASA had developed for the aerospace industry and applied it to the mattress industry. In 1991, their Tempur-Pedic Swedish Mattress came out, giving birth to Tempur World. It was a hit with consumers, and the new market for memory-foam mattresses was born.

Technical Innovation

Imagine an R & D lab developing new, cutting-edge technologies. That's technical innovation. Samsung is a perfect example of this. As its hardware sales struggle, Samsung has opened up its wallet to insure that it can stay competitive. It now spends over $12 billion a year on R & D. Most of this goes toward new products like smartphones, tablets, TVs, appliances, chips, displays, and cameras.

Business-Model Innovation

This is what most of today's startups do well. They don't have the resources of a leviathan like Samsung, so they tend to take off-the-shelf technology and innovate on the business model.

A good example of this is ClassPass, which sells a membership program that lets users pay a flat monthly fee to take unlimited fitness classes at different gyms and studios nearby. What they offer is a new way of doing business for existing services like yoga, Pilates, boxing, workouts, and more. It's essentially a one-stop shop for all the gym classes in your area. The technology needed to implement ClassPass is nothing special. The innovation lies in how they changed the model for browsing and purchasing classes.

Design Innovation

Design innovation is about designing products and services that surprise and enchant customers. It involves everything from the look and feel of a product to the user experience. The goal is to develop products and services that are so much more appealing than anything else on the market that they come to define their category and force competitors to become copycats.

Whole Foods Market is a great example of this. They completely redefined what a supermarket should be by focusing on everything from organic produce to creating a distinct and engaging experience for the shopper. When Whole Foods Market first launched, customers instantly knew they were not in an ordinary market. It was upscale, meticulously arranged, and appealing to someone who was willing to pay more for food they felt good about. Since then many large supermarket chains have felt compelled to copy Whole Foods Market in order to compete.

This same approach was used to craft every element of the Tesla Roadster, Model S and Model X. At its core, design thinking has allowed companies to outinnovate competitors by reimagining how a product looks, performs, and feels to the customer.

Frugal Innovation

Frugal innovation is all about driving down price so that products can be sold to low-income customers, primarily in emerging markets. Frugal innovation focuses on removing complexity and streamlining production, so products that used to be out of reach for much of the population become affordable. In essence, this creates a whole new market.

Tata Motors has done this in India with its minicar, which sells for $2,500 and up. Indians who never dreamed of owning a car can now afford to buy one. This has permanently altered the auto industry. Similar frugal innovations are springing up across Asia, Africa, and South America. There's a frugal fridge that uses no electricity and sells for only $50, cheap amphibious bicycles for weathering monsoons, and Android tablets for $35.

The other aspect of frugal innovation is relying on razor-thin margins and nontraditional distribution channels. Xiaomi did this in China with its iPhone clone, which sold for less than half the price of Samsung's Android phones and was only available online when it launched.

Sustainable Innovation

This is innovation with a focus on sustainable development. This environmentally friendly approach makes efforts not to deplete the earth's natural resources unnecessarily. For example, Starbucks has the goal of ethically sourcing 100 percent of its coffee beans; Dell has committed to reducing the energy intensity of its products by 80 percent; and Coca-Cola pledged to reduce its water use by 20 percent.

Another example of sustainable innovation is the startup Everplane, whose mission is to minimize the water and energy used to create clothing. They reveal everything to shoppers, from where the materials are sourced to the working conditions in factories to the complete environmental impact. Nothing is kept secret.

Open-Source Innovation

This is the idea of using crowdsourced talent to innovate. Whether it's Android, GitHub, Docker, Red Hat, WordPress, or one of the other open-source projects, this is how some of the most innovative software is developed today. But it's not limited to software. You can open-source hardware, research, design, and anything else that requires crowdsourced talent to produce.

Open Innovation

Open innovation, not to be confused with open-source innovation, is all about using external ideas, talent, and technologies to build your business, while simultaneously permitting outsiders to access internal ideas, talent, and technologies. In short, it's the uninhibited exchange of resources with partners in a collaborative building process.

The concept is that one company can't do everything by itself. To succeed in today's hypercompetitive world, you must harness the energy, ideas, and know-how of third parties. These third parties can be software developers, artists, scientists, service providers, and other companies. Many large corporations do this through exposing their application programming interfaces to third-party developers, open-sourcing their software, or allowing third parties to do business through their platforms.

Although open innovation has achieved buzzword status in the corporate world, it's much easier to say than do. Open innovation requires a company to completely rethink how it does business. Most companies tend toward secrecy. R & D labs are traditionally isolated from the outside world. Managers are worried about the competition stealing their precious ideas and intellectual property. To make open innovation work, a company needs to abandon this way of thinking and embrace collaboration, with the knowledge that only by sharing information and exposing value can they attract the outside talent necessary to make big leaps forward.

Product Innovation

When people think of innovation, they usually think of product innovation. Develop the next iPhone, and you'll conquer the world. Product innovation is about coming up with new products and line extensions, as well as improving the quality, features, and value of existing products.

Ecosystem Innovation

This is where you innovate on a product's ecosystem. It involves improving how products and services connect together to create a single system.

Apple is brilliant at ecosystem innovation. Think of how the iPhone, iPad, and iPod all share the same ecosystem, which includes the App Store, iTunes, iOS operating system, standardized ports, and so on. The ecosystem is often more important than the product itself. When done right, it increases the core value of the product and makes it more difficult to copy.

Service Innovation

This is where you innovate on the services surrounding a product, making the product easier to understand, use, and enjoy. Innovations around service can take an average product and raise it above the competition by providing customers with an exceptional out-of-the-box experience, customer support, and follow-up. This is often the way companies distinguish themselves from their competitors. The Geek Squad at Best Buy stores is a good example of service innovation.

Brand Innovation

Brands are not static. They are always changing, and smart companies must continually innovate to improve upon their brands. Brands can take a commodity and transform it into a highly valued product. But building and innovating on a brand requires a deep understanding of the customers, public perception, culture, and market. Brands are affected by everything from price to advertising, PR, customer service, channel partners, employee behavior, and the company's reputation. An example of a company that has done an amazing job at brand innovation is Under Armour, as it transformed itself from a one-trick pony, known for T-shirts that boost muscle performance and wick moisture, into one of the leading brands for men's and women's athletic apparel and shoes.

Channel Innovation

You need to analyze how your product gets into the hands of customers, including sales reps, websites, mobile apps, retail stores, distributors, affiliate programs, channel partners, and so on. How can you innovate on these sales and distribution channels? A company that built its reputation on channel innovation is Xiaomi. Its relentless focus on direct-to-consumer sales over the web helped it become one of the world's largest smartphone makers, when practically everyone else was focused primarily on traditional retail channels.

Profit-Model Innovation

In most industries, the dominant profit model goes unchallenged for years—or decades. But clever innovators often challenge industry assumptions about what to charge, how to collect revenues, and what to offer. It's about digging deep, engaging with customers, and figuring out what customers really value and how you can alter the revenue streams and pricing. T-Mobile's constant "uncarrier" tactics have illustrated some of the most successful profit-model innovation in the last decade, as they forced the big incumbents, Verizon and AT&T, to radically alter their models and stop trying to lock consumers into multiyear contracts.

Structure Innovation

With structure innovation, you analyze your company's assets and figure out new ways to create value from them. These can be hard assets (computers, machinery, etc.), human assets (researchers, salespeople, etc.) or intangible assets (patents, trademarks, etc.). You can use equipment in new ways to increase safety, reorganize entire departments to be more efficient, or thwart competitors through patent litigation. Many private equity firms look for opportunities where they can acquire a company, bring on a new management team, and engage in structure innovation to create value from a company's assets.

Process Innovation

This is where you work to improve the processes through which products are created or delivered. This can include significant improvements in production, testing, delivery method, support, and other key areas of your business. If done right, these become your "secret sauce" that competitors will have a difficult time replicating. This is what Tesla is attempting to do with its new, giant battery plant in Nevada.

Experience Innovation

How do customers perceive your products? What are they feeling? How can you construct emotionally engaging experiences that bring them deeper into your fold? These are the types of questions you need to ask when engaged in experience innovation. The goal is to create a tighter bond between your customers and your products. Customers tend to stick with what they love, and the innovator has to play the role of Cupid.

Bonobos launched Guideshop to provide a more personal shopping experience for its customers. This is an experiment blending online and offline. At every Bonobos Guideshop, the customer can make a one-hour appointment to try on clothes with the help of a personal guide. Once the customer places an order, the clothes are shipped directly to the customer's home. They aren't purchased in the store.

Network Innovation

More companies are engaging in network innovation, where they leverage other companies' core competencies. These include technologies, offerings, brands, channels, and processes. If another company is better than you at something, why do it yourself? The right strategic partnerships, whether short- or long-term, can allow you to execute faster, cheaper, and with less risk. The challenge is to rethink how you do business, understand your strengths, and take advantage of third parties to give you an edge over the competition.

Vizio, the upstart electronics maker known for its low-priced TVs, is a brilliant example of a company that has employed network innovation to outmaneuver much larger incumbents like Samsung and Sony. By outsourcing nearly everything, Vizio has built a global electronics business with less than four hundred employees, compared to Samsung Electronics, which has more than three hundred thousand employees.

Endnotes

1. Viguerie, Patrick, Sven Smit, and Mehrdad Baghai. *The Granularity of Growth: How to Identify the Sources of Growth and Drive Enduring Company Performance.* Hoboken: John Wiley & Sons, 2008.
2. Rigoglioso, Marguerite. "Jeffrey Pfeffer: Untested Assumptions May Have a Big Effect," interview with Jeffrey Pfeffer, *Insights by Stanford Business*, June 1, 2005. https://www.gsb.stanford.edu/insights/jeffrey-pfeffer-untested-assumptions-may -have-big-effect (accessed May 4, 2017).
3. McKinney, Steve. "Admit and Test Your Assumptions." McKinney Consulting. April 29, 2015. http://mckinneyconsulting.com/index.php/the-mckinney-blog/34 -admit-and-test-your-assumptions (accessed May 6, 2017)
4. Elliott, Seth. "Avoiding Bad Assumptions." LinkedIn. April 28, 2016. https:// www.linkedin.com/pulse/avoiding-bad-assumptions-seth-elliott (accessed May 6, 2017).
5. Rao, Jay, Joseph Weintraub. "How Innovative Is Your Company's Culture?" *MIT Sloan Management Review* vol. 54 no. 3 (Spring 1993), March 19, 2013. http:// sloanreview.mit.edu/article/how-innovative-is-your-companys-culture/ (accessed May 6, 2017)

Index

About the Author

Always innovating on his life, Steven Hoffman, known as Captain Hoff, has tried more professions than cats have lives, including serial entrepreneur, venture capitalist, angel investor, mobile studio head, computer engineer, filmmaker, Hollywood TV exec, published author, coder, game designer, manga rewriter, animator, and voice actor.

Hoffman was also the chair of Producers Guild Silicon Valley Chapter, Board of Governors of the New Media Council, and founding member of the Academy of Television's Interactive Media Group.

After starting three venture-funded startups in Silicon Valley, Hoffman launched Founders Space with the mission to educate and accelerate entrepreneurs and intrapreneurs. Founders Space has become one of the top startup accelerators in the world with more than fifty partners in twenty-two countries. Hoffman has trained hundreds of startup founders and corporate executives in the art of innovation and routinely works with the world's largest global corporations and venture funds. He's also a limited partner in August Capital.

Hoffman has a BS from the University of California in electrical computer engineering, and an MFA from the University of Southern California in cinema television production. He currently resides in San Francisco but spends most of his time in the air, visiting startups, investors, and incubators all over the world.